Dedicated to

To my Late BABA JI Grandfather and

"MAA"- "PAPA JI"

Source : UN cartographic section.

Map 1: Political Map of Mangolia

Contents

Preface

Aristotle described "*man as a political animal*". In this context, one may find that friendship and relations between human beings have existed since the beginning of human creation. Gradually, these relations between people have developed into groups and organisations which made policies for safeguarding their interest. Similarly, in the international system all states have their own foreign policies to safeguard their national interest. The foreign policy of a state can be termed as a strategy to deal with external environment in order to not only safeguard national interest but also survive in the ongoing international system. However, due to the globalisation and transnational activities, particularly in the post Cold War period, foreign policy changes have been noticed in several states worldwide to suit the interest of the nation. Mongolia is an example of such foreign policy changes through high-level, decision-making processes ever since the country opted for reforms in its internal and external affairs taking into consideration the national interest.

Having a rich historical legacy with proud traditions of statehood and foreign relations Mongolia is one of the least densely populated countries in the world. It possesses a landmass of 1,566,500 kilometers, with a mere population of 2,712,315 people.[1] Geographically, positioned as a landlocked country it is surrounded completely by Russia and China. Since Mongolia is known as the birthplace of Chinggis Khan, arguably the most authoritative ruler the world has ever known, his empire stretched from the Eastern edge of Asia to the far reaches of Central Europe, and from parts of Southern Indonesia to the frigid arctic of Siberia. This is the largest of any empire in the world's history. In the centuries that followed the height of the

Mongol empire, the nation experienced multiple periods of transition. After the fall of the Mongol Empire in the 14th century, Mongolian history was dotted with few significant events for nearly two centuries. The rhythmic lifestyle of nomadic herders set the pace of life, as opposed to the warring hordes that had dominated the region in previous centuries. Then in the 17th century, an extended period of Chinese influence and occupation began, fueling a rivalry between these two nations that endures even today. Not until the early 1900s did Mongolia gain complete autonomy from China, but this autonomy was quickly undermined with the commencement of Russian/Soviet manoeuvering. This finally resulted in Mongolia's independence in 1921 with an identity of it becoming the second Communist state in the world after the Soviet Union.[2]

From 1921 to 1991, Mongolia remained under the Soviet influence or more precisely "under Soviet control,", though it was never officially part of the former USSR. But after the collapse of the Soviet Union in 1991, Mongolians wasted little time in manifesting their independent status once again. Today, Mongolia is a democratic country with a free-market economy that has made an impressive transition from its Soviet socialist system to a burgeoning nation with an ambitious and optimistic outlook on the future.[3] In fact, the post-1921 revolution era witnessed Mongolia depending on former Soviet Union in its internal and external policies thereby affecting its sovereign and independence status. This in turn also affected its cultural and political identity as an Asian nation. But the year 1986 was a turning point as Gorbachev's policy of *Glasnost* and *Perestroika* and the ensuing process of reforms and restructuring in Soviet domestic and foreign policy had inevitable impact over Mongolia. Not only did Soviet reforms influence Mongolia but also Gorbachev's 1986 seminal Vladivostok speech to change Soviet foreign policy particularly towards Asia provided Ulaanbaatar an opportunity to carry out reforms independently in its own domestic and foreign policy. The process of Soviet style reforms and restructuring through *Il tod* and *Orchilan baigalalt* began in Mongolia, which permitted the government in particular and the people in general to have more open discussions on the on-going problems and past mistakes.

Significantly, in the late 1980s, the close relationship between Mongolia and the former Soviet Union was much the same as it had been since the 1920s. At that time, Mongolian foreign policy stressed on consolidating the "fraternal alliance" with the Soviet Union and close cooperation with the members of the Warsaw Pact and COMECON (Council for Mutual Economic Assistance).[4] The two countries had direct links among ministries, agencies, departments, and party organisations. The Mongolian ambassador to the Soviet Union also served on the ruling Mongolian People's Revolutionary Party (MPRP) Central Committee. In 1985, Batmunkh became General Secretary of the MPRP just as Gorbachev was elected as General Secretary of the Communist Party of the Soviet Union (CPSU).[5] The two leaders pledged to uphold and strengthen the Mongolian-Soviet alliance. Gorbachev's "new thinking" in foreign policy matters soon became evident, which raised major concerns, on the part of Mongolian leaders, particularly regarding a warming of relations between the Soviet Union and China. Soviet foreign minister Eduard Shevardnadze visited Mongolia in 1986, shortly after celebrations marking the Twentieth anniversary of the signing of the 1966 Mongolian-Soviet Treaty of Friendship, Cooperation, and Mutual Assistance and its extension for ten years. He emphasised that "the period of strained relationship with China is now behind us. The Soviet Union is for normalising and improving relations with the Chinese republic on condition that the principle of not harming third countries be observed." One clear purpose of the Soviet formula of "not harming third countries" was to reassure Mongolia that the Soviet Union did not plan initiatives toward China that would compromise or endanger Mongolia's national security or expose that country to Chinese encroachments.[6]

In July 1986, Gorbachev extended the new direction in foreign affairs in a speech on Asian security delivered in Vladivostok. He indicated Soviet interest in improved Moscow-Beijing relations, and he included a plan to withdraw Soviet troops from Mongolia, a major factor in Soviet diplomatic initiatives designed to meet China's conditions for normalisation of relations. Shortly after the Vladivostok initiative, Mongolian officials began talks with the United States diplomats on the establishment of diplomatic ties with Washington which could offer a greater degree of manoeuverability in the increasingly complex international setting in Asia.[7] In January 1987, diplomatic ties were established with the United States, and the Soviet Union announced its intention to withdraw one division of troops from Mongolia. Both actions were in favour of Mongolia as it began to pursue its independent policy, particularly in foreign affairs. Mongolia further broadened its diplomatic horizons by hosting delegations from twenty-one communist and workers' parties for the Consultative Meeting of Communist and Workers' Parties of Asia and the Pacific Region, the first regional gathering of this type in July 1986. The theme of this meeting was "peace, security and good-neighbourly cooperation in Asia and the Pacific region." As Mongolia expanded its contacts in the international community, Gorbachev continued to extend his Asian initiatives, a development directly affecting Mongolia's national interests.

In a speech delivered on September 16, 1988, at the Southeastern Siberian city of Krasnoyarsk, Gorbachev presented a seven-point program designed to enhance security in the Asia-Pacific region and to promote his view of a multi-polar approach to resolve issues in foreign relations. The so-called Krasnoyarsk initiative indicated both Soviet intentions to play a major role in the region and that China also must be included in regional development plans. This was considered as reassuring Mongolian leaders that Soviet proposals of involving China were not to threaten Mongolian national security. The challenge for Mongolia's foreign policy makers was to comply with Soviet initiatives, about which they had little choice, but to do so in a manner that suggested that Mongolia was acting as an independent country, shaping a foreign policy that served its national interests. At the same time, the Soviet Union could not appear to be overlooking the interests of its ally Mongolia while making its overtures to China.

This mild restriction on Soviet behaviour had helped to reassure Mongolia that continued Soviet protection and strategic support were reliable. This ensured Mongolia to continue with reforms initiatives that started in 1986. The rapidity of change brought out in Mongolia was largely due to the willingness and a welcoming acceptance of the reforms urgently required for the prosperity of the Mongolian people not only in the domestic political, social and economic fields but also in the foreign affairs. It further gained momentum after the collapse of the former Soviet Union in 1991 and the end of the Cold War which also altered the geopolitical environment of Mongolia and left it in a great power vacuum.[8]

However, that vacuum-political, economic and ideological-enabled Mongolia to achieve three major desired results. Firstly, for the first time in nearly seven decades it allowed Mongolia to open itself to the outside world and pursue an independent multi-pillared foreign policy. Secondly, Non-Aligned Movement (NAM) admitted Mongolia as a full-fledged member, something that could not have been possible during the Soviet time as it would have eroded the solidarity of the socialist block. And thirdly, Mongolia declared to engage itself in the broad perspectives of maintaining a balance in its relations with Russia and China, rather than giving importance to only one of them. In general, the emergence of new situation under the impact of political reforms and economic restructuring especially during 1990-1992 brought Mongolia at a crossroad where it had to consider its future development in the framework of new geopolitical realities. "Several academics and the policy planners are of the opinion that a critical reappraisal of Mongolia's own policy, both internal and external, could help the country change many of the existing policies which were considered to have held back development in domestic and foreign affairs".[9]

To begin with, during the reform process, a new constitution was adopted in 1992 by replacing the 1960 constitution, which made considerable changes to Mongolia's political system as well as foreign policy. Soon Mongolia conducted a major review of its foreign and security policy also. Since Mongolia's foreign policy and national security concerns are interlinked, the country adopted its own independent documents entitled "Concept of Foreign Policy" and "Concept of National Security" on quite a new basis in 1994. The new foreign policy what Mongolia describes as a "multi-pillar" foreign policy adopted during the reform period aimed first of all at developing long-term, stable and good neighbourly relations with its neighbours, particularly Russia and China. The policy core was not to adopt the line of either of these two neighbours but maintain a balanced relationship with both of them. As such Mongolia signed Treaties on Friendly Relations and Cooperation with Russia in 1993 and with China in 1994. Based on the universal principles of mutual respect for each other's sovereignty and territorial integrity, non-aggression, non-interference in internal affairs and peaceful co-existence, these agreements laid a legal foundation for the bilateral relations with these two nations.[10]

Mongolia's foreign policy in the political field is an important instrument for ensuring and strengthening its national security. In developing its relations with other countries. Mongolia has followed universally recognised principles and norms of international law as defined in the Charter of the United Nations. In sum, Mongolia's foreign policy is based on mutual respect for sovereignty, territorial integrity and inviolability of frontiers, right to self-determination, non-interference in internal affairs, non-use of force, settlement of disputes by peaceful means, respect for human rights and freedoms, and equal and mutually beneficial cooperation with other countries. While pursuing its multi-pillar foreign policy, Mongolia upholds peace and tries to avoid confrontation with other countries keeping in mind its national interests first and foremost. At the same time, it is committed to respect the legitimate interests of other countries and its partners. Besides, as per the directions of its reformed foreign policy, it also ensures itself not to interfere in the disputes between its two neighbouring countries unless the disputes affect Mongolia's national interests.[11]

Another major breakthrough in the country's history due to changes in domestic and foreign policy occurred in June 1996, when the third multi-party elections for the Parliament were held. The majority of voters preferred the opposition democrats over the Communists who had won the previous two elections held in 1991 and 1992. Soon the democrats were able to take the power for the first time in the history by acquiring two thirds of the votes. The reform process which was initiated in 1986 gained its momentum during the election campaigns. The 1996 election demonstrated that Mongolia was undergoing democratic changes, not only for the sake of politics but also for the entire society that wished to broaden the country's outlook in the international arena. Hence, the new government of democrats began focussing on implementing its new foreign policy objectives as outlined in the "1994 Concept of Mongolia's Foreign Policy" to attract more overseas partners who could be a reliable ally in international affairs besides helping to set right Mongolian economy through investments in major sectors.

This book contains six chapters including conclusion:

The first Chapter *"Introduction to Mongolia's Foreign Policy"* brings theoretical framework of foreign policy in general and conceptualise it in the Mongolian context. It has also deal with the background of the Mongolian foreign policy in the pre-1986 period, the beginning of the reform period in Mongolia under the direct impact of Gorbachev's reform policies, Vladivostok initiative to change Soviet Asian policy and its influence on Mongolia, and changes occurred in Mongolia's foreign policy to come out of Soviet orbit until the collapse of the former USSR.

The Second Chapter "*Changing Mongolia's Foreign Policy: Domestic Factor*" comprises on analysing various domestic factors responsible for changes in the foreign policy of Mongolia. Its highlight the post-Soviet reform initiatives following the peaceful movement for introduction of democracy and market economy, its impact on intellectual debates within the country for securing national interests of sovereignty and identity as well as resolving internal issues confronting the existing policies in foreign affairs. The adoption of a new constitution (1992) which provided new directions to Mongolia's domestic and foreign policies are also dealt with.

The third chapter of this dissertation namely "*Mongolia's Foreign Policy changes: External Factors*" is paying attention to various external factors that influenced the changes in post-Soviet Mongolia's foreign policy. Its analyse the emergence of new geopolitical situation in Mongolia's external environment following the Soviet collapse, national security issues in the new scenario, need to ensure financial assistance from the external forces to rebuild economy, and leadership initiatives towards revamping the prevailing foreign policy to suit national interests. Besides, it has also highlights the linkages between national security and foreign policy taking into consideration the initiatives of major external powers in ensuring Mongolia's security-both economic as well as strategic.

The fourth Chapter "*Multi-Pillar" Foreign Policy of Mongolia*" encompasses the adoption of the new post-Soviet Mongolia's foreign policy (1994) and the determinants of this "multi-pillar" foreign policy. It's also discuss its implications by focussing on the state of relations with the three most important external powers- Russia, China, and the US, apart from highlighting the roles of international financial institutions in the context of foreign policy objectives. In addition, this chapter deliberates upon the 1996 parliamentary elections that cleared the way for the democrats to form the government which started focussing on implementing the country's new foreign policy objectives to attract more overseas partners.

The fifth chapter "***India–Mongolia relations: Future prospective***" discusses about the India- Mongolia relations in detail and also discusses about the future prospective of the relations.

And the last concluding chapter "*Conclusion*" has given an overview of the whole book, besides highlighting its relevance for future bilateral and multilateral ties in the context of national security, both economic and strategic. The objectives of this book are the following:

The objectives of this book is to examine the nature of pre-1986 Mongolia's foreign policy and stages of its changes in the post-1986 period, to study various domestic and external factors influencing the evolution of post-communist Mongolian foreign policy, to understand the determinants of new Mongolian foreign policy and their implications for relations with the outside world, to observe whether Mongolia's foreign policy is still influenced by outside actors, particularly the actions and events of neighbouring powers: Russia and China. And also to evaluate whether Mongolia's landlocked geography is a challenge for its national security and how far Mongolian foreign policy would be able to ensure its security.

Subhash Kumar Baitha
Feb, 2014, New Delhi

References

1. http://www.mtac.gov.tw/mtacbook/upload/09505/0701/3.pdf.
2. http://itgel.org/history_of_mongolia.htm.
3. *Ibid.*
4. http://www.photoglobe.info/ebooks/mongolia/cstudies_mongolia_0145.html.
5. http://www.bored.com/ebooks/World_Reference/historical%20context%20 %20country%20studies/mongolia/mongolia. txt.
6. *Ibid.*
7. http://www.mongabay.com/reference/country_studies/mongolia/GOVERNMENT.html.
8. http://www.bored.com/ebooks/World_Reference/historical%20context%20-%20country%20studies/mongolia/mongolia.txt.
9. http://www.mtac.gov.tw/mtacbook/upload/09511/0202/2.pdf.
10. http://www.ub-mongolia.mn/facts-mongolia/political-system.html.
11. http://www.mongolianembassy.us/eng_foreign_policy/the_concept_of_foreign_policy.php?

Acknowledgments

Writing this book has been an awe-inspiring task for me. This book has been kept on track and been seen through to completion with the support and encouragement of numerous people including my well-wishers, my friends, colleagues and various institutions. I would like to thank all those people who made this book possible and an unforgettable experience for me. This book would not have been possible without the support of these people.

First and foremost, I express my deepest gratitude to my Ph.D. Supervisor Dr Sharad K. Soni for his gracious and expert guidance in the preparation of the manuscript.

A book like this relies on the input and patience of many colleagues. Those of particular aid have been: Renu, Preeti, Ajeet, Nayan, Soni, Pawan, Ritesh, Bhaskar, Avinash, Devideen and Gaurav. I would also like to extend my huge, warm thanks to my elder brother Sunil Kumar Gautam (IRS) for his love, care and support.

I am also eternally grateful to my family, especially my mother (Devpati Devi) and father (Madan Chaudhary), for all the love, motivation and guidance they have continually and unconditionally given me. I am immensely indebted to my aspirational *Bhaiya* and *Bhabhi* (Sushil and Reena), who have taken all the burden and work load at home and given me all the support and love throughout my work till accomplished. For their strong faith and belief they have bestowed on me since the beginning of my studies. I would like to express my heart-felt gratitude to my younger brothers Sudama, Santosh,

Rajesh and Antosh. Words are inadequate to express my deep sense of gratitude towards my sister-in-laws Vineeta, Babita and Khushboo. Thank you for your support, encouragement and care. Above all I owe special indebtness to my loving sisters Mala, Renu, Roshani, Nandini, Arrika, Arapana and Amrita, who stood on their toes in course of completion of this book. I extend heartily and special thanks to my brother in-law Kamlesh Baitha for cheering and encouraging me, he helped me a lot to work for hours together tirelessly. It is also a pleasure to mention my loveable nieces Priyanka, Priya, Preeti, Prince, Rahul, Rishu, kishu (Golu) and Viraj who indirectly encourage me with their love.

I would like to also make a special mention about Rahul and Rohit whose support over the years has been greatly appreciated with whom I started this work and many rounds of discussions on my project with them helped me a lot.

In course I must have missed many names worth mentioning and I am really thankful to them for all cooperation extended to me. For those of you whose names I did not mention here, I offer my apologies but know that those that have made this experience so special will never been forgotten.

Last but not the least, I express my sincere and heartfelt thanks to the Publisher, GenNext Publications, Delhi for enduring with the hardships till the publication of this book.

Subhash Kumar Baitha
February, New Delhi, 2014

Abbreviations

ADB	Asian Development Bank
ARVIN	Association, Resources, Vise, Information, and Negotiation
BDC	Business Development Consultation
CAV	Center Against Violence
CBO	Community-Based Organisation
CCC	Customs Co-operation Council
CEAF	Civic Engagement Analytical Framework
CEDAW	Convention on the Elimination of All Forms of Discrimination Against Women
COMECON	Council for Mutual Economic Assistance
CRC	Communications Regulatory Commission
CSC	Community Scorecard
CSO	Civil Society Organisation
DP	Democratic Party
DV	Domestic Violence
EIA	Environmental Impact Assessment
ESCAP	Economic and Social Commission for Asia and the Pacific
FAO	Food and Agriculture Organisation
GOM	Government of Mongolia
HLCSC	Household Livelihoods Capacity Support Council
IAEA	International Atomic Energy Agency

ICAO	International Civil Aviation Organisation
IDA	International Development Association
IFAD	International Fund for Agricultural Development
IFC	International Finance Corporation
ILO	International Labour Organisation
IMF	International Monetary Fund
INGO	International Non-Governmental Organisation
INTERPOL	International Criminal Police Organisation
IPU	Inter-Parliamentary Union
ITU	International Telecommunications Union
LIF	Local Initiatives Fund
MAPSSD	Mongolian Association for Primary and Secondary School Development
MDC	Motherland Democracy Coalition
MFN	Most-Favoured-Nation
MGP	Mongolian Green Party
MMFA	Mongolian Ministry of Foreign Affairs
MNPP	Mongolian National Progress Party
MOECS	Ministry of Education, Culture, and Science
MOFE	Ministry of Finance and Economics
MOJHA	Ministry of Justice and Home Affairs
MONE	Ministry of Nature and Environment
MP	Member of Parliament
MPRP	Mongolian People's Revolutionary Party
MRPA	Mineral Resource and Petroleum Authority of Mongolia
MRTV	Mongolian Radio and Television
MSDP	Mongolian Social-Democratic Party
MSWL	Ministry of Social Welfare and Labour
MT	Mongolian Togs

NAM	Non-Aligned Movement
NCAV	National Center Against Violence
NGO	Non-Governmental Organisation
NHRC	National Human Rights Commission
NTR	Normal Trade Relations
ODA	Official Development Assistance
ORM	Ongi River Movement
OSF	Open Society Forum
PETS	Public Expenditure Tracking Survey
PPA	Poverty Partnership Agreement
PRC	People's Republic of China
PSMFL	Public Sector Management and Finance Law
ROC	Republic of China
SLP	Sustainable Livelihoods Programme
SWOT	Strengths-Weaknesses-Opportunities-Threats
TAF	The Asia Foundation
TAN	Training in Advocacy for NGOs
UMENGO	Union of Environmental NGOs
UN	United Nations
UNCCD	*United Nations Convention to Combat Desertification*
UNDP	United Nations Development Programme
UNESCO	United Nations Educational, Scientific and Cultural Organisation
UNHRC	*United Nations Human Rights Council*
UNICEF	United Nations Children's Fund
UNIDO	United Nations Industrial Development Organisation
UNO	*United Nations Organisations*
UPU	Universal Postal Union
US	*United States*

USAID	United States Agency for International Development
USSR	Union of the Soviet Socialist Republics
WB	World Bank
WHO	*World Health Organisation*

1

Introduction to Mongolia's Foreign Policy

Mongolia's 70 years alliance with the former Soviet Union came to an abrupt end after disintegration of the USSR in 1991. This allowed fundamental changes in Mongolian foreign policy to take place. Today Mongolia's foreign policy is dominated by a need to secure sovereignty and economic independence.[1] However, before dealing with the main subject of Mongolia's foreign policy it is necessary to understand the foreign policy in the theoretical framework, particularly in the context of international relations theory. This will enable us to have a clear understanding of the subject. This chapter is also focussing on theoretical tools provide the basis to acquaint with the general patterns underlying the world of international politics. Since foreign policy guides the official external relations conducted by a particular State in international relations, the three main approaches of international relations theory, namely; idealism, realism, and constructivism becomes the core assumptions to analyse the linkages between international relations and foreign policy.

1.1 Background of Mongolia's Foreign Policy

In 1206 AD, a single Mongolian state was formed based on nomadic tribal groupings under the leadership of Chinggis (*Genghis*) Khan. He and his immediate successors conquered nearly all of Asia and European Russia and sent armies as far as Central Europe and Southeast Asia. Chinggis Khan's grandson Kublai Khan, who conquered China and established the Yuan dynasty (1279-1368 AD), gained fame in Europe through the writings of Marco Polo. Although Mongol-led confederations sometimes exercised wide political power over their conquered territories, their strength declined rapidly after the Mongol dynasty in China was overthrown in 1368. The Manchus, a tribal group which conquered China in 1644 and formed the Qing dynasty, were able to bring Mongolia under Manchu control in 1691 as Outer Mongolia when the Khalkha Mongol nobles swore an oath of allegiance to the Manchu emperor. The Mongol rulers of Outer Mongolia enjoyed considerable autonomy under the Manchus, and all Chinese claims to Outer Mongolia following the establishment of the republic rested on this oath. "In 1727, Russia and Manchu China concluded the Treaty of Khiakta, delimiting the border between China and Mongolia that exists in large part today".[2]

As Manchu authority in China waned, and as Russia and Japan confronted each other, Russia gave arms and diplomatic support to nationalists among the Mongol religious leaders and nobles.[3] The Mongols accepted Russian aid and proclaimed their independence of Chinese rule in 1911, shortly after a successful Chinese revolt against the Manchus. By agreements signed in 1913 and 1915, the Russian Government forced the new Chinese Republican Government to accept Mongolian autonomy under continued Chinese control, presumably to discourage other foreign powers from approaching a newly independent Mongolian state that might seek support from as many foreign sources as possible.

The Russian revolution and civil war provided Chinese warlords an opportunity to re-establish their rule in Outer Mongolia, and Chinese troops were dispatched there in 1919. Following Soviet military victories over White Russian forces in the early 1920s, and the occupation of the Mongolian capital Urga in July 1921,[4] Mongolia was declared as independent. The Mongolian People's Republic was proclaimed on November 25, 1924 and governmental power under the Communist regime began to be consolidated by the Mongolian People's Revolutionary Party (MPRP). Several factors characterised the country in the post -1921 period: The society was basically nomadic and illiterate; there was no industrial proletariat; the aristocracy and the religious establishment shared the country's wealth; there was widespread popular obedience to traditional authorities; the party lacked grassroots support; and the government had little organisation or experience. In an effort at swift socio-economic reform, the Leftist government applied extreme measures that attacked the two most dominant institutions in the country, the aristocracy and the religious establishment. Between 1932 and 1945, the excess zeal, intolerance, and inexperience led to anti-Communist uprisings.[5] In the late 1930s, purges directed at the religious institution resulted in the desecration of hundreds of Buddhist institutions and imprisonment of more than 10,000 people.

After the World War II, secured in its relations with Moscow, the Mongolian Government shifted its focus to post-war development.[6] International ties were expanded, and Mongolia established relations with North Korea and the new Communist governments in Eastern Europe. It also increased its participation in Communist-sponsored conferences and international organisations. Mongolia became a member of the United Nations in 1961. In the early 1960s, Mongolia attempted to maintain a neutral position amidst increasingly contentious Sino-Soviet polemics; this orientation changed in the middle of the decade. "Mongolia and the Soviet Union signed an agreement in 1966 that introduced large-scale Soviet ground forces as part of Moscow's general build-up along the Sino-Soviet frontier. During the period of Sino-Soviet tensions, relations between Mongolia and China deteriorated. In 1983, Mongolia systematically began expelling some of the 7,000 ethnic Chinese living in Mongolia. Many of them had lived in Mongolia since the 1950s, when they were sent there to assist in construction projects".[7]

During the winter after the fall of the Berlin Wall in 1989, peaceful protests led to the resignation of the politburo in March 1990, and Mongolia's first multi-party elections were held in July 1990. In the democratic era that followed the 1990 elections, Mongolia sought to maintain good relationships with its two immediate neighbours as well as with democratic countries further afield (referred to as "third neighbours"), including the United States. Mongolia also engaged more actively in international organisations including the UN, International Atomic Energy Agency (IAEA), and Association of South-east Asian Nations (ASEAN) Regional Forum and sought membership in the Organisation for Security and Cooperation in Europe (OSCE).[8]

1.2. Impact of Gorbachev's Reforms on Mongolia's Foreign Policy

Mikhail Gorbachev became General Secretary of the Communist Party of the Soviet Union on March 11, 1985 with the new leadership, the conduct of Soviet foreign policy improved. A skillful public relations effort had become an important component of Moscow's diplomacy, but the substance of the USSR.'s international behaviour also changed considerably. Gorbachev himself increasingly talked about the need for "a new approach" in addressing the problems of the world. At the 27th Party Congress in February 1986 he said, "It is not only in internal affairs that the turning point has been reached.[9] It characterises external affairs as well. The changes in contemporary world development are so profound and significant that they require a rethinking and comprehensive analysis of all factors involved.[10] The situation of nuclear deterrence demands the development of new approaches, methods and forms of relations between different social systems, states and regions".

In a speech in Vladivostok in July 1986, Gorbachev was even bolder, claiming that "the current stage in the development of civilization is dictating the need for an urgent, radical break with many of the conventional approaches to foreign policy, a break with the traditions of political thinking".[11] The foreign policy changes under Gorbachev went beyond words. He reshuffled the national security leadership, bringing younger and less doctrinaire officials to key positions and giving himself more personal control over decision-making. "The new team quickly distinguished itself not only in launching Gorbachev's "charm offensive" but also by introducing a wide variety of foreign policy initiatives ranging from arms control proposals to overtures to China".[12]

Gorbachev implemented the policies of *perestroika* and *glasnost*. The atmosphere of reforms in the Soviet Union prompted similar reforms in Mongolia also. Following mass demonstrations in the winter of 1990, the MPRP began to loosen its controls of the political system. The Politburo of the MPRP resigned in March, and in May the constitution was amended, deleting reference to the MPRP's role as the guiding force in the country, legalising opposition parties, creating a standing legislative body, and establishing the office of President. On July 29, 1990, the first free, multi-party elections in Mongolia were held. The election results returned a majority for the MPRP, which won with 85 per cent of the vote.[13] It was not until 1996 that the reformed MPRP was voted out of office by the democrats for the first time in the contemporary history of Mongolia.

The USSR withdrew its troops stationed in Mongolia, and its technical and financial assistance, between 1987 and 1992[14]. Subsequently, the foreign and defense policy of Mongolia was also changed. The impact of Mongolia's internal and external policies changes was that the country declared: "Maintaining friendly relations with the Russian Federation and the People's Republic of China shall be a priority of Mongolia's foreign policy activity.[15] It shall not adopt the line of either countries but shall maintain in principle a balanced relationship with both of them and shall promote all-round good neighbourly co-operation.

1.3. Changes in Mongolia's Foreign Policy before the Period of 1991

Major changes in the foreign policy of Mongolia were seen between 1986 and 1991 first as a result of Gorbachev's reform policies and then due to the collapse of the Soviet Union.[16] The diplomatic relations established with USA, in 1987 was a very significant event in Mongolia's foreign policy changes. Then Mongolia's relations with China started normalising. In that sense changes in Mongolian foreign policy cannot be understood without keeping in mind Mongolia's peculiar international position but before that it is also necessary to understand the role of Mongolian revolution on the country's foreign policy priorities. The Mongolian revolution of 1921 had a very important role to play in Mongolian foreign policy. The meaning of the revolution to the life of the Mongols should be evaluated not in comparison with Western standards, but bearing in mind the problems of life and survival in Mongolia before the revolution. It is true that if the Bolshevik revolution had not taken place in Russia, the Mongol nationalists could never have become really revolutionary, and their mission to Russia would only have been a repetition of what happened in 1911. It is doubtful whether the Mongols could have become even 'bourgeois' revolutionaries. There had been practically no way for them to be influenced by the ideology of Western democracy; and in any case, Western 'democracy' was introduced in Asian countries predominantly in the form of imperialism and colonialism, allying itself with the local feudal and conservative elements.[17] The other neighbour, China, especially in the north, was not yet liberated from the Warlord struggles; and the only philosophy which confronted Bolshevism was Lamaism which had nothing to offer in the way of changing the existing order of society (Isono 1976:394).

As already highlighted, there were two major developments that took place in Mongolia's foreign policy initiatives under the influence of Gorbachev's reform policies. For the first time Mongolia diversified itself to come closer to the United States and established their diplomatic relations in 1987. On the other side normalisation of relations with China also began to be witnessed at about the same time. These two events provided Mongolia a self-confidence to pursue its own independent foreign policy away from the one that was influenced by the Soviet Union. Though in terms of geography Mongolia's international position remained same, in terms of security its international position began to change that after the soviet collapse in 1991 became even more pronounced.

Developments on the international front in 1991 demonstrated Mongolia's commitment to integration as an active participant in the Asia-Pacific community and to strengthening ties with the European Community.[18] These developments were consistent with Mongolia's foreign policy stance as a non-aligned nation (Sheldon R. Severinghaus 1995:75).

Mongolia's recognition of South Korea set its new foreign policy direction. Pyongyang reacted by recalling its ambassador but then sent a new envoy a few weeks later, making Mongolia the first state to achieve diplomatic relations with both governments. Mongolian delegations travelled throughout the world in search of new political, economic, social, and cultural ties, and to promote tourism. Several countries in East Asia agreed to new cooperative relationships; even Taiwan, which formally maintains that Mongolia belongs to the Republic of China, contemplated agricultural and vocational assistance to Ulaanbaatar. Mongolian leaders focussed primarily on the Soviet

Union and China. P. Ochirbat concluded a successful state visit to China in May 1990, and numerous delegations with China were exchanged. Mongolia reopened a consulate in the capital of Inner Mongolia, Hohhot. But despite warm words of friendship and understanding, the Chinese remained wary of the impact of changes in Mongolia on Inner Mongolia. According to a Mongol oppositionist leader, when a delegation from Inner Mongolia attended meetings of the Democratic Party, Beijing protested (William R. Heaton 1991:56).[19]

Mongolia President P. Ochirbat affirmed in November 1990 that all Soviet combat units would be withdrawn from Mongolia by the end of 1991 and all support units by 1992. Mongolia, he said, "would abolish its formal alliance with the USSR and join the non-aligned movement as soon as Soviet troops withdrew". Relations with the West improved. US Secretary of State James Baker visited Mongolia in August 1990, the first high-ranking American to visit since Vice-President Wallace in 1944. Subsequently in October1990, Mongolian Foreign Minister Gombosuren met with Secretary Baker in the US to sign a bilateral investment treaty. Delegations were exchanged with Japan, the UK, France, and other Western countries as Mongolia emphasized its desire to play a more substantial role in the world community (William R. Heaton 1991:56). A rapid resurgency of traditional culture accompanied the opening up of Mongolia's political process as it sought to reduce the influence of Soviet-style communism and the use of traditional symbols to foster national consciousness.

At the domestic level, Ghengis Khan received new attention as a historical figure. The government announced that the traditional script abolished in the 1940s would be restored, taught in the schools, and used in all official correspondence by 1995. Freedom of religion was proclaimed, and Buddhist monasteries were reopened. The Buddhists formed a political party that claimed to have 80,000 members. Thus, 1990 witnessed significant change for the Mongolian People's Republic, though it remained under Communist party control (Heaton 1991:56). As the Heaton described, As Heaton described, "It was a year of reform and upheaval but not as yet revolution". The next three chapters discuss Mongolia's foreign policy in the post-1991 period or more preciously after the collapse of the Soviet Union and the end of the cold war.

1.4: Mongolia's Foreign Policy within Theoretical Prism

1.4.1: Origin and Development of International Relations Theory

The situation of the First World War opened new perspectives in the way the states conducted their relations with one another in the international arena. Before this, a majority of international lawyers believed that the right to declare war without any external approval was inherent in the nature of state sovereignty (Brown and Ainley, 2005:9).[20] Theologians and canon lawyers of the Middle Ages considered wars as just and, that is to say, regular and lawful. For that specific reason, theologians and canon lawyers tried to establish the exercise of war as a legal doctrine and an ethical principle (Brierly, 1945:19; Dugard, 2005:501).[21] The consequences of the First World War were indeed disastrous not only to the states that were attacked, but also to its initiators. Hundred millions of people died, regimes fell, and economies collapsed. How could such a disaster happen, and what solutions needed to be adopted in order to prevent it from happening again? These were the questions that early students of International Relations had to deal with.[22] This step marked the beginning of the theorising about international relations.

The importance of theorising about international relations has to do with the fact that phenomena we need to investigate does not speak for themselves. Halliday, Burchill and Linklater (2005:11)[23] gives three reasons to explain why theories are needed. First, there needs to be some preconceptions of which facts are significant and which are not. Second, any set of facts, even if accepted as true and significant, can yield different interpretations. Third, no human agent, academic or not, can rest content with facts alone because all social activity involves moral questions which cannot be decided by facts. In sum, we theorise because sometimes we ask questions that we are not able to answer without previous reflection, without an appropriate abstract thought.

There are some definitions of theory of different scholars like Hollis and Smith (1990)[24] say that theories attempt either to explain and predict behaviour or to understand the world 'inside the heads' of actors. Theories analyse and try to clarify the use of concepts such as the balance of power (Butterfied and Wight 1966).[25] Theories explain the laws of international politics or recurrent patterns of national behavior (Waltz 1979).[26] Theories are traditions of speculation about relations between states which focus on the struggle for power, the nature of international society and the possibility of a world community (Wight 1991). Theories are empirical data to test hypotheses about the world such as the absence of war between liberal-democratic states (Doyle 1983).[27] Theories criticize forms of domination and perspectives which make the socially constructed and changeable seem natural and unalterable (critical theory), Theories reflect on how the world ought to be organised and analyse ways in which various conceptions of human rights or global social justice are constructed and defend.[28] As the above suggests, different kinds of theories are engaged in the field of International Relations. The diversity of theory comes from the nature of the question we ask. Sometimes, the question is about how things work, or why things happen. Sometimes, the question is about what we should do, either in the sense of what action is instrumental to bringing about a particular kind of result or in the sense of what action is morally right.[29] Sometimes, the question is about what something or other means, how it is to be interpreted (Brown and Ainley 2005:7).

1.4.2 Mongolia's Foreign Policy and its Linkages on International Relations

The field of International Relations can be defined as the study of how authority and power is used to organise and manage trans-border relations between actors, and how this contributes to the establishment, maintenance and transformation of order in the world system (McGowan, Cornelissen and Nel, 2006:12).[30]

On the other hand, Foreign Policy is the sum of official external relations conducted by an independent actor in international relations (Hill, 2003:3). Hill explains that the phrase 'an independent actor' enables the inclusion of phenomena such as the European Union; external relations are 'official' to allow the inclusion of output from all parts of the governing mechanisms of the state or enterprise while also maintaining parsimony with respect to the vast number of international transactions now being conducted; policy is the 'sum' of these official relations because otherwise every particular action could be seen as a separate foreign policy; the policy is 'foreign' because the world is still more separated into distinctive communities than it is a single, homogenising entity.[31]

The idea of foreign policy implies that everything that a given state generates officially at the international level takes into consideration the values and principles that its political leaders wish to display[32]. From these two definitions, one can say that International Relations and Foreign Policy are closely linked. While the former scrutinises trans-borders relations between all international actors including states, INGOs, NGOs, and MNCs and tries to understand what influence these relations may have in the establishment, maintenance and transformation of order in the world system, the later seems to be specifically interested in how, officially, states interact with one another.[33]

Idealism is a term with several related meanings. It comes via *idea* from the Greek *idein*, meaning "to see". The term entered the English language by 1796. In ordinary use, as when speaking of Woodrow Wilson's political idealism, it generally suggests the priority of ideals, principles, values, and goals over concrete realities. Idealists are understood to represent the world as it might or should be, unlike pragmatists, who focus on the world as it presently is. In the arts, similarly, idealism affirms imagination and attempts to realise a mental conception of beauty, a standard of perfection, in opposition to aesthetic naturalism and realism[34]. Besides the fact that Britain, France, and Germany were to be blamed for the destruction on the battlefields of the First World War, there came a realisation that something wrong with the system of International Relations that needed to be revised. Carr (1966:2)[35] revealed that the war of 1914-18 brought an end to the idea that war was a matter which affects solely professional soldiers and dissipated the corresponding impression that international politics could safely be left in the hands of professional diplomats. Subsequently, a great number of thinkers such as Sirs Alfred Zimmern and Philip Noel-Baker and politicians, mostly from America and Britain, gave thought as to how to change the system to prevent a recurrence (Burchill and Linklater 2005:6). For these thinkers, revising international relations was necessary because the old assumptions and prescriptions of power were flawed. The rationale here was that peace would come about only if the classical balance of power were replaced by a system of collective security in which states transferred domestic concepts and practices to the international sphere. From the early 1900s to the late 1930, liberal thinking on international relations impacted significantly on the theory and practice of international relations. Its adherents were motivated by the desire to prevent war.[36] The First World War shifted liberal thinking towards the recognition that peace is not a natural condition, as its followers thought, but one that needed to be constructed and protected (Youla C. 2009).

Writers such as Sir Alfred Zimmern, S.H. Bailey, Philip Noel-Baker, and David Miltrany in the United Kingdom, and James T. Showell, Pitman Potter, and Parker T. Moon in the United States, to whom the term idealists was applied, assumed that the system of international relations that had given rise to the Great War (1914-1918) was "capable of being transformed into a fundamentally more peaceful and just world order; that under the impact of the awakening of democracy, the growth of the international mind, the development of the League of Nations, the good works of men of peace or the enlightenment spread by their own teachings, it was in fact being transformed; and that their responsibility as students of international relations was to assist this march of progress to overcome the ignorance, the prejudices, the ill-will, and the sinister interests that stood in its way" (Bull, 2001:58).[37]

The main assumptions of idealism are outlined below. This is important as it is imperative to assessing what aspects of Mongolia's foreign policy are characterised as idealist, and whether, in fact, idealism was the main driving force behind the country's international relations during this time. Firstly, idealists recognise the fact that international politics take place in an anarchical arena. However, they do not agree that the absence of a central authority above all actors condemns them to a perpetual competition of one against all, as contended by realists. While they do believe that there is competition in the international system, they hold, as Nel (2006:33)[38] states, that humans learn from their experience. Once they realise that all-out confrontation on a specific issue leads only to mutual disappointment and losses, they become willing to consider options that provide some chances for mutual gains, even if these gains are not the maximum the states aimed for at the beginning. Although the international system is anarchic, it has never been anomic (without rules) (Little, 2001:299).[39] Little considers that an important dimension of globalisation has been the establishment of worldwide regimes to foster rule-governed activity within the international system. As a result, there is now no international intercourse devoid of regimes, where states are not circumscribed, to some extent or other, by the existence of mutually accepted sets of rules. In connection with this, idealists posit that the absence of war cannot always be explained in terms of an existence of a balance of power. It can also be the result of the fact that states share a number of values. This explains why idealists tend to favour co-operation between states on an increasing range of issues such as global security, health, economic development, environment, and so forth. But, for them, co-operation between states needs to take place in a well-structured environment in which states can trust each other.[40] In this regard, the respect for international law and international organisations appears to be of a great importance (Youla 2009).

Secondly, idealists assert that morality plays an important role in international affairs. They point to the historical record to prove their point. Since the establishment of the modern state system, states have established many international moral principles and regimes through cooperation with one another. Religious freedom has been recognised, slavery has been outlawed and abolished, humane rules of warfare have been accepted, a universal Declaration of Human Rights has been accepted by most states in the world, torture has been outlawed, and the world community has taken steps to punish perpetrators of genocide (Nel, 2006:34).[41]

The idea that the state should respect the human rights of its citizens, as Schmitz and Sikkink (2002:518)[42] declare, is an old one dating back to the struggles for religious freedom and the secular writings of Kant, Locke and Rousseau. The US Bill of Rights and the French Declaration of the Rights of Man and of the Citizens were the most significant early transactions of efforts to give the individual special and inalienable protections.[43] What has emerged more recently, Schmitz and Sikkink argue, is the idealist-driven idea that not only states, but individuals, can be subjects in international law and that human rights should be an integral part of foreign policy and international relations.

Thirdly, idealists claim that non-state actors are also important entities in international politics. Idealists agree that the state is a very important actor in international affairs, but they refuse to regard it as necessarily the most important. In today's world of diverse and complex challenges, global governance involves a variety of international actors including states, IGOs, NGOs, MNCs, transnational social movements, and individuals.[44] In light of how the balance between states and non-state actors has shifted over the past few decades, idealists believe that any interpretation of international relations must now take the significance of non-state actors.

Finally idealists maintain that the agenda of international politics is extensive and not dominated primarily by military-security issues as suggested by realists. For idealist adherents, foreign affairs agendas have expanded and diversified over recent decades such that economic and social issues are often at the forefront of foreign policy debates (Viotti and Kauppi, 1993:8).[45] The problems of energy, resources, environment, pollution, the uses of spaces and the seas now rank with questions of military security, ideology, and territorial rivalry which have traditionally made up the diplomatic agenda (Keohane and Nye, 1997:3).[46]

As the above suggests, there is an increasingly wide-ranging agenda in international affairs, with political, economic, and social issues that are as, or more, important than military-security issues. In summary, democracy, the rule of law, human rights, collective security, and co-operation are some of the subjects that are very important in the idealist lexicon. After the collapse of the League of Nations, which, sometimes in the history of the field of international relations, is mistakenly considered as the end of the idealism tradition by some writers, certain fundamental idealist principles remained. Mongolia foreign policy priority also based on a number of these fundamental tenets constitutes the core principles of what subsequently became known as liberal institutionalism. In short, liberal institutionalists, like idealists before them, insist on international institutions to carry out a number of tasks that the state cannot perform on its own. By so doing, they have been in the process of perpetuating the idealist tradition (Youla 2009).[47]

In this contest we can say that, Mongolia's foreign policy based on its national interests in one hand and maintaining friendly relations with international community in terms of economic, political and security interest in other.

Realism is the view that world politics are driven by competitive self-interest. Realists believe that there are no universal principles with which all states may guide their actions. Instead, a state must always be aware of the actions of the states around it and must use a pragmatic approach to resolve problems as they arise[48]. Carr asserts in his book entitled 'The twenty years' crisis: 1919-1939' that the three essential tenets implicit in Machiavelli's doctrine constitute the foundation stones of the realist philosophy. "First, history is a sequence of cause and effect, whose course can be analysed and understood by intellectual effort, but not (as the idealists, or utopians as he renamed them, believe) directed by imagination. Second, theory does not create practice, but practice theory. Third, politics are not a function of ethics, but ethics of politics". From this quote, Carr seems to suggest that the purpose of a theory should be to collect, classify and analyse existing facts in order to draw interferences, and not the other way around as, according to him, idealists did.[49] In the same vein, Morgenthau (1973:3) notes that the test by which a theory must be judged is not a priori and abstract but empirical and pragmatic. A theory, according to Morgenthau, must be judged not by some preconceived abstract principle or concept unrelated to reality, but by its purpose, which is to bring order and meaning to the plethora of phenomena that exist in the real world (Youla 2009).

If the purpose of a theory is to collect and analyse existing facts, this, according to Carr (1966:5), does not apply to idealism. Carr explains that idealists paid little attention to existing facts or analyse of cause and effect, but rather devoted themselves whole-heartedly to the elaboration of visionary projects. The combination of the decline of liberal thinking in the late 1930s and the outbreak of World War II revitalised the realist perception of the role of power, defined as capability relative to other states. Keohane (1986:9)[50] states that since 1945, discussions of foreign policy have been carried on in the language of political realism that is, the language of power and interests rather than ideals or norms. In the same vein, Morgenthau characterises international politics as the struggle for power. According to him, this could be understood by assuming that statesmen "think and act in terms of interest defined as power" (Carr 1966:29). The idea of power being the most important thing in international relations lasted until the Cold War. Despite the fact that the Cold War was a period of conflict, tension and competition between the United States and the Soviet Union and their respective allies, no real war occurred during that period. Many realists attributed the absence of war to the bipolar nature of the post-war international system. With the end of the Cold War, most realists agreed that bipolarity had come to an end, although they disagreed about when and why it happened. Drawing on classical realism's apparent failure to develop an operational measure of polarity that could distinguish cause from effect, Waltz built a formal deductive theory of international relations which he called neorealism. Waltz's theory emphasises the importance of the structure (anarchy) of the international system and its role as the primary determinant of state behaviour. With above mentioned view, Mongolian foreign policy highlighted national interest in the ground of multi-bases foreign policy and avoiding confrontation with any other countries. In the concept of Mongolian foreign policy,[51] it is pointed out Mongolia will not interfere in the disputes between its neighbouring countries unless the disputes affect Mongolia's national interests. Mongolia is guided by universally recognised principles and norms of international law as defined in the Charter of the United Nations, including mutual respect for each other's sovereignty, territorial integrity and inviolability of frontiers, right to self-determination, non-interference in internal affairs, non-use of force, settlement of disputes by peaceful means, respect for human rights and freedoms, and equal and mutually beneficial cooperation. In this regards this document says that, foreign policy of Mongolia shall uphold peace, strive to avoid confrontation with other countries and pursue a multi-base policy.

Neo-realism is outlined by Kenneth Waltz in his 1979 book "*Theory of International Politics*". Waltz argues in favour of a systemic approach: the international structure acts as a constraint on state behaviour, so that only states whose outcomes fall within an expected range survive.[52] Neo-realism is distinctive from traditional or classical realism in a number of ways. Lamy (2001:185-186)[53] mentions three of them. Firstly, neo-realist believes that the effects of structure are as important as the actions and interactions of states in the international system.[54] According to Waltz, structure is defined by the ordering principle of the international system, which is anarchy, and the distribution of capabilities across units, which are states (Youla 2009).

Form neo-realist adherents, these two elements participate in shaping all foreign policy choices and, therefore, must be considered in our attempts to explain international politics. Secondly, contrary to realists who see power as an end in itself, neo-realist think that power is more than the accumulation of military resources and the ability to use this power to coerce and control other states in the system. In the neo-realist lexicon, power is simply the combined capabilities of a state. States are differentiated in the system by their power and not by their function. Power gives a state a place or position in the international system and that shapes the state's behaviour thirdly, neo-realists reject classical realists view on how states react to the condition of anarchy. Lame explains that to classical realists, anarchy is a condition of the system, and states react to it according to their size, location, domestic politics, and leadership qualities. Neo-realists, in contrast, suggest that anarchy defines the system. All states are functionally similar units, meaning that they all experience the same constraints presented by anarchy and strive to maintain their position in the system. Consequently, neo-realists believe that what results in differences in policy between states is the combination of differences in their power and capabilities. The importance of Waltz's theory, as Keohane (1986:15) points it, lies less in his initiation of a new line of theoretical inquiry or speculation than in his attempt to systematise political realism into a rigorous, deductive systemic theory of international politics.[55] In this sense, the Waltzian synthesis is referred to as neo-realism to indicate both its intellectual affinity with the classical realism of E.H. Carr, Hans Morgenthau, and Reinhold Niebuhr and its elements of originality and distinctiveness (Youla 2009). Realists believe that only states with power have a better chance of surviving than states with less power because, as Morgenthau (1966:29) points out, international politics, like national politics, is a struggle for power. Realists focus on material power mainly in the form of military strength. According to Viotti and Kauppi (1993:56), however, economic factors are also very important to realists because they affect national power or capabilities. These two authors observe that industrial countries that effectively combine technology with capital, skilled labour and raw materials not only enjoy a higher standard of living but also tend to have more leverage in their relations with others (Youla

2009).[56] In addition to trade, financial, and monetary influence that flows from a strong economy, military capabilities are usually greatest in states with advanced industrial economies.

"Realist believe that states are self-interested oriented and that their behaviour is largely shaped by the anarchic structure of the international system (Mearsheimer, 1994:5)".[57] For this reason, they recommend states to make use of all necessary means to safeguard or increase their interests while dealing with others. In short, realism emphasises the constraints on politics imposed by human selfishness ('egoism') and the absence of international government ('anarchy'), which require the primacy in all political life of power and security (Gilpin, cited in Donnelly 2005).[58] In this regard, unlike idealists, realists do not believe in the natural harmony of interests among states. Thirdly, realists are very skeptical about the role of morality in international affairs. Realist supporters frequently speak of a dual moral standard: one moral standard for individual citizens living inside the state and a different standard for the state in its external relations with other states. The exclusion of morality from foreign policy is an important feature of realism. Beyond the appeals to anarchy and egoism, many realists argue that morality is inappropriate in foreign policy because international politics is a distinct realm of human endeavour with its own standards and rules (Donnelly, 2000:161-164). For realist adherents, the nature of the environment within which international politics take place has created a necessary condition for state leaders to act in a way that would be unacceptable or immoral for the individual. For this reason, realists consider the act of cheating, lying and killing as moral duties of state leaders, since their task is to preserve the life of the state and the ethical community it contains (Dunne and Schmidt, 2001:144). Fourthly, the anarchic character of the international system has given an exclusive emphasis to the principle of self-help (or self-interest). According to Waltz (1979:102)[59] "the state among states conducts its affairs in brooding shadow of violence". This is, he explains, because "some states may at any time use force, all states must be prepared to do so or live at the mercy of their militarily more vigorous neighbours". Among states, the state of nature is a state of war. Contrary to domestic politics where a wide range of institutions and mechanisms seek to ensure the welfare of individuals, at the international level these are either non-existent or extremely weak. Related to this, realists posit that each state actor is responsible for ensuring their well-being and survival. In this sense, they do not think it is prudent for a state to entrust its safety and survival to another actor or international institution such as the League of Nations or the United Nations because, as Machiavelli stated, today's friend can quickly become tomorrow's enemy (Dunne and Schmidt, 2001:144).[60]

The principle of self-help is also strengthened by the fact that realists view the state as a unitary actor, that is to say that it faces the world as an integrated unit (Viotti and Kauppi, 1993:32).[61] The idea behind this is that political differences within the state are ultimately resolved authoritatively such that the government of the state speaks with one voice for the state as a whole. This emphasis on the unitary nature has led to the belief that the state is essentially a rational actor. A rational foreign policy decision-making process, as Viotti and Kauppi explain, "Would include a statement of objectives, consideration of all feasible alternatives in terms of existing capabilities available to the state, the relative likelihood of attaining these various objectives under consideration, and the benefits or cost associated with each alternative".[62] In brief, it assumes that any chosen behaviour can be understood as optimising material self-interest (Neuman, 1998:5).

In this context, we find that, within anarchical environment, Mongolia has shaped its foreign policy choices and accumulated its ability to use control other states in the system. This denotes its sovereignty in international anarchical system and strengthening national interest on the ground of choices and ability formulated by her foreign policy documents.

Constructivism is the claim that significant aspects of international relations are historically and socially contingent, rather than inevitable consequences of human nature or other essential characteristics of world politics.[63] The end of the Cold War opened a space for alternative explanatory perspectives and prompted critically inclined scholars to move away from a narrowly defined meta-theoretical critique (Reus Smit 2005:195). By the beginning of the 1990s, a new generation of young scholars emerged and initiated a new line of enquiry or speculation about world politics called constructivism. The writings of Friedrich Kratochwil (1989), Nicholas Onuf (1989) and Alexander Wendt (1987, 1992) established constructivist ideas as a genuinely radical alternative to conventional IR theories (Brown and Ainley, 2005:49). The leads of constructivist followers to the conclusion that the social world is constructed, not given. States may be self-interested but they continuously define what that means (Youla 2009).[64] In other words, the identities and interests of states that rationalists take as given and which they see as resulting in international relations are not in fact given but are things that states have created (Smith, 2001:244).[65]

Despite the divisions amongst constructivists regarding certain issues, all of them have, according to Reus-Smit (2005:196),[66] sought to articulate and explore three core ontological propositions about social life, propositions which, they claim, illuminate more about world politics than rival rationalist assumptions. First, to the extent that structures can be said to shape the behaviour of social and political actors, be they individuals or states, constructivists hold that normative or ideational structures are just as important as material structures. Where neo-realists emphasise the material structure of the balance of military power, constructivists argue that systems of shared ideas, beliefs and values also have structural characteristics, and that they exert a powerful influence on social and political action. This, they argue, is because (1) "material resources only acquire meaning for human action through the structure of shared knowledge in which they are embedded" (Wendt, cited in Adler, 2002:100),[67] and (2) "normative and ideational factors are thought to shape the social identities of political actors". In this sense, social facts, which are facts only by human agreement and which account for the majority of the fact studied in IR, differ from other physical facts, because unlike the latter, their existence depends on human consciousness and language (Adler, 2002:100).[68] In the same vein, Brown and Ainley (2005:49)[69] posit that mistaking a social fact for a brute fact is a cardinal error, because it leads to the ascription of a natural status to conditions that have been produced and may be, in principle, open to change.[70] For Brown and Ainley, if we treat 'anarchy' as a given, something that conditions state action without itself being conditioned by state action, we will miss the point that 'anarchy' is, as Wendt declares, what states make of it and that it does not, as such, dictate any particular course of action (Youla 2009).

In the field of international relation, anarchy means there is no centralised political authority above sovereign states', though it may, mean chaos. Viewed in this context, the possibility exists that within an anarchical framework norms can emerge. Second, contrary to rationalists who believe that actors' interests are exogenously determined, meaning that actors, be they individuals or states, encounter one another with a pre-existing set of preferences, constructivists argue that understanding how actors develop their interests is crucial to explaining a wide range of international political phenomena that rationalists ignore or misunderstand. In order to explain interest formation, constructivists focus on social identities of individuals or states.[71] Third, constructivists assert that agents and structures are mutually constituted. The construction of cognitive frames is an essential component of norm entrepreneurs' political strategies, because, when they are successful, the new frames resonate with broader public understandings and are adopted as new ways of talking about and understanding issues. However, in constructing their frames, norm entrepreneurs face firmly embedded alternative norms and frames that create alternative perceptions of both appropriateness and interest.[72] As van der Westhuizen (2004:5)[73] declares, the potential receptivity of a norm is enhanced when it fits with the normative practices and beliefs of the actor; if the arguments are held to be congruent with the self-conceptualised identity of the actor; and if the argument matches with existing social structures that are a consequence of the belief systems through which societies are ordered. In other words, new norms never enter a normative vacuum, but instead emerge in a highly-contested normative space where they must compete with other norms and perceptions of interests. To promote their norms at the international level, all norm entrepreneurs need some kind of organisational platforms. Sometimes, these platforms are constructed specifically for the purpose of promoting the norm, as are many NGOs and IGOs. But, whatever their platforms,[74] norm promoters and the organisations they inhabit usually need to secure the support of state actors to endorse their norms and make norm socialisation a part of their agenda, and different organisational platforms provide different kinds of tools for entrepreneurs to do this (Finnemore and Sikkink, 1998:899-900).

The second stage, norm cascade, is characterised more by a dynamic of imitation as the norm leaders attempt to socialise other states to become norm followers. Framing new norms is essential to overcome extrinsic constraints, but, as van der Westhuizen (2004:4) comments, the minimum extrinsic requirement is that an argument must be heard and intrinsic barriers include the fit with dominant belief systems, notions of identity and social institutions. The exact motivation behind this varies with the norm and the entrepreneur. Finnemore and Sikkink comment that for many of the social norms of interest to political scientists, these motivations include empathy, altruism, and ideational commitment. Empathy, they declare, exists when actors have the capacity for participating in another's feelings or ideas. Such empathy may lead to empathetic interdependence, where actors are interested in the welfare of others for its own sake, even if this has no effect on their own material well-being or security. Altruism exists when actors actually take action designed to benefit another even at the risk of significant harm to the actor's own well-being. Ideational commitment is the main motivation when entrepreneurs promote norms or ideas because they believe in the ideals and the values embodied in the norms, even though the pursuit of the norms may have no effect on their well being (Youla 2009). At the end of this phase, norm internationalisation occurs.

Norm internationalisation is the final stage of the "life cycle" of a norm. At the far end of the norm cascade, norms may become so widely accepted that they are internationalised by actors and achieve a "taken-for-granted" quality that makes conformance with the norm almost automatic. Internationalised norms can be both extremely powerful (because behaviour according to the norm is not questioned) and hard to discern (because actors do not seriously consider or discuss whether to conform). Completion of the "life cycle" is not, as Finnemore and Sikkink declare an inevitable process. Many emergent norms fail to reach a tipping point. In summary, as the above suggests, constructivists are not interested in how things are, nor in how they ought to be, but in how did they become what they are. Taken in this context, constructivism appears totally different from idealism and realism. From a constructivist perspective, international structure is determined by international distribution of ideas. Shared ideas, expectations, and beliefs about appropriate behaviour are what give the world structure, order, and stability.[75] Norms channel and regularise behaviour; often limit the range of choice and constrain action (Finnemore and Sikkink, 1998:894).

When the above mentioned theoretical framework of foreign policy is conceptualised in the Mongolian context, theory of "realism" seems to be most appropriate. This is more so because Mongolia's foreign policy is based on pragmatism, i.e., Mongolia follows pragmatic approach in the conduct of its foreign policy, which was adopted in 1994. This has been quite a different foreign policy from what was there in Mongolia in the pre-1986 period. Therefore, in order to understand Mongolia's foreign policy in the post -1986 period, *i.e.* during the reform period, there is a need to have a look on pre-1986 foreign policy and the systematic changes occurred in it before the collapse of the former Soviet Union.

Notes and References

1. http://www.mtac.gov.tw/mtacbook/upload/09505/0701/3.pdf
2. US Department of State Diplomacy in Action, *Bureau of East Asian and Pacific Affairs*, January 6, 2012, http: //www.state.gov/r/pa/ei/bgn/2779.
3. http://www.state.gov/r/pa/ei/bgn/2779.htm.
4. http://www.scoop.co.nz/stories/WO0903/S00062.htm.
5. U.S. Department of State Diplomacy in Action, *Bureau of East Asian and Pacific Affairs*, January 6, 2012, http: //www.state.gov/r/pa/ei/bgn/2779.
6. http://www.state.gov/r/pa/ei/bgn/2779.htm.
7. *Ibid.*
8. *Ibid.*
9. http://www.foreignaffairs.com/articles/41714/dimitri-k-simes/gorbachev-a-new-foreign-policy.
10. Permanent Mission of Mongolia to the United Nations, Concept of Mongolia's Foreign Policy, 1994.
11. *Ibid.*
12. http://www.foreignaffairs.com/articles/41714/dimitri-k-simes/gorbachev-a-new-foreign-policy.
13. http://www.uniblogger.com/en/Mongolian_People's_Republic
14. Mongolia, Landmine Monitor Report 2000.
15. Permanent Mission of Mongolia to the United Nations, Concept of Mongolia's Foreign Policy, 1994.

16. When USSR collapsed in 1991 and many changes happened in international relations.

17. Fujiko Isono. "The Mongolian Revolution of 1921", Modern Asian Studies, 07/1976.

18. This is according to NSC Secretary J. Enhsaihan, as reported in Mongol Messenger, August 9, 1994.

19. "We need a Popular Revolution," interview with G. Bosigt by Lajos Kormendi, Nep-szabadsag (Budapest), 18 September 1990; FBIS, DR/AP, 26th September 1990.

20. Brown, Chris, and Kirsten Ainley. Understanding International Relations. 3rd ed. New York: Palgrave MacMillan, 2005.

21. Dugard, J. (2005) International Law: A South African Perspective (3rd ed.).

22. Youla Christian (2009), Thesis presented in partial fulfillments for degree of Masters of Arts (International Studies), Stellenbosch University.

23. http://scholar.sun.ac.za/bitstream/handle/10019.1/1592/Youla,%20 C.pdf.txt?sequence=2.

24. Baylis and S. Smith (eds). *The Globalisation of World Politics: An introduction to international relations,* (2nd ed.) Oxford: Oxford University Press.

25. http://scholar.sun.ac.za/bitstream/handle/10019.1/1592/Youla,%20C. pdf.txt?sequence=2.

26. Waltz, K.N. (1979), *Theory of International Politics*, California: Addition-Wesley Publishing Company.

27. http://frenndw.files.wordpress.com/2010/03/thi-theories-of-international. pdf.

28. http://us.macmillan.com/CMS400/uploadedFiles/PalgraveTrade/Non Menu_Items/TheoriesofInternational.pdf.

29. http://www.palgrave.com/Pdfs/1403946647.pdf.

30. http://scholar.sun.ac.za/bitstream/handle/10019.1/1592/Youla,%20C.pdf.txt?sequence=2.

31. Youla Christian (2009), Thesis presented in partial fulfillments for degree of Masters of Arts (International Studies), Stellenbosch University.

32. *Ibid.*

33. *Ibid.*

34. http://dictionary.reference.com/browse/idealism dated on 28 may 2012.

35. http://scholar.sun.ac.za/bitstream/handle/10019.1/1592/Youla,%20C.pdf. txt?sequence=2.

36. *Ibid.*

37. Bull, H. (2001) "The theory of international politics 1919-1969" in Andrew Linklater. International Relations: Critical Concepts in Political Science (Vol I). London: Routledge.

38. Nel, P. (2006) "Theories of International Relations" in P. J. McGowan, S. Cornelissen and P. Nel (eds). Power, Wealth and Global Equity: An International Relations Textbook for Africa (2nd ed). Cap Town: UCT Press.

39. Little, R. (2001) "International Regimes" in J. Baylis and S. Smith (eds). The Globalisation of World Politics: Introduction to international relations. (2nd ed.) Oxford: Oxford University Press.

40. Youla Christian (2009), Thesis presented in partial fulfillments for degree of Masters of Arts (International Studies), Stellenbosch University.

41. Nel, P. (2006) "Theories of International Relations" in P. J. McGowan, S. Cornelissen and P. Nel (eds). Power, Wealth and Global Equity: An International Relations Textbook for Africa (2nd ed). Cap Town: UCT Press.

42. Schmitz, H.P. and Sikkink, K. (2002) "International Human Rights" in W. Carlsnaes, T. Risse and B.A. Simmons. Handbook of International Relations. London: SAGE Publications.

43. *Ibid.*

44. *Ibid.*

45. Viotti, P. R., and Kauppi, M. V. (1993) International relations theory: realism, pluralism, globalism. New York : Macmillan, 1993.

46. Keohane, R.O. and Nye, J.S. (1989) Power and Interdependence: World Politics in Transition (2nd ed.). Scott, Foresman and Company.

47. Youla Christian (2009), Thesis presented in partial fulfillments for degree of Masters of Arts (International Studies), Stellenbosch University.

48. Ashley, Richard K. (1981) "Political Realism and the Human Interests," *International Studies Quarterly* 25: 204-36.

49. Youla Christian (2009), Thesis presented in partial fulfillments for degree of Masters of Arts (International Studies), Stellenbosch University.

50. Keohane, R.O. (1986) Neo-realism and its critics. New York: Columbia University Press.

51. Embassy of Mongoliya in the Uk http://www. embassy ofmongolia. co.uk/index.php?option=com_content& view=article &id=59& Itemid=76&lang=en.

52. Waltz, Kenneth Neal (1979). Theory of International Politics. Reading, MA: Addison–Wesley Pub. Co.

53. Lamy, S.L. (2001) "Contemporary mainstream approaches: neo-realism and neo-liberalism" in J. Baylis and S. Smith (eds). The Globalisation of World Politics: Introduction to international relations. (2nd ed.) Oxford: Oxford University Press.

54. Youla Christian (2009), Thesis presented in partial fulfillments for degree of Masters of Arts (International Studies), Stellenbosch University.

55. Youla Christian (2009), Thesis presented in partial fulfillments for degree of Masters of Arts (International Studies), Stellenbosch University.

56. *Ibid.*

57. Mearsheimer, J. (1994) "The False Promise of International Institutions". International Security, 19:5-49.

58. Donnelly, J. (2000) Realism and International Relations. United Kingdom: Cambridge University Press.

59. Waltz, K.N. (1979) Theory of International Politics. California: Addition-Wesley Publishing Company.

60. Dunne, T. and Schmidt, B. C. (2001) "Liberalism" in John Baylis and Steve Smith (eds.) The Globalisation of World Politics: Introduction to international relations. (2nd ed.) Oxford: Oxford University Press.

61. Viotti, P. R., and Kauppi, M. V. (1993) International relations theory : realism, pluralism, globalism. New York : Macmillan, 1993.

62. Neuman, S.G. (1998) International Relations Theory and the Third World . London: Macmillan.

63. Patrick Thaddeus Jackson and Daniel H. Nexon, "Whence Causal Mechanisms? A Comment on Legro" in *Dialogue IO* Vol. 1, 2002.

64. Youla Christian (2009), Thesis presented in partial fulfillments for degree of Masters of Arts (International Studies), Stellenbosch University.

65. Smith, S. (2001) "Reflectivist and constructivist approaches to international theory" in J. Baylis and S. Smith (eds). The Globalisation of World Politics: An introduction to international relations. (2nd ed.) Oxford: Oxford University Press.

66. Reus-Smit, C. (2005) "Constructivism" in S. Burchi ll, A. Linklater, R. Davetak, J. Donnelly, M. Paterson, C. Reus-S mit and J. True. Theories of International Relations (3rd ed.) Houndsmills: Palgrave Macmillan.

67. Adler, E. (2002) "Constructivism and International Relations" in Carlsnaes, T. Rise, and Beth A. Simmons (eds). Handbook of International Relations. London: SAGE.

68. Adler, E. (2002) "Constructivism and International Relations" in Carlsnaes, T. Rise, and Beth A. Simmons (eds). Handbook of International Relations. London: SAGE.

69. Brown, C. and Ainley, K. (2005) Understanding International Relations. London: Palgrave.

70. Youla Christian (2009), Thesis presented in partial fulfillments for degree of Masters of Arts (International Studies), Stellenbosch University.

71. Student papers from 08-Nov-2009, Submitted to University of Oklahoma on 2009-11-08.

72. Development.net/Projekte/Nachhaltigkeit/DVD_10_Footprint/ Material/pdf/Puschkarsky_2009_GFN_ Norm_of_Sustainability. pdf, http://www. conservation.

73. Van der Westhuizen, J., Taylor, I. and Nel, P. (1999) "of Rogues, Rebels, Renegades and Reformist: South African Multilateralism in Context" in South Africa's Multilateral Diplomacy and Global Change: The limits of Reformism. Ashgate: Aldershot.

74. Schmitz, H.P. and Sikkink, K. (2002) "International Human Rights" in W. Carlsnaes, T. Risse and B. A. Simmons. Handbook of International Relations. London: SAGE Publications.

75. Finnemore, M. and Sikkink, K. (1998) "International Norms Dynamic and Political Change" in International Organisation, Vol. 52, No. 4:887-917.

2

Changing Mongolia's Foreign Policy: Domestic Factor

With Mongolia's borders secured and relations with neighbours stable, in the post-soviet period, Mongolia began focussing on a number of pressing domestic socio-economic issues. Unemployment, poverty[1], rapid urbanisation and the ensuing social displacement posed potential threats to the long-term stability and economic prosperity (Soni 2006:38). And Mongolia had no option but to take such measures that could help the country progress both at the domestic as well as foreign affairs levels at a time when globalisation was becoming the order of the day.[2] In that sense introduction of democracy and market economy brought about significant changes in Mongolia's domestic policy which ultimately influenced the country's foreign policy as well.

2.1 Democracy and Market Economy in Mongolia

The 1990 unrest in Mongolia was a peaceful democratic revolution that started with hunger strikes to overthrow ruling Communist government and eventually move towards democratic changes by adopting a new constitution. It was spearheaded by mostly younger people demonstrating on Sukhbaatar Square in the capital Ulan Bator. It ended with the authoritarian government resigning without bloodshed. Some of the main organisers were Sanjaasurengiin Zorig, Erdeniin Bat-Uul, Bat-Erdeniin Batbayar, and Tsakhiagiin Elbegdorj.

Finally, the peaceful revolution revived the thousand year-old parliamentary tradition of Mongolia. This was the beginning of the end of the 70-year period of socialism in Mongolia. Although a multi-party system was established, the Mongolian People's Revolutionary Party (MPRP) actually remained in power until 1996. Nevertheless, reforms were implemented and the transition to a market economy begun.

In fact, the revolution was inspired by the reforms in the former Soviet Union and by the similar revolutions in Eastern Europe in late 1989.[3] The Mongolian People's Party took power in Mongolia in 1921. Over the following decades, Mongolia was always very closely aligned with the Soviet Union, who in turn guaranteed Mongolia's independence from China. After the ousting of Yumjaagiin Tsedenbal in 1984, and inspired by Mikhail Gorbachev's reforms in the Soviet Union, the new leadership under Jambyn Batmönkh implemented economic reforms, but failed to appeal to those who, in the late 1989, wanted broader changes.[4]

As such the first small scale public protests occurred on December 10, 1989, in front of the Cultural Center for Youth. The protesters called for Mongolia to follow the Soviet Union and adopt *perestroika* and *glasnost*. Dissident leaders demanded free elections and economic reform. On January 14, 1990, the protesters, having grown from two hundred to some 1,000, met at the Lenin Museum in Ulan Bator.[5] A demonstration at Sukhbaatar Square on January 21 followed. After then came weekend demonstrations in January and February and the forming of Mongolia's first opposition parties. On March 7, 1990 ten dissidents assembled at Sukhbaatar Square and went on a hunger strike. Thousands of supporters joined them. On March 9, 1990, the Communist MPRP government resigned. The new government announced Mongolia's first free parliamentary elections, which were to be held in July 1990.[6] Unrest also spread to the other industrial centers in Erdenet and Darkhan, and to the province centers, notably Moron in Khovsgl.

However, the opposition parties failed to win a majority in the 1990 elections. There had been 430 seats in the Great Khural, and the opposition parties had been unable to nominate enough candidates as they mustered only 346. Also, the MPRP enjoyed a strong position in the countryside. Consequently, the MPRP won 357 seats in the Great and 31 (out of 53) in the Small Khural.

Nonetheless, the new MPRP government under D. Byambasuren shared power with the democrats, and implemented constitutional and economic reforms. As these reforms coincided with the dissolution of the Soviet Union, which had until 1990 provided significant economic aid to Mongolia's state budget, the country did experience harsh economic problems: enterprises were closed down, inflation rose, and basic foodstuffs had to be rationed for a time. The first election win for the opposition was the presidential election of 1993, when the opposition democrat's candidate P. Ochirbat won.[7] In 1996, the opposition for the first time succeeded in winning the majority in the State of Great Khural also.

During Socialist times, Mongolia did not have any political opposition groups. Noblemen along with monks were commonly persecuted. Even the highest Buddhist monk was a former university professor, which the Mongolian People's Revolutionary Party (MPRP) sent to serve as Hamba Lama to the monastery Gandan. Therefore, socialism or communism was accepted by all as a social stratus in Mongolia. Suddenly in the late 1980s, Mikhail Gorbachev's perestroika, or restructuring, occupied the thoughts of many Mongolian intellectuals. Many forbidden topics suddenly became open for discussion. The MPRP did not have a clear idea of how to deal with the news of change from the Soviet Union. The MPRP alone with other Communist parties were rigid and conservative. What is significant note here that the MPRP waited but did not receive clear instructions from the Communist Party of the Soviet Union about what to do? For the first time since 1921, the governing party did not have any instructions from Moscow and so it fell into a total depression.[8]

Many Mongolian intellectuals saw that time as an opportunity to change their lives. For the most part, life was miserable with pathetic dreams of winter coats or tiny apartments. In terms of employment, the system of career growth in socialist Mongolia was very restricted. First of all, it required party membership. Unfortunately, the dream of party membership in the MPRP was forbidden for children of government officials, artists and professors. "Even Vladimir Lenin stated that these were the most unreliable parts of the social strata. Therefore, if you were a factory worker or herder, oddly, then you were welcomed for the most part to join the party".

When Democratic movements first popped up in Mongolia, they were mainly limited to universities and other academic institutions. Most current leaders of the Democratic Party (DP) joined these movements much later.[9] At that time, the future of the democratic movements was precarious at best though Mongolians saw what happened in other socialist countries, especially in Asia and this resulted in taking place several events as the domestic level which saw Mongolia's transition to democracy and market economy from communism and state controlled economy.

Mongolia has been one of the most interesting of the economies in transition from central planning during the 1990s. Massive external shocks in 1989 and 1990 led unexpectedly and suddenly to what was possibly the largest ever peacetime decline in a country' s gross national expenditure. At the same time Mongolia embraced democracy and rapid economic reform, which exacerbated the decline in output and high inflation. Despite expectations of a political backlash, the 1996 elections produced a pro-reform government which accelerated economic liberalisation. By the late 1990s Mongolia was pursuing a policy of almost complete free trade and had one of the most flourishing democracies in Asia.[10]

Mongolia is an exception for its level of democratisation compared to its distance from the possible spatial influences of the West (Kopstein and Reilly 2000: 9-12).[11] Outside these socio-economic, cultural, and general geographical concerns, Mongolia serves as an exception to broader regional trends. Uzbekistan, Turkmenistan, Tajikistan, Kazakhstan, and Kyrgyzstan have had significant difficulties in establishing even basic democratic institutions and procedures, and have had persistent problems with the violation of fundamental human rights (Fish 1998 and Reilly 2000),[12] while Mongolia's process of democratisation has not been subject to undue interference from either Russia or China (Fish 1998 2001; Fritz 2002; Sabloff 2002).[13] The most remarkable feature of Mongolia is the peaceful manner in which it achieved a transition from a centrally-controlled political system to a democracy with flourishing political parties and a participating electorate.[14] The advent of unprecedented political freedom and a stable, open political system augurs well for future economic growth and improved quality of life (UNDP, 1997: 29).

The introduction of democracy and market economy in Mongolia also lies into fact that the 1980s saw a major growth spurt as Mongolia was more tightly integrated into the Council for Mutual Economic Assistance (CMEA) international planning system. With large inflows of capital, inputs and technology from Eastern Europe and the Soviet Union, net imports amounted to a massive 30 per cent of GDP. Industry, and especially mining, developed rapidly. Mongolia was so completely integrated both politically and economically with the Soviet Union that it acquired the label of the 16th republic'. This world was turned upside down in the second half of 1989 with the collapse of communism in Eastern Europe and the effective disintegration of the CMEA. Soviet ties were maintained, but the flow of assistance declined in 1990 as the USSR itself experienced growing economic difficulties. In 1991, as the Soviet Union dissolved, Mongolia suffered a huge negative economic shock. Not only did net inflows cease, but also supply chains broke and the favourable terms of trade arising from underpriced Soviet oil and other supplies and overpriced payments for Mongolian copper exports came to an end.[15] The combined shock has been estimated at equal to loss of around half of gross national expenditure (Pomfret 1993; Boone 1994).

Despite its vassal status, Mongolia had the advantage over the other 15 other Soviet republics that it was already a sovereign state with internationally recognised borders, national institutions and the trappings of statehood. As the elections were held in July 1990, the victorious President Orchirbat terminated the People's Republic and embarked on a programme of rapid price liberalisation and voucher-based privatisation (Pomfret 2000).[16]

Though the Parliament was dominated by the successor to the Communist Party, it neither halted economic reform nor prevented the drawing up of a new constitution in 1992 under which Mongolia has had a democratic system with peaceful alternation of power.[17] In that sense it can be said that even the Communist party in Mongolia got itself reformed to support the implementation of democracy and market economy.

2.2 Economic Reforms and International Institutions

As Mongolia embarked on democratic transition in 1990s, these were also years of hyperinflation, a rapidly depreciating exchange rate and incipient dollarisation. Living standards noticeably declined, as the guaranteed services of the old system deteriorated and the greater availability and variety of goods promised by advocates of market-based reforms were scarcely visible. In the medium term, however, macro-economic performance improved as positive GDP growth was recorded in 1994 and inflation began to abate. Both the characterisation of Mongolia as a rapid reformer in the early 1990s and the interpretation of its economic performance as short-term pain prior to long-term gain were questioned. Murrell (1996) argues that price reform was liberal in proclamation but partial in practice.[18] The privatisation process was also dramatic in announcement, with beautiful vouchers engraved with Chinggis Khan's head issued to the population and a prominently renovated stock exchange building, but after a promising start in 1991 the privatisation programme grounded to a halt in mid-1992; little privatisation occurred beyond the small-scale, and the stock exchange was quiescent.[19] Financial reform was initiated with the replacement of the monobank by a two-tier banking system in 1991, but this step was followed by substantial disintermediation due to lack of public confidence in the banking system and the financial sector remained in poor shape throughout the 1990s (Hahm and Yener 1998; IMF 1999:26-35).[20]

The relationship between policy and performance was attenuated by the role of aid and copper. Mongolia's apparent liberalism and geostrategic location made it a favoured aid recipient, especially when aid was measured on a per capita basis. The large inflows reduced the need for domestic adjustment to maintain balance of payments equilibrium.[21] Mongolia was also helped by buoyant world markets for copper, by far its largest export, in the early and mid-1990s. Lower copper prices in 1996 reduced the GDP growth rate and raised questions about the sustainability of Mongolia's post-1994 growth (Pomfret 2000),[22] which itself was evidence that the democracy was at work and there was no threat to economic reform initiatives.

The Democratic Coalition was not only reformers, but also they were radical reformers. The new government' s first step was to free energy prices as the price of coal went up by 48 per cent, electricity by 60 per cent and heating by 40 per cent. Import duties were abolished and other forms of protection removed.

In July 1997 Mongolia acceded to the World Trade Organisation. Subsidies were reduced or abolished and public administration was streamlined. The Law on Housing Privatisation passed by Parliament in October 1996 was delayed by presidential veto but eventually became a law in February 1997 and 25,000 flats were privatised in Ulaanbaatar in 1997. In 1997; in 1996 thirteen enterprises had been privatised and yielded revenue of 1.5 billion to grogs, while in 1997,236 privatised enterprises yielded 15.5 billion to grogs (IMF 1999: 85). Sales tax coverage was extended, income taxes streamlined, and fees for service introduced to increase government cost recovery. Social sector spending was reformed, e.g. by introducing a health insurance system, although some reforms were not radical. The overall picture of the Mongolian economy by 1997 was that the first phase of post-Soviet development was complete. The economy was clearly market-based, although financial sector reform was still required and some large enterprises were still in need of restructuring (Richard Pomfret 2000).[23] Economic reforms opened Mongolia to the rest of world, which helped to change old mind-set for bringing changes Mongolian foreign policy.[24]

2.3 Debates on National Interest

Once having distinction of being the second Communist state of the world after the erstwhile Soviet Union, Mongolia's transition to a democratic state structure has not been an easy task since it remained isolated from the outside world except the Soviet Union for almost seven decades. The turning point, however, was Gorbachev's 1986 Vladivostok initiative for removing tension and conflict in the Asia-Pacific region, which also altered the then political status of Mongolia as a "buffer" in the Sino-Soviet relations.[25] Emergence of new geopolitical situation as well as impact of domestic political reforms and economic restructuring particularly during 1990-1992 compelled both the leadership and intellectuals in Mongolia to debates on national interest. Finally, they reached a consensus to consider Mongolia's future development and security issues in the framework of new realities.[26] As such, a major review of its foreign and security policy was undertaken in June 1994, which resulted in the formulation of three very important documents i.e., Concept of National Security, Concept of Foreign Policy and Military Doctrine (Soni 2006).

These three documents were interlinked in terms of their basic objectives, *i.e.* safeguarding the country's national interests both internal as well as external in order to ensure overall advancement of its people. However, much attention was paid on the perceived threats from specific internal and external situations while defining the national goals in these documents. One striking feature, "so Soni describes, is that the previously made commitments to strengthen international Communist order went into oblivion and instead the pursuit of fundamental national interests described as "pragmatic realism" came into focus". Thus, National Security of Mongolia was termed as being "multi-faceted" by the former Mongolian President N. Bagabandi during his speech delivered on April 6, 1998 to the opening session of the *State Great Hural* (Mongolian Parliament). He stressed that "within the framework of activities aimed at ensuring the national security, it is a pressing task to create favourable external conditions for the existence of Mongolia, strengthen friendly relations with influential countries and carry out a multi-pillared foreign policy".[27]

What was important was that the adoption of the National Security Concept marked a fundamental change in Mongolia's post-Cold War security thinking. According to the provisions laid down in this Concept, "the vital national interests of Mongolia consist in the existence of the Mongolian people and their civilization, in the country's independence, sovereignty, territorial integrity, inviolability of State frontiers, relative economic independence, sustainable ecological development and national unity." [28] In this sense, Mongolia's national security has been defined on quite a new basis in terms of a number of primary areas of concern such as security of the existence of Mongolia, security of the social order and state system, security of citizens' rights and freedoms, economic security, scientific and technological security, security of information, security of Mongolian civilization, security of the population and its gene pool, and ecological security.[29] So, any policy with regard to Mongolia's security concerns revolves around its national interests in the first place, depending upon how constructively the policy and strategy can achieve the defined goals (Soni 2006).

The National Security Concept also suggest that in its foreign relations Mongolia shall exercise "political realism and consistently principled approach, accord top priority to vital national interests and other national considerations, seek to secure many partners in its international relations and promote a non-aligned policy so long as it does not threaten the country's vital interests."[30] Following this comprehensive approach Mongolia began pursuing an open foreign policy with a commitment to "promote the policy of consultation with influential countries on issues of strengthening world peace and security, of developing international cooperation, of enhancing the country's strategic significance and fostering strategic interests of major powers in Mongolia." Furthermore, in its relations with developing and land locked countries, Mongolia follows the line of jointly defending and promoting the shared interests on the international field (Soni 2001:11-14).[31] Mongolia is also made committed to ensure the security of its existence by strictly observing the policy of not allowing the use of the country's territory against other States; ensuring its Nuclear-Weapon-Free status at the international level and making it an important element of strengthening the country's security by political means.

It is worth mentioning here that Mongolia's security thinking also depends on its active foreign policy that too focuses on the national interests. According to the Foreign Policy Concept, "the priority of Mongolia's foreign policy shall be safeguarding of its security and vital national interests by political and diplomatic means, and creating a favourable external environment for its economic, scientific and technological development."[32] In order to achieve this objective Mongolia's approach was set to secure maximum benefits offered by international and regional multilateral cooperation. Hence by adopting a "multi-pillar" foreign policy Mongolia not only discarded the lopsided attitude of the Cold War period but also opted for a non-aligned policy in order to make its presence in the world felt as a developing country. Until 1996, it "broadened its diplomatic outlook and the scope of its international activities by adhering to the principle of flexible priorities in foreign policy implementation" (Soni 2006).

"Pragmatism", as part of quite a new thinking, has been one of the main characteristics of Mongolia's foreign policy. Therefore, the country began relying on ongoing international political reality as well as on the international legal system besides following the trends of international economic development. However, the key issue involving Mongolia's foreign policy priorities was to ensure the security and prosperity of the country both internally and externally by "forming with influential countries in the region and in the world a network of relationships based on the interdependence of political, economic and other interests."[33] As such, Mongolia established new partnership with global and regional powers within the framework of its multi-pillared and multi-dimensional foreign policy, so as to ensure its security in terms of state as well as socio-economic and civilian interests (Soni 2002).[34]

The third document, which became the guiding principles of preserving the country's strategic interest, is the Military Doctrine. It was adopted at a time when Mongolian leadership acknowledged that although the prospects for mutual understanding, trust and partnership came to be prevailed in international relations with the end of the Cold War, the danger of war and armed conflicts had not been fully eliminated and a collective security system had not yet been formed either at the global or regional level. Mongolia, thus, needed a guiding principle, which has been enshrined in this military doctrine to avoid any kind of danger militarily. Significantly, the document asserts that Mongolia's international relations had "shifted from predominantly political and military fields to economic, scientific-technological and informational fields, in other words, from geopolitics to geo-economics."[35] Mongolia thus pledged that it would never engage in a conflict except if invaded and that the country would never enter into any military bloc so long as its independence and sovereignty were not threatened.[36]

In fact, the military doctrine was been formulated on the basis of broader security issues particularly in the Asia-Pacific region, and hence the objective of Mongolia's defence policy was to participate in the creation of collective security systems. Though Mongolia engaged itself in various dialogues on broader regional security issues in order to find a worthy place in the regional cooperation, it still wished to do much.[37] Nevertheless, Mongolia's foreign policy and national security interests had a reflection of both the internal politics as well as regional dynamics, and therefore, relations with the outside world had significant roles to play in future (Soni 2001:11-14).

2.4 Political, Economic and Social Issues

2.4.1: Sovereignty as a Factor in Mongolia's Foreign Policy

Mongolia's position between Russia and China, and the history of Soviet influence meant that it had rarely satisfied the conditions for full sovereignty, i.e., autonomy in foreign policy making and exclusive control of internal affairs. Its position in the post-Soviet period as a small 'developing' nation means that it is a relatively insignificant player on the global arena, which was true at least in the period before 1996. Thus, Mongolia began relying on global institutions to give voice to its opinions, and recognition and guarantees of its sovereign status. Mongolia is a member of over twenty different international groups or organisations, the most important in this respect being the United Nations (UN) to which Mongolia became a member of in 1961 after fifteen years of campaign. The Mongolian Ministry of Foreign Affairs (MMFA) declared that Mongolia's membership was 'the most viable guarantee of its independence and sovereignty'. "If Mongolia ever faces a threat and decides to refer the matter to the UN Security Council, the US, along with other members of the security council would consider appropriate steps to be taken" (Tumerchuluun 1999:286).[38] This threat of action was to act as a deterrent to any country considering directly threatening Mongolia's territory.

Mongolia now actively participates in UN processes and actions, most notably are the recent UN sponsored peacekeeping activities, in particular the contribution of 250 military personnel[39] to assist with reconstruction in Iraq. Not only are international institutions important but individual nations. Ginsburg (1999:250) states that Mongolia has 'aggressively courted' Europe, US and Asia in the search for a 'third neighbour[40]' to guarantee national security. Initially there was optimism that the US or Japan might prove to be such a 'neighbour', however political realism has set in and as authors such as (Ginsberg 1999), and Bruun and Odgaard (1997b) conclude, it is the international community as a whole that guarantees Mongolia's security and survival, rather than one individual nation (Telford 2004:57).

2.4.2 Sovereignty and Identity as a Factor in Mongolia's Foreign Policy

Mongolia is a relatively ethnically homogenous nation comprised of 86 per cent of Khalakh Mongols (Mayhew, 2001:34) and a small Kazak minority. Its culture is very distinct from both Chinese and Russian cultures. Traditionally, a nomadic society, there was a conflict in foreign policy making between those who saw Mongolia's future in embracing this traditional identity and forging closer ties to Central Asia with its similar culture, Soviet history and economic ties (Campi 2003b), and those such as the former Prime Minister Enkhbayar, who believed nomadism to be uneconomic in a modern market economy that Mongolia was trying to become (Batbayar 2002) and as such ties with 'modern' countries in Northeast Asia was to be encouraged. Even Mongolia began identifying itself as a Northeast Asian country.

However, despite the greater potential for investment, trade and security, Campi (2003b:48)[41] warned that "tying itself mainly to Northeast Asia will not work economically and militarily, because Russia and China are the main developing economies which overwhelmingly attract investment money and trade, therefore, Mongolia should reinforce links with Central Asia". So, the relative importance accorded to Mongolia's different identities, both modern and traditional, impacted the priority it placed on relations with neighbouring regions. The 'Concept of Foreign Policy' indicates that the reality was priority to the Asia Pacific region, not Central Asia as confirmed by the fact that there were higher levels of diplomacy and trade with this region and interestingly plans to 'Latinise' the Cyrillic alphabet.[42] This was thought to be the end of a significant common link between Mongolia, Russia and much of Central Asia (Telford 2004:59).[43]

2.4.3 Soviet Antiquity as a Factor for Changes in Mongolia's Foreign Policy

Mongolia's historical links with Russia also had a significant influence on changing its foreign policy. In 1991, there were considerable moves to make a clean break from Russian 'imperialism' but as Ginsburg (1999:248)[44] points out, the "top cadres and urban intellectuals shared a common cosmopolitan orientation and common formative experiences in the USSR". He found that virtually all the political elites between 1990 and 1998 had studied at some point in Russia or Eastern Europe. This common background means that their decisions were "inevitably a product of their formative experiences in Russia".[45]

This contributed to the attitude of distrust towards China and continuation of subservience towards Russia (Telford 2004:60).

2.4.4 Enhanced Presidential Role in Foreign Policy

Mongolia has historically been blessed and cursed by its geostrategic location between two great powers. President Elbedorj is now making it a priority for Mongolia to manage these problems ranging from historical disputes, energy security to corruption in order to chart out a prosperous and sustainable future for his country. The current Mongolian government's nuanced approach to its foreign policy is accruing benefits. Elbedorj continues to follow a policy similar to that of newly re-elected Turkish Prime Minister Tayyip Erdogan that advocates "zero problems" on its borders.[46] While Mongolia does not have to deal with the same problems as Turkey from a security perspective, the challenge of managing its relationships with China and Russia is considerable.

Earlier owing to the break with the USSR, which cut the country off from vital Soviet economic assistance, the leadership of Mongolia turned their attention to the world community, expanding their search for world partners and donors to replace the former patron. Six directions outlined in the Foreign policy concept listed the countries of the West and East, which the current leadership of Mongolia thought important partners. Besides the two neighbors, the USA, Japan, and Germany were regarded as high priority countries.[47] At the same time Mongolia sought friendly relations with countries as diverse as India, the Republic of Korea, Thailand, Singapore, Turkey, Denmark, the Netherlands, Finland, Austria, Sweden, and Switzerland. President P. Ochirbat, elected in 1993, pursued active diplomacy by travelling extensively to Europe and Asia, as well as to New Zealand and Australia. Ochirbat visited the Russian Federation in 1993; India, Thailand, Laos and Vietnam in 1994; Germany, Belgium, European Union and Hungary in 1995; France and Great Britain in 1996; Indonesia, New Zealand and Australia in 1997. He had also participated in the inauguration ceremony of the new Japanese Emperor Akihito in 1991 and in Moscow activities commemorating the 50th anniversary of Russian victory over Nazi Germany in 1995.[48]

Ochirbat's greatest diplomatic score was the summit meeting with President Yeltsin in Moscow in 1993 that produced a new bilateral treaty on friendly relations and cooperation. During the highly publicised visit a number of important documents including a Joint Statement on Stalinist purges of 1930s in Mongolia were signed between the two parties. The visit became a huge success domestically for two main reasons. First, the Mongols were still accustomed to linking their security with certain agreements, commitments and guarantees at the state level. Second, because of the overwhelming power of the Presidential post in Russia, the summit meeting with President Yeltsin and his signature on the bilateral treaty were the best tangible results hoped for by his Mongolian counterpart.[49] As the head of the National Security Council Ochirbat full-heartedly embraced the idea to turn Mongolia into a nuclear-weapon-free zone.

2.5 The Role of Civil Society in State Affaires

Although state-society relations have been influenced by a host of the external factors, discussed above, the characteristic political deference and passivity associated with the socialist legacy in Mongolia did not prevent the rise of mass pro-democracy movements that played a critical role in the transition to democracy in 1989-90 nor the creation of more than 5,300 registered NGOs that have been formed largely since the transition.[50] Post-transition relations between CSOs and public officials have been marked by the state's acceptance of an independent civil society. The transition is not unqualified, however; the CIVICUS report notes that CSOs continue to be "subject to occasional unwarranted government interference" (CIVICUS 2006:39). Methods of state control include the NGO registration process; control of information dissemination through state-owned mass media; and restrictions on public protests and demonstration; as well as intimidation, interrogation, and surveillance at the local level. The CIVICUS report also criticises the state's discriminatory dialogue with a small set of CSOs and selective legitimisation of CSOs by hand-picking "friendly" organisations for collaboration, a practice that leads to self-censorship by some civil society leaders (CIVICUS 2006:39–41).

In the late 1990s, the Mongolian branch of the World Wildlife Fund facilitated the establishment of the Union of Environmental NGOs (UMENGO). The Union served as an umbrella organisation with 30 members, including the Mongolian Association for Conservation, Nature and the Environment

(MACNE), the biggest environmental NGO in Mongolia. MACNE is a "legacy" NGO that was established in the socialist era as a governmental NGO (referred to as a GONGO) that still has strong ties to government. UMENGO initially benefitted from this close relationship with the Ministry of Nature and Environment.

2.6 Constructing Social Accountability through Media

The Mongolian media sector is characterised by lively, if sometimes not very professional, reporting from outlets that represent the full range of political viewpoints, although few outlets are politically neutral. In many respects, the challenges facing the Mongolian media are similar to those facing the media in other countries emerging from the oppression that characterised the period of socialist rule, although progress toward a free and responsible media has been hampered by Mongolia's relative poverty. In fact, the media played a key role in giving voice to the views and demands of citizens, as well as providing information to both ordinary citizens and decision makers. A free and effective media acts as a two-way conduit for communication between government and the citizenry.[51] So, the media played a crucial role in facilitating civic engagement for social accountability during early 1990s.

The relations between Mongolian media and civil society during the period of this study were generally sound. Most CSOs, particularly Ulaanbaatar based NGOs, were able to attract news coverage of their work. Several CBOs, such as the Ongi River Movement worked closely with the media over a number of years to build better relationships and thus ensured better coverage. Many CSOs have complained, however, that they were often required to pay for coverage. Furthermore, NGOs paid to broadcast their own productions, including various public interest programs, though they effectively relieved the media of the responsibility to produce it themselves.[52]

2.7 The Constitutional Remedies for Making New Mongolia

From 1924 to 1989 the Soviet Union exercised dominant control over Mongolia. During that period, Mongolia followed the Soviet model in politics and economics, and closely conformed to Moscow's foreign policy. Once the Soviet monolith began cracking and collapsing, the MPRP could no longer maintain its hegemony.

Mongolia had no written Constitution before 1924. In the period of autonomy after the December 1, 1911, proclamation of independence from Manchu rule, Qing law remained the guide for administration. A professional bureaucracy and various ministries were established. The post of Prime Minister was not created until October 1912. Two houses of a parliamentary type were formed in 1914, although their role was deliberative and they were convened and dissolved by the Bogd Khaan.[53] The Upper House, including high-ranking secular and ecclesiastical lords and departmental ministers, was chaired by the Prime Minister, while the Lower House consisted of less important nobles, lower-Ranking officials, and army officers (Sanders 1992:506-520).

In March 1921, Mongolian revolutionaries held the first Congress of the Mongolian People's Party (MPP) in Kyakhta on Soviet territory, and adopted a party program defining "anti-feudal goals". After the victory of the revolution and the installation of the people's government with Soviet Russian assistance in July 1921, a provisional *hural* (people's assembly) was set up as an advisory body.[54] The Bogd Khaan remained head of state, although his powers were limited by the Oath-Taking Treaty or Solemn Compact of 1921, which might be regarded as confirming a constitutional division of power. Following the Bogd Khaan's death in May 1924, it was decided to establish a republican regime without a President (Sanders 1992:506-520).[55]

Three months later, the first Great Hural met to proclaim the first constitution "an independent People's Republic in which all power belongs to the people" and who's main task was to "strengthen the new republican order." The first constitution comprised six chapters, opening with the Declaration of Rights of the People of Mongolia. Chapter 2 outlined the functions of the Great Hural, the Little Hural elected by the former, the Presidium, and the government. "Local self-government" in Chapter 3 provided for rural hurals modeled on the peasant Soviets set up in Soviet Central Asia. The right to vote and be elected was accorded by Chapter 4 to citizens over 18 years of age living by their own labor, but it disenfranchised "secular and ecclesiastical feudalists" and Lamas permanently resident in monasteries. Chapter 5 explained the national budget; while Chapter 6 described the state seal, arms, and flag.[56] This constitution represented a commitment to social transformation in the direction of socialism while bypassing capitalism (Sanders 1992:506-520).

In 1940, the Eighth Great Hural was convened to adopt Mongolia's second constitution, which was modeled on the Soviet Constitution of 1936. The second constitution defined the MPR as an "independent state of working people, herdsmen, workers and intelligentsia, which guarantees the country's non-capitalist road of development for the future transition to socialism." Article 95, highlighting the monolithic nature of the one-party state, described the MPRP as the vanguard of the working people and the core of all their organisations.[57] Amendments to the 1940 constitution introduced by the Ninth Great Hural in 1949 included direct elections, a secret ballot and universal suffrage following the restoration of political rights. These changes came into force for the 1951 elections, after which the sessions of the Great Hural were renumbered. The Little Hural was abolished.[58]

Mongolia's third constitution was adopted in July 1960 by the first session of the Great Hural (Fourth convocation). In 1940, Mongolia had been predominantly a livestock-raising country, but by 1960 it had developed a mixed agrarian-industrial economy and acquired a working class. It had collectivised herding and developed mining and light industry (Sanders 1992:506-520).[59] According to the preamble of the third constitution, Mongolia embarked on the path of building a Communist society. The guiding and directing force of society and of the state was the MPRP, which was guided in its activities by the all-conquering theory of Marxism-Leninism. "[60] The Great Hural was renamed the People's Great Hural in the third constitution (Sanders 1992:506-520).[61]

Amendments to the 1960 constitution subsequently extended the term of the People's Great Hural from three to four and then five years, and eventually fixed the number of deputies at 370. The important amendments of March 1990, introduced under the pressure for democratic reforms, abolished the reference to the MPRP as the "guiding and directing force of society and of the state." Further amendments in May 1990 created the posts of President and Vice-President and restored the Little Hural, or standing legislature, with 50 members after the July 1990 elections. The Law on political parties legalised membership in any political party and formalised registration procedures.[62]

2.8 The Fourth New Constitution, 1992

From 1990 to 1992, Mongolia initiated political reforms to eliminate the 'leading role' of the MPRP in the state. With the adoption of the new Constitution in January 1992 Mongolia entered a new era of democracy. Symbolically, the name of the country was changed from the 'People's Republic of Mongolia' to 'Mongolia'. The Constitution established a mixed political system, resembling a semi-presidential regime loosely modelled on France's Fifth Republic. The President is the head of state with power to veto parliamentary legislation, while the Prime Minister serves as head of government. The transitional bicameral parliament was consolidated into a unicameral body, the State Great Hural.[63] At the same time, the Constitution called for the formation of new political institutions including a National Security Council, a Constitutional Court, and a new body called the General Council of the Courts to oversee judicial administration and ensure the constitutionally declared goal of judicial independence (Sanders 1992: 506-520).[64]

The Constitution stipulated that the State Great Hural, a 76-member unicameral legislature, is the supreme organ of state and legislative power. It can enact laws dealing with domestic, financial, monetary, and foreign policy, and supervised their implementation, approved the budget, sets the dates for legislative and presidential elections, removes or relieves the President, appoints and replaces the Prime Minister and other officials accountable to the State Great Hural, determines the organisation and role of the National Security Council, holds national referenda, ratifies and vetoes international agreements, establishes and severs diplomatic relations, and declares a state of emergency or war (Batbayar 2003 :45-49). "The President, upon consultation with the Prime Minister, can propose dissolution of the State Great Hural, which requires a two-thirds majority of its members for approval".[65]

The President is elected by universal suffrage and is the head of state and the symbol of national unity. He may not concurrently serve as a member of the cabinet or the State Great Hural. Each parliamentary party or group of parliamentary parties may nominate a candidate for the presidential contest. A candidate who receives a majority of the popular vote is considered elected and the State Great Hural then passes a law recognising his or her mandate. The President has the power to veto all or parts of any legislation; a two-thirds majority of the State Great Hural is needed to override the veto. The President nominates the Prime Minister, in consultation with the majority party or a group of parties (Batbayar 2003:45-49).[66] He instructs the cabinet and issues decrees with policy guidelines that are effective only upon the Prime Minister's signature. The President represents Mongolia in foreign relations and enters into international treaties; serves as Commander-in-Chief and as head of the National Security Council; declares general or partial conscription; and can declare a state of emergency or war, with the State Great Hural's approval within seven days.[67] The Prime Minister leads the Government and is responsible to the State Great Hural for implementation of state laws. (Batbayar T.2003:45-49).[68]

One of the constitutional and legal debates that have persisted since 1996 is whether or not an MP can concurrently hold a ministerial post. At first, the decision was negative. This state of affairs was one factor that brought down the first government of the Democratic Coalition. Under debate also was the role of the President in vetoing or approving Prime Ministerial candidates. This question became the focus of the fierce debate when President Bagabandi (the MPRP) vetoed the Democratic Coalition nominee for Prime Minister seven times. Consecutively, (Batbayar 2003: 45-49).[69] As a result of these and other battles, the period was characterised by ineffective governance and government.[70]

Moreover, in the name of "defence of the state, national security and public order," Article 16:17 excludes the right to know "secrets that the state and its bodies shall protect according to the law," and declares that "secrets of the state, individuals or organisations which are not subject to disclosure shall be defined and protected by law." Parties and public organisations are obliged to uphold state security (Article 16:10), and there is some cause for concern that an individual could thereby protect his personal interests on the grounds of state security (Sanders 1992:506-520).[71]

There has been much debate in democratic circles about the president's power "to direct the Government on matters within the area of his competence" and the validity of a decree to this effect issued by him and counter-signed by the Prime Minister (Article 33:1). President Ochirbat and Prime Minister

Byambasuren were both old style MPRP Communists who held positions of authority in earlier governments. The setting of a minimum age limit of 45 years for the president also tends to favor older MPRP candidates, since most non-communist politicians are much younger (Sanders 1992:506-520).[72]

As independent Mongolia's first democratic Constitution came into force in 1992, Little Hural Social Democrat Hatanbaatar emphasised that a key feature of its adoption was the guarantee that its provisions would "not become empty declarations." It showed, he said, that Mongolia had "rid itself of communism and has embarked on the natural road of global development. It proves that Mongolia has taken the transition from a Communist-type one-party rule to a government combining the traditions of statehood and parliamentary rule."[73] The adoption of 1992 Constitution gave way to the adoption of national security concept and foreign policy concept.[74] As such, constitution played a significance role in changing the existing foreign policy of Mongolia.

In sum, in the case of Mongolia, a land-locked country situated between Russia and China, a coherent foreign policy was thought to be is indispensable in maintaining any political regime intact. An extraordinary degree of foreign policy consensus emerged in Mongolia in the 1990s reflected in such ideas as 'multi-pillar' foreign policy (Soni 2006)[75] and a 'balanced' relationship with two neighbours. The President, a weak and symbolic post-defined by the 1992 Constitution, emerged as a key foreign policy player in the Mongolian domestic political scene.[76] What has been found during the period of this research study is that there have been interrelations between foreign policy and domestic reforms and that domestic influence on foreign policy changes in Mongolia has been very significant.

Notes and References

1. Sharad K. Soni (2006), "*India's* New Role in East Asia: Implications for Mongolia", *The Mongolian Journal of International Affairs,* Number 13, p. 38.
2. *Ibid.*
3. http://en.wikipedia.org/wiki 1990_Democratic_Revolution_in_Mongolia.
4. *Ibid.*
5. http://medlibrary.org/medwiki 1990_Democratic_Revolution_in_Mongolia.

6. Morris Rossabi (2005), *Modern Mongolia: From Khans to Commissars to Capitalists*, University of California Press, pp. 1-28.

7. Ochirbat was originally a MPRP member, but when his party nominated an orthodox Communist as their presidential candidate, he agreed to run for the opposition.

8. http://ubpost.mongolnews.mn/index.php/2011-07-24-01-47-35/24-opinion/5026.

9. http://ubpost.mongolnews.mn/index.php/2011-07-24-01-47-35/24-opinion/5026.

10. http://www.findarticles.com/cf_dls/m3955/1_52/60139963/p1/article.jhtml?term=%2BDemocracy+%2BEurope.

11. Kopstein, J. and Reilly, D. (2000), 'Geographic Diffusion and the Transformation of the Postcommunist World', *World Politics*, 53 (10): pp. 1-37.

12. Kopstein, J. and Reilly, D. (2000), 'Geographic Diffusion and the Transformation of the Postcommunist World', *World Politics*, 53 (10): pp. 1-37.

13. Fritz, V. (2002), 'Mongolia: Dependent Democratisation', *Journal of Communist Studies and Transition Politics*, 18 (4): pp. 75-100.

14. United Nations Development Programme (New York); http://www.undp.org.

15. Boone, P. (1994), "Grassroots Macro-economic Reform in Mongolia," *Journal of Comparative Economics* 18(3): pp. 329-356.

16. Richard Pomfret, (2000): Transition and Democracy in Mongolia, *Europe-Asia Studies*, 52:1, pp. 149-160.

17. The post-1990 election results and voter turnout are summarised in UNDP (1997: 59). The Communist Party's successor won a landslide victory in the 1992 parliamentary elections but lost the 1996 parliamentary elections. Its candidate won the 1997 presidential election.

18. Pomfret (1993:95-97 or 1996:84-87) provides examples of government regulation of prices in order to alleviate the short-term impact of price increases.

19. Secondary trading did not begin until August 1995. Corporate governance remained a major problem throughout the 1990s, as lack of transparency in accounting or disclosure rules prevented the stock market from playing a role in promoting good management.

20. IMF (1999): Mongolia: Selected Issues, IMF Staff Country Report No.99/4, International Monetary Fund, Washington DC, January. http://citeseerx.ist.psu.edu/viewdoc/download?doi=10.1.1.41.1675 &rep=rep1&type=pdf.

21. The $250 million in soft loans and grants committed at the 1997 donors' meeting was equal to the annual state budget revenue. The actual budget equation in 1997 worked out at a deficit equal to 8.5 per cent of GDP, offset by aid disbursements equal to 12 per cent of GDP, so that the net domestic financing Requirement was a negative 3.75 per cent (IMF, 1999, p. 10).

22. Richard Pomfret, (2000): Transition and Democracy in Mongolia, *Europe-Asia Studies*, 52:1, pp. 149-160.

23. *Ibid.*

24. *Ibid.*

25. For more on Vladivostok initiative which has had direct bearing on Mongolia, see Sharad K. Soni, *Mongolia-Russia Relations: Kiakhta to Vladivostok* (Delhi: Shipra, 2002), pp. 218-221.

26. Soni, Sharad K. (2006), "Mongolia between Russia and China: Emerging Equation," in *Mongolica, An International Annual of Mongol Studies*, 17(38): pp. v 252-268.

27. *Collection of the Public Statements and Addresses of the President of Mongolia related to National Security and Defence Policies* (Ulaanbaatar, 2000), p. 14.

28. See, "Concept of National Security of Mongolia", in *National Security Council: Concept, Law and Regulations* (Ulaanbaatar, 2000), second edition, p. 82.

29. Soni, Sharad K. (2006), "Mongolia between Russia and China: Emerging Equation," in *Mongolica, An International Annual of Mongol Studies*, 17(38): pp. 252-268.

30. *Ibid.*, p. 89.

31. Soni. Sharad K. (2001), "Mongolia's Foreign Policy Priorities", *Himalayan and Central Asian Studies"*, 5(1): pp. 11-14.

32. "Concept of Mongolia's Foreign Policy", *The Mongolian Journal of International Affairs* (Ulaanbaatar), No.2, 1995, p. 71.

33. *Ibid.*

34. For detail see Sharad K.Soni (2002), *Mongolia-Russia Relations: Kiakhta to Vladivostok,* New Delhi: Shipra Publication.

35. J. Enkhsaikhan, "Mongolia's Security Policy: Regional and International Aspects," *The Mongol Messenger*, Vol. 18, No. 210, 14 July 1995 at http://www.indiana.edu/~mongsoc/mong/security.htm.

36. See, "The Fundamentals of the Military Doctrine of Mongolia", *Strategic Digest* (New Delhi), Vol. 26, No. 2, February 1996, pp. 193-195.

37. For detail see Sharad K. Soni (2001), "Mongolia's Foreign Policy Priorities", *Himalayan and Central Asian Studies"*, 5(1): pp. 11-14.

38. G. Tumerchuluun, (1999), "Mongolia's Foreign Policy Revisited: Relations with Russia and the PRC into the 1990s", in Kotkin, S. and Elleman, B. eds. *Mongolia in the Twentieth Century, Landlocked Cosmopolitan,* New York: M.E. Sharpe.

39. See FCO website.

40. 'The notion that Mongolia must find a nation or group of nations to counterbalance the traditional monopoly China and Russia exerted over Mongolia's foreign relations' (Campi, 2003b:30).

41. Campi, A. (2003a), Review of *Mongolia's Foreign Policy in the 1990s: New Identity and New Challenges* by Tsedendamba Batbayar. US.; Mongolia Advisory Group.

42. See UB Post, July 25th 2003.

43. Telford Sarah (2004), "To What Extent Does Post-1990 Mongolia Pursue an Independent Foreign Policy?" Research *Unit on International Security and Cooperation (UNISCI)*, Spain: Madrid.

44. Ginsburg, T. (1999), "Nationalism, Elites and Mongolia's Rapid Transformation", in Kotkin, S. and Elleman, B. eds. *Mongolia in the Twentieth Century, Landlocked Cosmopolitan,* New York: M.E. Sharpe.

45. Telford Sarah (2004), "To What Extent Does Post-1990 Mongolia Pursue an Independent Foreign Policy?" Research *Unit on International Security and Cooperation (UNISCI)*, Spain: Madrid.

46. Jonathan Berkshire Miller (13 July 2011), Mongolia: Looking East, Looking West, asiasentinel.com/index.php?option=com_content&task=view&id=3316&Itemid=373.

47. 'The concept of foreign policy' (1995), *The Mongolian Journal of International Affairs*, No 2:70–78.

48. TSEDENDAMBA BATBAYAR. "Foreign policy and domestic reform in Mongolia", Central Asian Survey, 3/1/2003.

49. For more on this initiative, see J. Enkhsaikhan, 'Mongolia's nuclear-weapon-free status: concept and practice', *Asian Survey*, March/April 2000: pp. 342–359.

50. In contrast with business associations and trade unions, women are well-represented in most professional associations and NGOs. In fact, they dominate certain areas such as health, education, poverty alleviation, and human as well as women's rights, leading some observers to refer to Mongolian civil society as "matriarchal" (CIVICUS 2006:19).

51. http://vle.worldbank.org/bnpp/files/TF053665MongoliaESWFINALweb.pdf.

52. While one CSO leader interviewed during the dissemination phase indicated that CSO-media relations are "not so good not very

developed" in Mongolia because "the media doesn't think the CSOs are important," another criticised the media for "not appreciating democratic values."

53. B. Shirendev, ed., History of the Mongolian People's Republic (Moscow: Nauka, 1973). The two houses were the Ulsyn Hurlyn deed dood tanhim (upper and lower houses) or Olnoogiyn ulsyn deed dood hoyor hural (upper and lower hurals).

54. Thomas E. Ewing, Between the Hammer and the Anvil? Chinese and Russian Policies in Outer Mongolia 1911-1921 (Bloomington: Indiana University Press, 1980), p. 35.

55. M. Sanjdorj, Ardyn Tdriyn Tutih (Ulan Bator: Academy of Sciences, 1974), pp. 79-83 details the sessions of the Ulsyn tur tsagiyn hural (provisional hural).

56. Sanders, Alan J.K. (1992), "Mongolia's New Constitution: Blueprint for Democracy", *Asian Survey,* 32(6): pp. 506-520.

57. Gerard M. Friters, Outer Mongolia and Its International Position (Baltimore: Johns Hopkins University Press, 1949) has the text (12 Chapters, 95 Articles).

58. For amendments, see I. Ya. Zlatkin, Mongol'skaya Narodnaya Respublika (Moscow: Academy of Sciences, 1952), pp. 349-66 (12 Chapters, 108 Articles.

59. Sanders, Alan J.K. (1992), "Mongolia's New Constitution: Blueprint for Democracy", *Asian Survey,* 32(6): 506-520.

60. Bugd Nayramdah Mongol Ard Ulsyn Undsen Huul' (Ulan Bator: State Publishing House, 1981).

61. Sanders, Alan J.K. (1992), "Mongolia's New Constitution: Blueprint for Democracy", *Asian Survey,* 32(6): pp. 506-520.

62. See also Alan Sanders, Asia Yearbook 1991 (Hong Kong: Far Eastern Economic Review, 1992), p. 172.

63. For more on the constitutional reform process, see Tom Ginsburg and Gombosuren Ganzorig, 'Constitutional reform and human rights', in Ole Bruun and Ole Odgaard, eds, *Mongolia in Transition: Old Patterns and New Challenges* (Curzon Press, 1996), pp 147–164.

64. Sanders, Alan J.K. (1992), "Mongolia's New Constitution: Blueprint for Democracy",*Asian Survey,* 32(6): pp. 506-520.

65. *Mongol Ulsyn Undsen Khuul* (The Constitution of Mongolia) (Ulaanbaatar, 1992), Chapter 3, Article 25.

66. Batbayar, T. (2003), "Foreign Policy and Domestic Reform in Mongolia." *Central Asian Survey* 22(1): pp. 45-59.

67. *Ibid.*, Articles 30, 31, and 33.

68. *Ibid.*, Article 38.

69. Batbayar, T. (2003), "Foreign Policy and Domestic Reform in Mongolia." *Central Asian Survey* 22(1): 45-59.

70. Sheldon R. Severinghaus (2000), 'Mongolia in 1998 and 1999', *The Asian Survey*, 40(1): pp. 132–134.

71. Sanders, Alan J.K. (1992), "Mongolia's New Constitution: Blueprint for Democracy", *Asian Survey*, 32(6): pp. 506-520.

72. *Ibid.*

73. Mongol Messenger, February 4, 1992.

74. *Ibid.*

75. Soni, Sharad K. (2006), India's New Role in East Asia: Implications For Mongolia, *The Mongolian Journal of International Affairs*, pp. 32-41.

76. *Ibid.*

3

Mongolia's Foreign Policy Changes: External Factors

Mongolia has a 3485 kilometers border with Russia and a 4677 kilometers border with China (Foreign Policy Blue Book 2000:18). Both countries have held imperial ambitions for Mongolia and today they are still the biggest threat to its sovereignty (Telford 2004).[1] As a part of reform process Mongolia's domestic and external scenario underwent a drastic change during the democratic transition, and that it's security and foreign policy objectives figured prominently among the country's think-tanks (Soni 2006:27-39).[2] It was then understood that Mongolia's national security could only be ensured by taking unilateral, bilateral and multilateral measures[3]. In June 1994, Mongolia made radical changes in its national security and Foreign policy objectives which were finally endorsed by the Mongolian Parliament. The main concerns for Mongolia's security at that time aimed at achieving favourable internal and external conditions for ensuring vital national interest.

3.1 Geopolitical Importance of Mongolia in Inner Asia

Without understanding the geography we cannot understand the foreign policy of any country as geographical location is one of the main factors to decide or shape the foreign policy. Every state is constrained by circumstances and seeks security of its boundary within a sea of ever-shifting limitations. A dominant influence on Mongolia's national security is geography. Its security has, for the past six centuries, been intertwined in its relations with Russia and China and in their relations with one another. Geographically the Mongolian land slopes from the high Altai Mountains of the West and the North to plains and depressions in the east and the south. Hutyen Orgil in the extreme Western Mongolia, where the Mongolian, Russian and Chinese borders meet, it is the highest point (4,374 meters). The lowest is 560 meters, an otherwise undistinguished spot in the Eastern Mongolian plain. The country has an average elevation of 1,580 meters. The landscape includes one of Asia's largest fresh water lakes (Hovsgol Nuur), many salt lakes, marshes, sand dunes, rolling grasslands, alpine forests, and permanent montane glaciers.[4]

Mongolia has three major mountain ranges. The highest is the Altai Mountains, which stretches across the Western and the Southwestern regions of the country on a Northwest to Southeast axis. The Hangayn Nuruu, mountains also trending Northwest to Southeast, occupy much of central and North-central Mongolia. These are older, lower, and more eroded mountains, with many forests and alpine pastures. The Hentiyn Nuruu, mountains near the Russian border to the Northeast of Ulaanbaatar, is still lower. Much of Eastern Mongolia is occupied by a plain, and the lowest area is a Southwest-to-Northeast trending depression that reaches from the Gobi region in the South to the Eastern frontier. The rivers drain in three directions: North to the Arctic Ocean, East to the Pacific, or South to the deserts and the depressions of Inner Asia. Rivers are most extensively developed in the North, and the country's major river system is that of the Selenge-Moron, which drains into Lake Baykal. Some minor tributaries of Siberia's Yenisey River also rise in the mountains of Northwestern Mongolia. Rivers in Northeastern Mongolia drain into the Pacific through the Argun and Amur (Heilong Jiang) rivers, while the few streams of Southern and Southwestern Mongolia do not reach the sea but run into salt lakes or deserts (Worden and Savada 1989).[5] Moreover, the vast geographical land of Mongolia has always been of strategic importance for the outside the world.

3.2 Emergence of New Geopolitical Environment

For centuries, Mongolia was a territorial buffer. When the Manchus conquered China and established the Qing Empire, they swept Mongolia into their realm. When the Qing collapsed, Moscow sucked Mongolia into its own expanding domain and, during the period of Sino-Soviet enmity from the mid-1960s to 1989, the Soviet Union stationed troops and military equipment in Mongolia to enhance its strategic advantage over the PRC. For Moscow, Mongolia was then a territorial buffer the particularities of Mongolian terrain underscored its salience as a shield behind which Russia felt more secure than if Mongolia had been in China's hands (Garver 1988, 217; Liu 2006, 342).[6] While Mongolia apparently sought Soviets' protection against the prospect of Chinese irredentist expansionism, its territory was used by Moscow to ensure shorter lines of attack on China than the Soviet Union would have otherwise had Mongolia offer a greater strategic depth in which the Soviet Union could combat a PRC assault, had Beijing launched an assault on the Soviet Union (Soni 2002).[7] During the period when Mongolia was under Moscow's thumb, it was nominally independent. In fact, it was a "satellite" of the Soviet Union and did not exercise autonomy commensurate with that of an independent state. Dependence on the Soviet Union brought Mongolia certain developments that Mongolians even now refer to as "civilisation," such as infrastructure associated with modernity and urbanisation. However, Mongolian's "paid with their freedom, their personal property, and their freedom to think" (Babaar 1999). Among the burdens of dependence was the expectation on Moscow's part that Mongolia's resources were available for exploitation.[8] In 1966, Moscow and Ulaanbaatar signed a twenty-year "Treaty of Friendship, Cooperation and Mutual Assistance" that heralded the transfer of 100,000 Soviet troops, tanks, and missile units to Mongolia where they were "ideally situated for an attack on the Chinese capital" (Dittmer 1992: 188; Soni 2002, 241).[9] This condition of remained intact until 1990, by which time the Soviet imperium was rapidly disintegrating.[10] Then, at just that grand juncture when former Soviet Republics, nominally independent states on the Soviet periphery, and even autonomous authoritarian regimes allied to the United States cascaded toward democracy, Mongolia declared itself a democracy and has, since that moment, consciously repositioned itself in the international community (Huntington 1991).

"As Mongolia has tried to establish itself within the international arena as an independent actor, it is reminded at every occasion of where it is located. Mongolia cannot escape its situation: landlocked between Russia and China. It is bound by the history of its own relations to each of its proximate neighbours, as well as to their history of relations with one another".[11] That history is, to a considerable degree, a product of interests arising from geography.

Samuel Huntington stressed on as a "third wave" of democratisation that reached Mongolia and accelerated in late 1989 (Huntington 1993).[12] A resolution was passed by Mongolia's Small Khural (legislature) on October 4, 1990, to establish a new constitution, and that Constitution took effect on February 12, 1992. With that, the Mongolian People's Republic was renamed, simply, Mongolia. Mongolia's legacy of dependence led it in independence to reach beyond geographic constraints to cultivate relationships with states far afield. Mongolia shifted from a "satellite" foreign policy of dependence on Moscow to what Ulaanbaatar describes as an "independent, non-aligned, multi-pillar, open" foreign policy (Embassy of Mongolia. Ulaanbaatar has adopted a plucky posture of gracious defiance, embodied in the "National Security Concept" and the "Concept of Mongolia's Foreign Policy," which articulated a policy of balance that is known as the "third neighbour" policy. [13]

Mongolia's foreign policy must be viewed in the context of the nation's landlocked position, sandwiched between Russia and China. The country's survival and growth have largely depended on its leaders' adroit management of this sensitive and strategic location.[14] In 1989 the principal motivations driving Mongolia's foreign policy were the preservation of territorial integrity, together with the projection of a substantial measure of political independence. Major goals included expanding and modernising the economy through aid and trade arrangements, and extending diplomatic and economic contacts with the international community.[15] By mid-1989, some indications of changes in Mongolia's foreign policy direction were visible, very likely in response to initiatives taken by Soviet leader Gorbachev. Operating within the context of the distinct improvements being made in Sino-Soviet relations, Mongolian leaders also began to demonstrate a more relaxed attitude toward China.[16] Furthermore, they seemed willing to explore new relationships with other Asian countries and to accelerate contact and deepening relationships with Western and Third World countries.

At that time the minister of foreign affairs was assisted in implementing foreign policy by a first deputy minister, two deputy ministers, and heads of specialised departments. Some key departments responsible for specific geographic areas covered (a) number one, the Soviet Union, Czechoslovakia, the German Democratic Republic (East Germany), and Poland; (b) remaining European countries; (c) East Asia and Southeast Asia; and (d) South Asia, West Asia, and Africa. Additional departments handled cultural affairs, treaties and archives, relations with international organisations, legal affairs, protocol, and the administration of diplomatic agencies, the press, and other matters.

However, a definite change in Mongolia's foreign policy came only after the break-up of the Soviet Union in 1991 and the end of the Cold War. This was more so due to the emergence of a new geopolitical situation in Mongolia that brought to an end of Mongolia's "buffer" status between the break-up of the Soviet Union created a power vacuum in Mongolia in terms of both the political and economic development. China, the other neighbour, thus came forward to fill this power vacuum, though the USA too appeared on the sense. This entire new geopolitical environment in Mongolia contributed much to make changes in the foreign policy in order to suit the demands of the day.

3.3 National Security Concern of Mongolia

The national security, of Mongolia represents the status when favourable external and internal conditions are secured to ensure vital national interests. Such national interests lay in the existence of the Mongolian people and their civilisation, in the country's independence, sovereignty territorial integrity, inviolability of State frontiers, relative economic independence, sustainable ecological development and national unity. The endurance of national security implies State policy aimed at creating all-round guarantees of protecting and strengthening of Mongolia's vital national interests, actions taken by the State, its agencies and functionaries to that effect as well as measures implemented by its citizens.

The national security of Mongolia consist the following main components:

- Security of the existence of Mongolia,
- Security of the social order and state system,
- Security of citizens' rights and freedoms,
- Economic security,

- Scientific and technological security,
- Security of information,
- Security of Mongolian civilization,
- Security of the population and its gene pool,
- Ecological security.

Taking into consideration all these components national security can be ensured by social, political, organisational, economic, diplomatic, military, intelligence and legal means, unilaterally or through the development of international cooperation. The main means of ensuring national security consists of taking measures designed to forecast and forestall the trends and the development of events on the basis of reliable information and thorough its evaluation and assessment. The main guarantors of national security are the people of Mongolia and the Mongolian State. International guarantees of national security consist of political, legal and moral-psychological components. They are secured and strengthened through the combination of unilateral, bilateral and multilateral measures.[17] Military-political security can be ensured through a collective security system by joint efforts or participation in such a system.

The duties to ensure national security are incumbent on the State Great Hural, the President of Mongolia, the National Security Council headed by the President, the Government, the central and local law enforcement and State administrative agencies. The legislative, executive, judicial and local self-governing bodies are obligated to implement, within their competence, the tenets of the national security concerns strengthened by the Constitution, legislation and other relevant legal acts. Political and public organisations, as well as citizens are obliged to strictly observe the legislation on ensuring national security and actively participate in the realisation thereof. The National Security Council is charged with the coordination of the strategies and tactics of the implementation of the security measures with due regard to existing circumstances. It monitors the state of safeguarding national security, and annually informs the State Great Hural thereon.[18] The organisations concerned provide for funds needed to implement all the related measures in their budgets. In cases of special measures, expenses are be covered by the State budget.

3.4 Linkages between Security and Foreign Policy

There are political and security motivations behind all agreements and policies, in addition to the hoped for economic and political benefits. Beginning here and now, Mongolia's national security both in theory and in practice are defined in terms of perceived success in multi-dimensional geo-economic balancing rather than the relatively simple geo-political and geo-strategic balancing that dominated both scholarly thought and practical actions since Mongolia's democratic revolution in 1990. Throughout Mongolia's two-decade period of democratic experience and real independence following almost 70 years of membership in the Soviet bloc which restrained freedom of action in the international arena its perception of and strategy for national security underwent significant changes. Despite the shift in substance from politics to economy, the core concern remained the same.[19] Mongolia began pursuing a strategy of diversifying its partners and more partners resulted in greater balancing opportunities and hence, a more guaranteed external security environment.

3.4.1 Security through Democratisation

Mongolia became the world's second socialist country in 1924, and was destined to become the first Asian nation to denounce the old system through a peaceful revolution in 1990.[20] The period of peaceful change between 1990 and 1994 marked a watershed in Mongolia's historical development, and the change had been no less dramatic in nature and in scope for having been achieved without violence and bloodshed.

The new Constitution of 1992 instituted a solid legal framework for genuine democratic reforms. Pluralism and a multi-party system became a reality. Free market rules were introduced to govern the economic life of the country. Mongolia joined the International Monetary Fund, the World Bank, the Asian Development Bank, and the World Trade Organisation. These developments were a breakthrough in the process of integrating Mongolia into the world economy, and that integration itself was a breakthrough. Having been dominated by China for two centuries and then by Soviet Union for seven decades, Mongolia learned a single indelible lesson in terms of national sovereignty and security that the nation should seek balanced, equidistant relations with its two neighbours while seeking wider recognition and global interaction to the utmost possible degree.[21]

However, Mongolia was considered one of the least likely cases to achieve a successful transition to democracy. M. Steven

Fish has noted that often a country's transition to democracy and its success are often assisted by a history of previous liberal governance, its political culture, prior experience with elements of a capitalist free-market economy, and even proximity to other democratic states. This helps explain the relative ease with which many East and Central European nations have undergone their transitions. Mongolia had none of these. It is because of these reasons that Fish described Mongolia's successful transition as "democracy without prerequisites." [22]

Now, it is widely believed that the initial assurance of national security was closely linked to, and exclusively depended on, the processes of liberalisation and democratisation. Mongolia had to become an open country to ensure international recognition. In doing so, Mongolia had to equally distance itself from the political domination of the then-still existing Soviet Union and post-Tiananmen China and move closer to the so-called "third neighbours," such as major democracies like the United States and Japan. This international recognition and, moreover, appreciation of Mongolia's transition to liberal democracy, served as the single most important factor of assuring national security in this otherwise unfavourable historical and geographical environment.

3.4.2 Security through Proactive Diplomacy

Mongolia's foreign policy achievements were direct results of its strategy of assuring maximum national security through democratisation. In 1994, the Parliament adopted two main documents based on the spirit of the 1992 Constitution.[23] First, the Foreign Policy Concept heralded fundamental changes in the *modus operandi* of the nation's engagement with the rest of the world as the end of the ideological confrontation of the Cold War opened up opportunities for Mongolia to pursue an independent foreign policy. In securing its interests, Mongolia pursues the following broad objectives:[24]

- maintaining friendly relations with both Russia and China;
- developing friendly relations with developed countries in both the West and the East;
- strengthening the nation's position in Asia and participating in the political and economic integration process in the region;

- seeking cooperation with international institutions such as the United Nations, its affiliated agencies, and international financial institutions;
- developing friendly relations with countries of the former socialist countries, including the newly, independent states;
- Promoting friendly relations and cooperation in the pursuit of common objectives with developing countries.

In addition, as a plausible counter-weight to the dominance of Russia and China, especially in the wake of their strategic partnership and like-mindedness in nearly all issues of concern to global and regional security, first Mongolian scholars and then practitioners coined the term and pursued the "Third Neighbour Policy," developing ever closer political, economic, cultural and security ties to developed democracies, including the United States, Japan, India, and European nations, as well as the international organisations.[25]

The National Security Concept, also legislated in 1994, demonstrates how a comprehensive, human-centered, development-oriented security approach can complement the nation's political will to pursue liberal democracy. Given the aforementioned foreign policy agenda and its ultimate success, the national security perception is based on the liberal institutionalist approach which many developing countries adhere to.[26] It is composed of nine areas of concern including security of the existence of state, security of constitutional order, security of national economy, security of information, security of population and genetic composition, security of the environment, security of Mongolian culture and way of life, security of science and technology and finally, most importantly, security of civil liberties.

Within this context of a pro-active foreign policy and liberal institutionalist approach to national security, Mongolia has offered a number of unique initiatives within the Northeast Asian region as active contributions to regional security. Mongolia declared its territory nuclear-free, a status recognised by the five permanent members of the United Nations Security Council, and proposed to expand the nuclear-free zone beyond its boundaries throughout Northeast Asia. Though sounding utterly unrealistic within the neighbourhood of nuclear Russia and China, this proposal was understood as Ulaanbaatar's call to Pyongyang to curtail its nuclear ambitions, which could destabilise the whole sub-region. As part of its multi-pillar foreign policy, the Mongolian government offered goodwill gestures and had a vested interest in maintaining stable relations with the two Korean states. Mongolia declared its interest in the peaceful resolution of the Korean crisis and its willingness to offer its contribution to the mutual understanding among the major actors of the region. In particular, it was declared that although North Korea faced difficulties in communicating to other actors, Mongolia's stable and friendly relations with the two Koreas, Japan, and the United States could serve as an asset in enhancing the mutual understanding and building the confidence. Mongolia was keen to become a full participant in the process of Asian regional integration and so it because is a member of the Association of Southeast Asian Nations (ASEAN) Regional Forum, and is now seeking ASEAN Dialogue Partner status and membership in Asia-Pacific Economic Cooperation (APEC) and the East Asian Community.[27]

In sum, the second half of the 1990s was marked by the strategy of proactive diplomacy, a more sophisticated tool of security assurance than merely a political democratisation. Having secured stable and harmonious relations with both Russia and China while pursuing greater visibility in the region, this was the period of strengthening the "third neighbour" concept. This stage was built upon democratisation, and commitments to ensure security through proactive diplomacy.

3.5 Impact of Relations with External Powers

3.5.1 Mongolia — Soviet Union/Russia Relations

Mongolia was a territorial buffer country. The Manchus occupied China and established the Qing Empire; and then they swept Mongolia into their kingdom. When the Qing collapsed, Moscow sucked Mongolia into its own expanding domain and, during the period of Sino-Soviet enmity from the mid-1960s to 1989, the Soviet Union stationed troops and military equipment in Mongolia to enhance its strategic advantage over the PRC.[28] Garver (1988, 217)[29] and Liu (2006, 342)[30] say that for Moscow, Mongolia was then a territorial buffer the particularities of Mongolian terrain underscored its salience as a shield behind which Russia felt more secure than if Mongolia had been in China's hands (Soni 2002).[31]

In the late 1980s, the close relationship between Mongolia and the Soviet Union was much the same as it had been since the 1920s. Mongolian foreign policy stressed consolidating the "fraternal alliance" with the Soviet Union and close cooperation with the members of the Warsaw Pact and Comecon. The two countries had direct links among ministries, agencies, departments, and party organisations. The Soviet Union encouraged direct contacts between Mongolia and the Buryatskaya Autonomous Soviet Socialist Republic and Tuvinskaya Autonomous Soviet Socialist Republics as well as the Central Asian Soviet republics. By 1985, the Soviet Union had consulates in the cities of Choybalsan; Darhan, where many Soviet-built factories were located; and Erdenet, the site of a Mongolian-Soviet joint copper and molybdenum mining enterprise. In August 1988, the only Mongolian ambassadorships with incumbents serving concurrently on the party Central Committee were assignments to countries of major concern to the Soviet Union: Albania, Afghanistan, East Germany, and Finland.[32] The Mongolian ambassador to the Soviet Union also served on the party Central Committee.

When Batmonh became general secretary of the Mongolian People's Revolutionary Party, an event followed closely by Gorbachev's election as general secretary of the Communist Party of the Soviet Union. The two leaders pledged to uphold and to strengthen the Mongolian-Soviet alliance. Gorbachev's "new thinking" in foreign policy matters soon became evident, however, and it no doubt raised major concerns, on the part of Mongolian leaders, particularly regarding a warming of relations between the Soviet Union and China. Soviet foreign minister Eduard Shevardnadze visited Mongolia from January 23 to 25, 1986, shortly after celebrations marking the twentieth anniversary of the signing of the 1966 Mongolian-Soviet Treaty of Friendship, Cooperation, and Mutual Assistance and its extension for ten years. Shevardnadze said that "the period of strained relationships with China is now behind us. The Soviet Union is for normalising and improving relations with the Chinese republic on condition that the principle of not harming third countries is observed." One clear purpose of the Soviet formula of "not harming third countries" was to reassure Mongolia that the Soviet Union did not plan initiatives toward China that would compromise or endanger Mongolia's national security or expose that country to Chinese encroachments (*Steve Mann 1989*).[33]

In July 1986, Gorbachev extended the new direction in foreign affairs in a speech on Asian security delivered in Vladivostok. He indicated Soviet interest in improved Moscow-Beijing relations, and he included a plan to withdraw Soviet troops from Mongolia, a major factor in Soviet diplomatic initiatives designed to meet China's conditions for normalisation of relations. Shortly after the Vladivostok initiative, Mongolian officials began talks with United States diplomats concerning another attempt to improve relations. Ulaanbaatar probably viewed prospective ties with Washington as offering a greater degree of manoeuverability in the increasingly complex international setting in Asia. In January 1987, diplomatic ties were established with the United States, and the Soviet Union announced its intention to withdraw one division of troops from Mongolia.[34] Both actions no doubt were the subject of lengthy substantive talks between Soviet and Mongolian leaders (*ibid*).

Mongolia further broadened its diplomatic horizons by hosting delegations from twenty-one Communist and workers' parties for the Consultative Meeting of Communist and Workers' Parties of Asia and the Pacific Region, the first regional gathering of this type, in July 1986. The theme of this meeting was "peace, security and good-neighbourly cooperation in Asia and the Pacific region." By hosting this meeting, Ulaanbaatar served Moscow's purposes of underscoring Gorbachev's new interest in Asia further highlighted by the attendance of a high-powered Soviet delegation. China declined to send a delegation, claiming that conditions were "not ripe," and the Democratic People's Republic of Korea (North Korea) did not attend either, probably as a gesture to China (*Steve Mann 1989*).[35]

As Mongolia expanded its contacts in the international community, Gorbachev continued to extend his Asian initiatives, a development directly affecting Mongolia's national interests. In a speech delivered on September 16, 1988, at the southeastern Siberian city of Krasnoyarsk, Gorbachev presented a seven-point program designed to enhance security in the Asia-Pacific region and to promote his view of a multi-polar approach to resolving issues in foreign relations. The so-called Krasnoyarsk initiative indicated both Soviet intentions to play a major role in the region and its awareness that China also must be included in regional development plans.[36] Observers speculated that the Soviets must have expended considerable effort in reassuring Mongolian leaders that Soviet proposals dealing with East Asia, particularly those involving China, did not threaten Mongolian national security (Worden and Savada 1989).

The challenge for Mongolia's foreign policy makers was to comply with Soviet initiatives, about which they had little choice, but to do so in a manner that suggested that Mongolia was acting as an independent country, shaping a foreign policy that served its national interests. At the same time, the Soviet Union could not appear to be overlooking the interests of its ally Mongolia while making its overtures to China. This mild restriction on Soviet behaviour had helped to reassure Mongolia that continued Soviet protection and strategic support were reliable. In any case, Mongolian compliance with the Soviet initiatives was evident in Gorbachev's address to the United Nations (UN) General Assembly on December 7, 1988. In it he announced that most Soviet troops stationed in Mongolia would be withdrawn. Subsequently, in February 1989, during talks between Batmonh and a Soviet deputy foreign minister, the latter explained that discussions to resolve questions connected with "the withdrawal from the territory of Mongolia of 75 per cent of Soviet land forces and other military sub units would soon begin." On March 7, 1989, the Soviets announced, probably as an additional concession to China on the eve of the May 1989 Sino - Soviet summit that withdrawal plans had been finalised (Worden and Savada 1989).[37]

While Mongolia became independent of the Soviet Union in 1990, then both countries (Beijing and Moscow) did not view Mongolia as a territorial buffer. However, Mongolia played the role of what might be called a geopolitical buffer. What Moscow and Beijing sought of Mongolia was not a barrier that could be subordinated by one to enhance the defense of the homeland territory from assault by the other, but a neutral region where each of the two neighbours could be assured of Ulaanbaatar's political pliability and an absence of menace.[38] It suited Beijing and Moscow that Ulaanbaatar was deferential to their own core interests, so long as Mongolia did not give precedence to the interests of one over the other. In that sense, Mongolia was still a buffer, but its role was defined politically and economically, rather than territorially, by its determination to be an unaligned zone of neutrality in a region with a fierce and bloody history of geopolitical friction. Wachmanb (2009) argue that if Mongolia were to align itself too closely to either of its proximate neighbors,[39] it would surely spark alarm. Should it lean too far toward Moscow or Beijing, the other would swiftly see Mongolia as a territorial buffer subject to exploitation by the other side (Worden and Savada 1989).

Immediately, after the break-up of the Soviet Union the declaration of friendship and good-neighbourly cooperation in 1991 between Russia and Mongolia was the first affirmation of their equality as sovereign states. However, relations with Russia were in decline for much of the 1990's because of Russia's internal economic and social problems (Batbayar, 2003).[40] It was not until Putin's[41] visit to Mongolia at the end of 2000 that relations began to revitalise. Understandably, Mongolia's relations first with the Soviet Union and then with Russia did impact foreign policy changes in Mongolia.[42]

3.5.2 Mongolia—China Relations

China and Mongolia established diplomatic relations on October 16, 1949. Despite some twists and turns in their relations over the past 60 years since the establishment of their diplomatic relations, neighbourliness and friendship have always remained the mainstream of Sino-Mongolian relations. In the second half of the 1990s in particular, their relations developed rapidly and made remarkable achievements. In 1994, both sides signed a treaty on Friendship and Cooperation, laying the political and legal foundation for the healthy and steady development of their relations.

Mongolian-Chinese relations historically have suffered because of China's claims to "lost territory" and Mongolia's fear of China's expansion because of overpopulation. Since 1984 improvement in Mongolia's relations with China lagged behind the more rapid advances in Sino-Soviet relations. An early indication of lessening of tensions, however, came in July 1984 when Ulaanbaatar sent to Beijing a delegation led by its deputy foreign minister, the first such visit in several years. The Mongolian representative met with China's minister of foreign affairs to discuss developing bilateral economic, cultural, trade, and technical relations. Also, the officials signed a document verifying the first joint inspection of the Mongolian-Chinese border. The warming atmosphere continued with the signing of an agreement on civil aviation in December 1985, followed by the resumption of direct Beijing-Ulaanbaatar air service in June 1986. A five-year agreement increasing levels of trade was signed in April 1986 (Worden and Savada 1989).[43]

Mongolian President Batmonh gave official sanction to improvements in Mongolian-Chinese relations in his address to the May 1986, nineteenth Congress. Displaying caution and restraint, Batmonh declared that Mongolia was pursuing consistently its "scrupulous policy" of normalising relations with China, with the qualification that the relationship should be based on equality and "non-interference in another's internal affairs." This evident uncertainty concerning national security was reflected in Mongolian press statements, just prior to Gorbachev's July 1986 address that announced Soviet troop withdrawals were under consideration. The press stressed that the disposition of Soviet a troop stationed in Mongolia was an internal matter between Mongolia and the Soviet Union, and that it was not a subject for discussion during any Sino-Soviet consultations.[44] An article appearing in the press shortly after Gorbachev's speech captured the Mongolian sentiment that "no country which borders on China feels secure" (Worden and Savada 1989).

Batmonh's initiatives were followed by an August 1986 visit to Mongolia of a vice foreign minister described as the highest ranking Chinese official to visit Mongolia in twenty years. This important meeting resulted in the signing of a consular agreement, the first since the establishment of diplomatic relations between the countries in 1949. This agreement was followed in 1987 by several key visits and events: a high-level delegation from China's legislative body, the National People's Congress, visited Mongolia in June; this visit was reciprocated in September 1988 by a delegation from the People's Great Hural, the first since 1960; a scientific and technical cooperative program for the 1987 to 1988 period was ratified in July; and a major Mongolian friendship delegation visited China in September 1987 reciprocated by a Chinese friendship delegation that went to Mongolia in July 1988 (Worden and Savada 1989).[45]

Other important points of discussion at the August 1986 meeting reportedly were "certain international issues of common concern." Japanese press reports indicated that the Mongolians had rejected a Chinese request at the meeting that all Soviet troops be withdrawn from Mongolia. In China's view, the presence of Soviet troops in Mongolia was a key "obstacle" to normalisation of relations between China and the Soviet Union. Maintaining that only a total troop withdrawal would be satisfactory, China refused to back down from this position. From the Chinese perspective, Mongolia once had been under China's domination; it was therefore particularly galling that Soviet troops were now massed in that area and were directed against China.

In 1988 security concerns and Mongolia's image as an independent country were especially visible in its foreign policy *vis-à-vis* China. The stationing of Soviet troops on Mongolia's border with China remained a major impediment to improve Sino-Soviet relations and Mongolian-Chinese relations. China now respects Mongolia's independence and sovereignty besides carrying out mutually beneficial cooperation in not only political and economic spheres, but also in the defence sector. Soni (2004) suggests that "Mongolia's security is not to be viewed in terms of Chinese threat".[46] Telford (2004)[47] also articulated that during

Table 1: Sino-Mongolian Bilateral Trade, 1987-1996

(Value in million US$)

Year	*China's Exports to Mongolia*	*China's Imports from Mongolia*	*Total value of Bilateral Trade*	*Trade Balance (+-)*
1	2	3	4 (2+3)	5 (2-3)
1987	20.27	4.61	24.88	15.66
1988	16.98	7.95	24.93	9.03
1989	19.86	8.67	28.53	11.19
1990	29.81	11.21	41.02	18.60
1991	25.96	20.07	46.03	5.89
1992	135.76	48.11	183.87	87.65
1993	81.59	69.36	150.95	12.23
1994	42.77	76.10	118.87	(-) 33.33
1995	62.91	99.04	161.95	(-) 36.13
1996	72.36	126.39	198.75	(-) 54.03

(*Sources:* Sharad K. Soni (2009), China Periphery Policy: implications for sino-Mongolian relations, *India Quarterly: A journal of international affairs, pp. 65:251*).

the 1990s Mongolian-Chinese relations considerably enhanced from a state of virtual non-existence to one of mutual cooperation, based on the "Treaty on Friendship and Cooperation" signed between China and Mongolia in 1994. Batbayar (2002)[48] attributes this warming of attitudes to the improvement in Sino-Soviet relations, the removal of Soviet troops from Mongolia and the collapse of the USSR. In contrast to Russia, China's influence over Mongolia was increasing. Campi (2004)[49] says that "during the past decade (1990s) Chinese aid has become significant". China also became the biggest investor in Mongolia, with $ US 281 million accounting for over 40 per cent of Mongolia's total FDI (Chinese Ministry of External Affairs)[50].

However, the most important issue from the Mongolian perspective has been a fear of Chinese expansion. The 'Concept of National Security' and 'Concept of Foreign Policy' both identify "*massive inflows of migrants from a neighbouring state*" as a real threat to national interests. In addition to several highly publicised maps originating in China and showing all or part of Mongolia integrated into China, there were Chinese plans for starting '*large-scale animal-husbandry operations*' in southern Mongolia (Kaplan, 2004)[51] and there was also fear that increases in Chinese investments would lead to economic, if not physical control over Mongolia (Bruun and Odgaard 1997a).[52]

Soni (2006)[53] articulated that the Cold War period saw stagnation in Sino-Mongolian economic and trade cooperation, while the post-Cold War period has brought an unprecedented growth especially in bilateral trade. Obviously, such situations impacted Mongolia's foreign policy as well.[54]

Political Relations

Mongolia is one of the first groups of countries that recognised the People's Republic of China. In 1962, both sides signed Sino-Mongolian Treaty on Friendship and Mutual Assistance, and in 1962, signed Boundary Treaty. In mid and late 1960s, their relations suffered ups and downs. In 1970s, the two countries restored to exchange of ambassadors. In 1980s, their relations saw gradual improvement. In 1989, their state and ruling party's (Chinese Communist Party and Mongolian People's Revolutionary Party) relations were normalised. Since then, their friendly relations and cooperation have consolidated and developed in such areas as the political, economic, cultural, educational and military. In 1990, China and Mongolia issued a joint communiqué, revised Sino-Mongolian Treaty on Friendship and Mutual Assistance in 1994, and signed Friendship and Cooperation Treaty between China and Mongolia based on the previous treaty. Both sides agreed to strengthen and develop friendly relations and cooperation on the basis of the five principles of peaceful coexistence.[55]

Chinese leaders who have visited Mongolia are as follows: Premier Zhou Enlai (in 1954 and 1960), Vice-President Zhu De (in 1956), President Yang Shangkuan (in 1991), Premier Li Peng (1994), Chairman of SC of the NPC Qiao Shi (in 1997), Vice-Premier-cum-Foreign Minister (in 1997), President Jiang Zemin (in 1999), Member of the SC of PB of Central Committee of the CPC-cum-Secretary of the Secretariat Wei Jianxin (2000), and President Hu Jintao (in June 2003).

Economic/Trade Relations and Economic/Technological Cooperation

In 1951, China and Mongolia established trade relations. In 1989, the two governments set up a committee on economic, trade, scientific and technological cooperation, and seven meetings have been held. In 1991, the two governments signed a new trade agreement, replacing inter-governmental credit trade with cash trade. In the same year, they signed an investment protection agreement. By the statistics from China's General Administration of Customs, in 2002, Sino-Mongolian trade volume totaled $US 363 million, of which China's exports accounted for $US 140 million and its imports $US 223 million.[56]

On the basis of equality and mutual benefit, China and Mongolia have developed economic and trade cooperation. By statistics from the Mongolian side, up to the end of 2002, there were 825 enterprises with Chinese investment in Mongolia. With its investment exceeding $US 281 million, China has remained Mongolia's biggest investor, reaching some 40 per cent of Mongolia's total foreign investment. In June 2002, Minister of Foreign Trade and Economic Cooperation Shi Guangsheng visited Mongolia.

Since 1985, the two countries have developed their border trade while developing trade between their governments. Border trade has been conducted between China's Inner Mongolia, Xinjiang Uygur and Ningxia Hui Autonomous Regions, Hebei and Jilin Provinces and Mongolia's related regions and departments.

Exchanges and Cooperation in the Cultural, Educational, Scientific and Technological Fields

China and Mongolia have stared cultural exchanges since 1951. Over the recent years, in accordance with the cultural exchange programmes between their governments, the two countries have conducted cultural exchanges and cooperation through many channels and tiers and in various forms. In 1994, Cultural Cooperation Agreement between China and Mongolia was signed. In 1997, Cultural Minister Liu Dezhong visited Mongolia as head of a cultural delegation of the Chinese Government, it is the first visit to Mongolia by China's cultural minister since the establishment of diplomatic relations between the two countries. In 1998, Mongolian Minister of Education Saihanbileg visited China as head of the government delegation, and both sides signed 1998-2000 Executive Plan for Sino-Mongolian Cultural Exchanges. In April 1999, Vice-Minister of Culture Ai Qing visited Mongolia as head of the Chinese Cultural Delegation. In April 2001, Assistant Minister of Culture Chang Keren visited Mongolia as head of the Chinese Cultural Delegation, and both sides signed 2001-2003 Executive Plan for Cultural Exchanges and Cooperation. In May 2001, Mongolian Director-General of Radio and Television Ganbold visited China.[57]

In 1987, China and Mongolia restored scientific and technological exchanges suspended for more than the previous 20 years, and signed 1987-1988 Plan for Scientific and Technological Cooperation. In 1989, the sci-tech cooperation delegation of the Mongolian government visited China. Since then, both sides have regularly held sci-tech cooperation meetings and signed annual sci-tech cooperation programmes. Between the end of August and start of September 1999, President of Chinese Academy of Sciences Lu Yongxiang visited Mongolia as head of the delegation of his academy. In November 2001, Vice-President of this academy visited Mongolia.

China and Mongolia started educational contacts in 1952. Over the years, they have witnessed smooth development in the educational exchanges and cooperation. In 1996, Mongolian Minister of Science and Education Tumur-Ochir visited China, and both sides signed 1996-2000 Educational Exchanges and Cooperation Programme between China and Mongolia. In 1998,

China and Mongolia signed Agreement on Mutual Recognition of Academic Degrees and Credentials between the Governments of the People's Republic of China and Mongolia. In 2000, they signed the Executive Programme on the Project for Helping the Mongolian Students Studying in China with Chinese Free Loan. Between 2002 and 2003, Mongolia sent to China 180 trainees and students while China had sent 15 trainees for further studies in Mongolia and a teacher for teaching Chinese. In May 2002, Vice-Minister of Education Zhang Tianbao visited Mongolia.[58]

Other Relations

Along with the development of the bilateral relations, consular relations have also developed between the two countries. In 1986, the two governments signed in Beijing Consular Treaty between China and Mongolia. In 1990, Mongolia reopened its consulate-general in Hohhot. In 1996, the Office of Mongolia's Hohhot Consulate-General in Eren started working. In 1997, the two countries signed the Agreement on Mongolia retaining its honourary consulate in Hong Kong Special Administration of China between the Governments of the People's Republic of China and Mongolia. At present, diplomatic, official and service passport holders are exempted from visas between the two countries. Development of Sino-Mongolian consular relations has played an active part in promoting economic and trade contacts and personnel exchanges between the two countries.[59]

In 1991, China and Mongolia signed the Agreement on Border Ports and their Management System between the Governments of the People's Republic of China and People's Republic of Mongolia. At present, both sides have 11 pairs of ports opened, of which China's Eren and Mongolia's Zamyn-Uud are open all year round and rest are only open in certain seasons.

There are now regular flights between Ulan Bator and Beijing opened by both sides. Mongolia has opened regular flights between Ulan Bator and Hohhot.

Major Bilateral Agreements

1. The Boundary Treaty between the People's Republic of China and People's Republic of Mongolia (signed on December 26, 1962).
2. The Consular Treaty between the People's Republic of China and People's Republic of Mongolia (signed on August 9, 1986).

3. The Treaty on Friendly Relations and Cooperation between the People's Republic of China and Mongolia (signed on April 29, 1994).

Thus, it's clear that the relations between Mongolia and China had dynamism with every passing dynasties ruling the Mongolian plateau. The Mongol-China relations which can be traced back to the legacy of the Mongol conquest in the 13th century when Cenghis Khan united the warring Mongol tribes into military force and led campaigns against settled regions of the Eurasian continent. They both had constant relationship since the recorded history of the region. Before Cenghis Khan, the Mongols lacked a sense of their identity as a people. His historic role was to endow them with such a strong sense of identification with his ancestral homelands, almost akin to modern nationalism, The success of Mongols armies over such an enormous area of Europe and Asia in such a short time is one of the wonders of history and we are bound to ask why they achieved so much. Mongol successes were because of the discipline and cohesion of army organisation. In 1271, Kublai Khan adopted the Chinese name Yuan (beginning) for his Mongolian dynasty. Of the 631 years from 1280 to 1911, China was under national rulers for 276 years and under alien rule for 355 years. The Mongols were the first alien people to rule the whole of China; the Manchus, who appeared in, were the second and the last. The unification under Mongol rule facilated the assimilation of the different peoples to create the multi-national character, which has been a source of China's strength. During the era of colonialism an acute social and political antagonism developed between China and Mongolia had been created by the antithesis of rising technique of railways, factories, mines, motor cars and electric power plants at the urban end and increasing reliance at rural end of the necessities of life (which earlier had nomadic mode of production). That failure, growing out of the forces inherent in their pastoral feudal structure, created a power vacuum on the Mongolian plateau. The Mongols were unable to present a united front to the combined threat from China and Russia. The concept of nation-state had not developed since they were just a land and cattle economy and party because there was little investment in the trade and industry. It was inevitable that the stronger of the two should fill the power vacuum.

3.5.3 Mongolia — US Relations

The US had significant role in influencing Mongolian foreign policy decisions. In 1986 Soviet foreign minister Shevardnadze gave Mongolia the 'green light' to establish independent diplomatic relations with the US. It did so in January 1987, spurred on by Gorbachev's decision to withdraw Soviet troops, the loss of whose protection they feared (Batbayar, 2003b:954).[60] The United States established diplomatic relations with Mongolia at a time, when it was still a Communist state, and since then has sought to expand bilateral cultural and economic ties. In 1991, following the signing of a bilateral trade agreement, President Bush restored Mongolia's most-favoured-nation (MFN) trading status now referred to as Normal Trade Relations (NTR) under the conditional annual waiver provisions of Title IV of the Trade Act of 1974 (Dumbaugh and Morrison 2009).[61] That NTR status was made permanent (PNTR) effective from July 1, 1999, obviating the annual trade status review process.[62]

United States officials were primarily interested in establishing ties because of Mongolia's strategic and geographic position in the Sino-Soviet relationship. Washington had considered establishing diplomatic relations in the past, but it had deferred to the Guomindang (Kuomintang), or Chinese Nationalist, government in Taiwan, which still claimed Mongolia as part of China. In the early 1970s, negotiations were reopened, and they were almost completed when the proceedings were broken off by Mongolia because of problems between the United States and the Soviet Union, including the Second Indo-China War (1963-75).

The establishment of Mongolian-United States relations reflected improvements in the United States-Soviet relationship also and it was consistent with Gorbachev's interest in dealing with all states that have substantial interests in Asia. The United States gained the diplomatic recognition of a strategically located country in Asia. The new Mongolian-United States relationship was assisted by the establishment of ties between China and the United States. For Mongolia the new relationship had given greater credibility to its political independence and sovereign status and increased its foreign policy options.

The Foreign Policy Blue Book (2000:23) states that 'the relationship with the two immediate neighbours remains a top priority in Mongolia's foreign policy, however from the country's development and national security perspective, the expansion of the relations with highly-developed countries is also a top priority agenda'. So development of relations with the US is fully consistent with the national interests of Mongolia. Perhaps at first glance Mongolia wouldn't seem to be a country of strategic importance outside of Russia and China, however as Kaplan (2003)[63] says "we live in an era when 'any place can turn out to be strategic" and after September 11th Central Asia, including Mongolia, became 'strategic' to the US. The USAID-21 website states that US interests in Mongolia "center largely on its strategic location between Russia and China, two traditional rivals that are also nuclear powers and important global players". China's rapid growth both militarily and economically[64] has been of great concern to the US, but "if we look beyond the present conflagrations in the Middle East, China looms as the greatest challenge to American power" (Kaplan, 2004).[65]

As Bruun and Odgaard (1997a:26) say 'for the Mongolians, there are historical reasons to see international aid as coinciding with larger, geopolitical interests. The sequence of Russian and Chinese aid reflected delicate balances between the superpowers to which the country had to submit but perhaps owed its survival as an independent nation' there is certainly an argument for this being the case today with the US replacing China and Russia. In the past, however, there were also attempts to bring US and Mongolia closer.[66]

As Scalapino points out, in 1919, the theocratic leader of Mongolia, Bogd Khan (Divine King), sent two letters to the American government which requested political recognition of an independent Mongolia and expressed his wish for an American Consulate to be established in the Mongolian capital of Urga (Scalapino 2005: 9). In April 1921, a United States Consular Office was established in the city of Kalgan (located in today's Inner Mongolia Autonomous Region in China).[67] However, following the Soviet revolution and Mongolia's inclusion under the Soviet umbrella, the United States rescinded its diplomatic ties, leaving the fate of the Mongol people and territory to be determined through Soviet and Chinese diplomatic processes. Although unsuccessful in the early twentieth century in securing US support, Mongolia noted America's interest in the region. The memory of this subsequently lingered throughout the socialist period, giving

Mongolia the confidence to once again reactivate relations with the US during the post-Cold War period.

Porter absorbs that Mongolia has three main areas of interest to improve relations with the US, that is: political independence, regional and global security, and economic growth. The most important factor in Mongolia-US relations is the realisation of Mongolia's "third neighbour" foreign policy. Third neighbor policy is something recently manifested and based on Mongolia's post-Cold War shift from socialism to liberal democracy. As both Russia and China have tussled over Mongol territory for over four hundred years, with both exercising great influence over it at different times, another "neighbour" or outside power is seen as essential in balancing the influence of both Russia and China and maintaining Mongolian independence. Although the "third neighbour" policy is essentially open to all nations who wish to develop relations with Mongolia, the Mongolian government views courting the US as its main priority[68].

On the other hand Soni (2006) understands that US interests in Mongolia centre largely on the following considerations:[69] (a) Mongolia's strategic location which could prove to be of vital importance for moderating Asian politics; (b) Mongolia provides a significant though fragile example of democratic reforms and economic restructuring in a potentially unstable part of the world; and (c) Mongolia consistently lends its strong support to the US stand on several international issues including those concerning ongoing war on terrorism[70]. So relations with the United States have had significant impact on Mongolia's foreign policy that can be seen through the adoption of a new independent concept of in the field of foreign affairs.

As a sovereign nation in her own right, due to membership of, and participation in multilateral organisations such as the UN, Mongolia has been able to make fully independent foreign policy decisions (Telford 2004).[71] Besides, relations with the Soviet Union/Russia, China and the US provided much needed bulwarks to changes the existing foreign policy and adopt a new one by taking into consideration the new geopolitical environment surrounding Mongolia and its national security interest.

Notes and References

1. Telford Sarah (2004), "To What Extent Does Post-1990 Mongolia Pursue an Independent Foreign Policy?" Research *Unit on International Security and Cooperation (UNISCI)*, Spain: Madrid.

2. Soni. Sharad K. (2006), "Mongolia's Security Thinking and Outside World: A Reappraisal", *Bimonthly Journal of Mongolian and Tibetan Current Situation*, 15 (6): pp. 27-39.

3. For detail see Sharad. K. Soni (2006), *Mongolia-China Relations: Modern and Contemporary Times*, New Delhi: Pentagon Press.

4. student papers from 29-May-2012. Submitted to Associatie K.U.Leuven on 2012-05-29.

5. http://hovdtour.mn/index.php/page/34/0/show.

6. Garver, J. (1988), *Sino-Soviet Relations, 1937–1945: The Diplomacy of Chinese Nationalism*. Oxford: Oxford University Press.

7. Soni. Sharad K. (2002), *Mongolia-Russia Relations: Kiakhta to Vladivostok,* New Delhi: Shipra Publication.

8. Baabar, B. (1999) . *History of Mongolia*. Cambridge, UK: The White Horse Press.

9. Soni. Sharad K. (2002), *Mongolia-Russia Relations: Kiakhta to Vladivostok,* New Delhi: Shipra Publication.

10. Huntington, S. P. (1993), "The Clash of Civilizations". *Foreign Affairs,* 72(3).

11. *Ibid.*

12. *Ibid.*

13. Ministry of Foreign Affairs (2006), "Concept of Mongolia's Foreign Policy," *Diplomatic Bluebook 2006*, Ulaanbaatar.

14. http://www.bored.com/ebooks/World_Reference/historical%20 context%20—%20country%20studies/mongolia/mongolia.txt.

15. http://countrystudies.us/mongolia/63.htm.

16. http://www.photoglobe.info/ebooks/mongolia/cstudies_ mongolia_0143.html.

17. http://www.embassymon.at/policy_2.html.

18. *Ibid.*

19. Munkh-Ochir Dorjjugder (2009), *Same Rules, New Dimensions For Mongolia's National Security: Adapting to the New Geo-Economic Environment,* Associate Senior Analyst, Institute for Strategic Studies, National Security Council of Mongolia.

20. http://www.brookings.edu/opinions/2009/10_mongolia_ dorjjugder.aspx

21. *Ibid.*

22. Student papers from 11-Feb-2009), Submitted to University of Tasmania on 2009-02-11

23. Munkh-Ochir Dorjjugder (2009), *Same Rules, New Dimensions For Mongolia's National Security: Adapting to the New Geo-Economic Environment,* Associate Senior Analyst, Institute for Strategic Studies, National Security Council of Mongolia.

24. *Ibid.*

25. *Ibid.*

26. *Ibid.*

27. *Ibid.*

28. Wachmanb Alan M. (2009), *Mongolia's Geo-political Gambit:Preserving a Precarious Independence While Resisting "Soft Colonialism",*The East Asia Institute (EAI) is a non-profit and independent research organisation in Korea, Tufts University.ellows.

29. Garver, J. (1988), *Sino-Soviet Relations, 1937–1945: The Diplomacy of Chinese Nationalism.* Oxford: Oxford University Press.

30. Liu Xiaoyuan (2006),*Reins of Liberation: An Entangled History of Mongolian Independence, Chinese Territoriality, and Great Power Hegemony,* Stanford: Stanford University Press.

31. Soni. Sharad K. (2002),*Mongolia-Russia Relations: Kiakhta to Vladivostok,* New Delhi: Shipra Publication.

32. http://www.photoglobe.info/ebooks/mongolia/cstudies_ mongolia_ 0145.html.

33. *Ibid.*

34. *Ibid.*

35. *Ibid.*

36. Worden R. L. and Savada A. M. (1989), *Mongolia: A Country Study.* Washington: GPO for the Library of Congress.

37. *Ibid.*

38. *Ibid.*

39. Worden R. L. and Savada A. M. (1989), *Mongolia: A Country Study.* Washington: GPO for the Library of Congress.

40. Batbayar, T. (2003), "Foreign Policy and Domestic Reform in Mongolia", *Central Asian Survey*, 22(1):172-204.

41. President of Russia.

42. *Ibid.*

43. Batbayar, T. (2003), "Foreign Policy and Domestic Reform in Mongolia", *Central Asian Survey*, 22(1): pp. 172-204.

44. Worden R. L. and Savada A. M. (1989), *Mongolia: A Country Study.* Washington: GPO for the Library of Congress.

45. *Ibid.*

46. *Ibid.*

47. Sharad K. Soni (2005), "Mongolia-China Relations: Post-Cold War Scenario", in Mahavir Singh, ed.,*Asia Annual 2004,* Delhi: Shipra Publications, Kolkata, p. 234.

48. Telford Sarah (2004), "To What Extent Does Post-1990 Mongolia Pursue an Independent Foreign Policy?" Research *Unit on International Security and Cooperation (UNISCI)*, Spain: Madrid.

49. Batbayar, T. (2002), "Mongolia's New Identity and Security Dilemmas", *The Mongolian Journal of International Affairs*, 8(9): pp. 3-11.

50. Campi, A. (2004), *Modern Mongolian-Chinese Strategic Relations: Challenges for the New Century*. U.S.: Mongolia Advisory Group.

51. Telford Sarah (2004), *To What Extent Does Post-1990 Mongolia Pursue an Independent Foreign Policy?* Research Unit on International Security and Cooperation (UNISCI), Madrid, Spain.

52. Kaplan, R. D. (2004). 'The Man Who Would be Khan', The Atlantic Monthly. March. [Online] Available at http://www.theatlantic.com/issues/2004/03/kaplan.htm.

53. Bruun, O and Odgaard, O. (1997b), "Consolidating Independence", in Bruun, O. and Odgaard, O. eds. *Mongolia in Transition: Old Patterns, New Challenges,* Curzon: Routledge.

54. Soni. Sharad K. (2006), *Mongolia-China Relations: Modern and Contemporary Times*, New Delhi: Pentagon Press.

55. *Ibid.*

56. China Daily (2010), China-Mongolia Relations, update on 27 May 2010 fmprc.gov.cn

57. China Daily (2010), China-Mongolia Relations, update on 27 May 2010 fmprc.gov.cn

58. *Ibid.*

59. *Ibid.*

60. *Ibid.*

61. Batbayar, T. (2003), "Foreign Policy and Domestic Reform in Mongolia", *Central sian Survey*, 22(1): pp. 172-204.

62. Dumbaugh K. and Wayne M. Morrison (2009), Mongolia and U.S. Policy: Political and Economic Relations, CRS Report for Congress, www.crs.gov.

63. See Section 2424 of The Miscellaneous Trade and Technical Corrections Act of 1999, enacted as P.L. 106-36, effective on July 1, 1999, by Presidential Proclamation 7207.

64. Kaplan, R. D. (2004). 'The Man Who Would be Khan', The Atlantic Monthly. March. [Online] Available at http://www.the atlantic.com/issues/2004/03/kaplan.htm.

65. 'Buoyed by spectacular economic development, China is rapidly increasing its military spending and vigorously moving forward with the modernisation of its armed forces' (Huntington, 1993).

66. Telford Sarah (2004), To What Extent Does Post-1990 Mongolia Pursue an Independent Foreign Policy? Research Unit on International Security and Cooperation (UNISCI), Madrid, Spain.

67. Bruun, O and Odgaard, O. (1997b), "Consolidating Independence", in Bruun, O. and Odgaard, O. eds. *Mongolia in Transition: Old Patterns, New Challenges,* Curzon: Routledge.

68. The United States chose to open its Consulate Office in the city of Kalgan instead of Urga mainly due to the perceived commercial benefits that were available in Kalgan (Chinese Inner Mongolia) as opposed to Urga (Outer Mongolia).

69. For more detail see Ron A. Porter, *Realpolitik in Mongolia-US Relations* http://r cube.ritsumei.ac.jp/bitstream/10367/947/1/6-RJAPS26_Realpolitik%20in%20Mongolia US%20Relations.pdf.

70. See, "Mongolia" at www.usaid.gov/regions/ane/newpages/one_pagers/mong01a.htm.

71. Soni, Sharad K. (2006), "Mongolia's Security Thinking and Outside World: A Reappraisal", *Bimonthly Journal of Mongolian and Tibetan Current Situation*, 15 (6): pp. 27-39.

4

"Multi-Pillar" Foreign Policy of Mongolia

Since Mongolia is a land-locked country situated between Russia and China, a coherent foreign policy is indispensable in maintaining any political regime intact. An extraordinary degree of foreign policy consensus emerged in Mongolia in the early Genghis1990s reflected in such ideas as 'multi-pillar' foreign policy (Soni 2006)[1] and a 'balanced' relationship with two neighbours. The idea behind adopting such a foreign policy was to make constructive relations with all nations, seeking independence from its two giant neighbours, and avoid dependence on any single partner. After the collapse of the USSR, Mongolia became one of the so-called "Nationalising States". During that time, a new genealogy of nationhood and a model of political succession were forming; though Mongolia has been leading its succession since the times of Genghis Khan, the epoch of the Great Mongolian State. In nationalist discourse the following people are distinguished in the history as the key personalities: Genghis Khan as the founder of the State, Zanabazar, Mongolian Leonardo da Vinci, and Sukhe-Bator, the revolution leader of 1921 (Kaplonski 2004).[2] However, in contemporary Mongolia to a number of personalities have been describe neither as nationalists who contributed significantly nor only to the democratic transition of the country but also to the emergence of a new foreign policy.

The emergence of new "multi-pillar" foreign policy owes much to the reform process. With the influence of USSR, Mongolia lunched Soviet style reforms and restructuring through Iltod and Orchilan baigalalt in 1988, this allowed the government to discuss several problems and mistakes committed by the Mongolian leaderships. Thus, the reforms were required not only in domestic political, social and economic fields but also in the foreign affairs. In the meantime as discussed in previous chapters., the demise of the former USSR in 1991 and the end of the Cold War altered the geo-political environment of Mongolia and left it in a great power vacuum. It was then the reform process towards democracy and market economy that warranted a drastic shift in the strategies, purpose and priorities of the country's foreign policy. Hence, Mongolia abandoned "Satellite State" foreign policy and developed an independent, non-aligned, multi-pillar, open foreign policy based on its national interests.[3]

4.1 Determinants of Mongolian Foreign Policy

The disintegration of the world socialist system and the Soviet Union has dramatically changed the external situation of Mongolia which used to be aligned with them. The major changes taking place in Mongolia's two neighbouring countries had a direct impact on its external environment. The restructuring and reforming of the country's political, social and economic systems provided it with favourable conditions for conducting a foreign policybased on realism and its national interests. [4] The concept of Mongolia's foreign policy has taken in to account the following:

"Independent and sovereign Mongolia, in terms of its state structure, is a unitary State upholding rights, freedoms and free economy; in political and geographical respects, it is a developing country in Asia, land-locked between two great powers. Mongolia's foreign policy shall be based on its national interests, as defined in its Constitution; the country's specific external and internal situation constitutes the basis for determining its foreign policy objectives, principles and priorities. Mongolia's foreign policy objectives reside in ensuring its independence and sovereignty by following the trends of human society's advancement, maintaining friendly relations with all countries, strengthening its position in the international community and forming with influential countries in the region and in the world a network of relationships based on the interdependence of political, economic and other interests. Mongolia shall pursue an open and non-aligned policy. While following a policy of creating realistic interest of the developed countries in Mongolia, it will seek to avoid becoming overly reliant or dependent on any particular country. In formulating Mongolia's foreign policy and determining its priority directions and objectives, flexible approach shall be applied, paying close attention to the development of international relations and to the regional and world political situations. The priority of Mongolia's foreign policy shall be safeguarding of its security and vital national interests by political and diplomatic means, and creating a favourable external environment for its economic, scientific and technological development.[5] Considerations of foreign relations shall be in political, economic, scientific, technological, cultural and humanitarian fields of foreign policy.

4.1.1 Mongolia's foreign policy in the political sphere

Mongolia's foreign policy in the political field is an important instrument for ensuring and strengthening its security.[6] Thus as the concept of foreign policy says, its results will be measured first and foremost by how the country's security and independence interests are met, and to what extent its international position has been strengthened and its prestige enhanced. In developing its relations with other countries, Mongolia will be guided by universally recognised principles and norms of international law as defined in the Charter of the United Nations, including mutual respect for each other's sovereignty, territorial integrity and inviolability of frontiers, right to self-determination, non-interference in internal affairs, non-use of force, settlement of disputes by peaceful means, respect for human rights and freedoms, and equal and mutually beneficial cooperation. In this regard the concept of Mongolia's foreign policy says that, "foreign policy of Mongolia shall uphold peace, strive to avoid confrontation with other countries and pursue a multi-base policy. While always championing its national interests, it will at the same time respect the legitimate interests of other countries and its partners". It shall pursue a policy of refraining from joining any military alliance or grouping, allowing the use of its territory or air space against any other country, and the stationing of foreign troops or weapons, including nuclear or any other type of mass destruction weapons in its territory. Mongolia shall seek to guarantee its interests in the international arena through bilateral and multi-lateral treaties and agreements. Mongolia shall respect and observe international law, and fulfill in good faith its obligations under international treaties. As a member of the world community Mongolia shall strive to make active contribution to the common cause of settling pressing regional and international issues. In doing so, it shall be guided primarily by its national interests, values and fundamental principles.[7] Above mentioned points are for strengthening national interest, and avoiding confrontation with other countries to pursue a multi-bases foreign policy.[8]

Batbayar and Soni have discussed six directions as guidelines for implementing Mongolia's foreign policy[9] as such Mongolia is guided by the following directions:

(a) Maintaining friendly relations with the Russian Federation, People's Republic of China shall be priority directions of Mongolia's foreign policy activity. It shall not adopt the line of either country but shall maintain in principle a balanced relationship with both of them and shall promote all-round neighbourly cooperation. In doing so, the traditional relations as well as the specific nature of our economic cooperation with these two countries will be taken into account.

(b) The second direction of Mongolia's foreign policy activity shall be developing friendly-relations with highly developed countries of the West and East such as the United States of America, Japan and the Federal Republic of Germany. At the same time, it will also pursue a policy aimed at promoting friendly-relations with such countries as India, the Republic of Korea, Thailand, Singapore, Turkey, Denmark, the Netherlands, Finland, Austria, Sweden, Switzerland and at creating and bringing to an appropriate level their economic and other interests in Mongolia.[10]

(c) The third direction of Mongolia's foreign policy activity shall be strengthening its position in Asia and securing a constructive participation in the political and economic integration process in the region. Within the framework of this objective, greater attention shall be given to Asia and the Pacific region, in particular to North-East and Central Asia. Mongolia shall take an active part in the process of initiating dialogues and negotiations on the issues of strengthening regional security and creating a collective security mechanism. It will strive to become a member of the Asia, Pacific Economic Cooperation

Forum (APEC).[11] Prerequisites for participating in regional integration shall be created primarily through expanding and promoting bilateral relations with the countries of the region.

(d) The fourth direction of Mongolia's foreign policy, activity shall be promoting cooperation with the United Nations Organisation and its specialised agencies, and with international financial and economic organizations, including the International Monetary Fund, the World Bank and the Asian Development Bank[12].

(c) The fifth direction of Mongolia's foreign policy activity will be developing friendly relations with countries of the former socialist community, as well as the newly-independent states. When developing relations with these countries, a flexible approach will be adopted, reinforcing the positive legacy of our past relations while at the same time taking into account the potential of promoting relations in conformity with the new circumstances. Particular attention will be given to promoting relations with Poland, Hungary and the Czech Republic in Eastern Europe as well as with Kazakhstan, the Ukraine, Belarus, Kyrgyzstan and Uzbekistan.

(f) The sixth direction of Mongolia's foreign policy activity shall be developing friendly-relations with developing countries and cooperating with them, as much as possible, in the solution of common objectives. Beyond the framework of bilateral relations with these countries, this task will be realised mainly through cooperation within the framework of international organisations and movements, such as the United Nations, the Group of 77 and the Non-Aligned Movement.

It further says that the placement of Mongolia's plenipotentiary (diplomatic) representatives abroad shall be carried out with due regard to directions of foreign political relations so as to ensure conditions for their implementation. Assignment of highly qualified and competent personnel from the economic, scientific and technological spheres to Mongolia's diplomatic missions abroad shall be deemed a matter of principle.

4.1.2 Mongolia's Foreign Policy in the Economic Sphere

The fundamental objective of Mongolia's policy is concerning foreign economic relations lies in the optimal use of external factors to adequate solutions to long-term and current economic goals in the light of the concept of sustainable development and in eventually securing a proper place for its economy in regional economic integration. In developing economic relations and cooperation with foreign countries, Mongolia, while safeguarding against any adverse impact on its economic security and against becoming dependent on any given country, shall pursue a policy designed to ensure conditions leading to equality, mutual benefit and faithful fulfillment of obligations, freedom political and other pressures, based on the principles and norms of international economic relations. In the implementation of projects connected with establishing economic, customs and trade special zones, joint ventures or enterprises with full foreign investment or with granting concessions, their political and economic consequences shall be thoroughly examined to ensure that they do not adversely affect the country's economic security and that they will bring economic gains.[13]

In selecting partners in the implementation of projects of crucial importance to the national interests, political interests shall have a significant role to play. External debt issues shall be settled without detriment to national economic security, and loans will be accepted on the basis of a thorough assessment of guarantees of their repayment and effective utilisation.

In developing foreign economic relations, Mongolia shall adhere to the following main guidelines: [14]

(a) Foreign economic activities should be focussed on enhancing the country's potential, increasing export resources, developing economic infrastructure and producing import substituting goods;

(b) Mindful of the need to modernise the economy, presently dominated by raw materials production, and to develop basic sectors conducive to building a rational structure, measures will be taken to achieve the most effective level of processing minerals as well as raw materials of animal and plant extraction and to produce that are competitive on the world market;

(c) Pursuing the policy of modernising existing industries by re-equipping them with advanced technology and techniques, and developing export-oriented industries such as food, light, mining and chemical industries as well as bio-technology and new products on the basis of raw materials available in the country ;

(d) In enhancing its export potential, Mongolia shall promote cooperation with foreign countries in the fields of processing mineral resources, including gold, copper, molybdenum, uranium, and of manufacturing finished products thereof, as well as in the area of full processing agricultural raw materials and producing goods which are capable of competing on world market;

(e) Expanding markets for Mongolia export commodities;

(f) Developing fuel, energy, transportation, communication and other necessary components of economic infrastructure and creating favourable conditions for securing access to sea ports and transit to them;

(g) Integrating in the international transportation, information and communication networks, particularly those in Northeast Asia;

(h) Pursuing a policy of securing foreign assistance and technology for developing small and medium industries oriented towards the production of import substituting goods;[15]

4.1.3 Mongolia's foreign policy in science and technology

The main objective of foreign relations in the scientific and technological fields lies in making full use of external factors to build and enhance a modern national scientific, technical and technological potential capable of serving as a driving force for the effective development of the national economy and industry and able to be competitive at regional, continental and global levels.[16] Thus, Mongolia shall apply the principle of benefitting from world scientific and technological achievements to enrich the pool of national endowment and intellectual capacity which are congruous with the national human and natural resources, the level of social theory and thought as well as with the unique culture of its pastoral livestock breeding economy.

In implementing its scientific and technological foreign policy, Mongolia adheres to the following basic guidelines:

(a) While Introducing advanced technology and methods into production and services, priority will be given to the selective introduction of research-intensive technology. Greater attention will be paid to introducing technologies related to processing mineral resources, raw materials of animal and plant extraction, and use of renewable energy sources;

(b) Gearing the national scientific and technological information system to the international information network; and

(c) Developing bilateral and multilateral cooperation in the field of intellectual property as well as science and technology.

4.1.4 Cultural and humanitarian foreign policy

The main objective of the cultural and humanitarian foreign relations resides in protecting the culture and the way of life of Mongols, endowing their unique cultural heritage and enriching it with the achievements of world culture, restoring national historical and cultural assets, recovering cultural and art relics from abroad, in using cultural cooperation for the purpose of educating and training skilled personnel capable of working in new conditions, introducing Mongolia to foreign countries, expanding the ranks of well-wishers and supporters of Mongolia, encouraging Mongolian studies in other nations and promoting mutual understanding and trust. In promoting cultural and humanitarian cooperation, the concept of foreign policy says that Mongolia will practice both Government and people's diplomacy, and apply the principle of respect for human rights, freedoms, equality and mutual benefit. In developing humanitarian relations with foreign countries, Mongolia adheres to the following guidelines[17]:

(a) Safeguarding the rights, freedoms, legitimate interests and the security of Mongolian citizens residing or travelling abroad through the promotion of broad cooperation with foreign countries in the legal sphere;

(b) enhancing contacts and cooperation with Mongolian nationals residing abroad and mutual support in preserving and developing the Mongolian language, culture, and traditions as well as securing their contributions to Mongolia's progress and growth;

(c) Taking preventive measures to thwart the influence of reactionary movements and groups prejudicial to the national security of Mongolia and the unity of its people;

(d) Giving priority to training in developed countries of Mongolian students, managerial personnel and specialists in the field of market economy, politics, law, management and marketing as well as in the leading areas of the country's scientific and technological fields. In doing so, Mongolia shall seek to benefit from specialised funds of international organisations and developed countries, scholarships of public and private universities and institutes for the purpose of training students, upgrading specialists, arranging degree studies, training highly skilled workers as well as for using the services of foreign lecturers and scholars of excellence;

(e) Studying the advanced methods and technology of training and management of foreign countries in general education and vocational training with a view to applying them flexibly in a way suiting the specific conditions of the country;

(f) In restoring and protecting Mongolia's historical, cultural and natural heritage and assets and in sharing them with other nations, Mongolia shall cooperate with Asian countries which have similar historical, religious and cultural legacies as well as with other interested countries, UNESCO and other related international organisations;

(g) Promoting active relations with international organisations, foundations and non-governmental institutions in the field of education, culture, arts, sports and information, acceding to relevant treaties, establishing and promoting direct ties between similar organisations, encouraging the exchange of scholars, teachers, creative workers, representatives of the media and sportsmen, taking part in international cultural, art and sport events, and organising such measures in the country[18]; and

(h) Promoting cooperation designed to help bring about favourable external conditions for ensuring the country's ecological security, maintaining its ecological balance and protecting nature".[19]

4.2 Implementation of Foreign Policy through Democratic Elections

At the end of the 1990s, the democratic camp was highly fragmented. Several new parties were formed. Mongolia modelled its elections since 1951 after the Soviet Union's system of allowing only one political party to exist in the country the Mongolian People's Revolutionary Party (MPRP), which was the Communist party body, and the only party allowed, to rule until 1990. Following the Soviet policy of *Perestroika* and the democratic uprisings in Eastern Europe, Mongolia successfully led political transition, and for the first time, it made significant strides towards its electoral reform, by introducing multi-party elections for the 1990 parliamentary election? The country's multi-party system developed in the following years with the first opposition coalition parties, the so-called Democratic Union Parties, forming prior to the elections of 1996 wherein they scored a dramatic victory over the MPRP which broke 75 years of Communist party rule.[20]

4.2.1 Timeline of Mongolian Democracy

- 1990 - Street demonstrations force resignation of the Mongolian People's Revolutionary Party (MPRP) Politburo. Political parties are legalised. Elections to the Great Hural (parliament) are won by the MPRP, but 19 of the 50 seats in a new standing legislature go to non-Communists.
- 1992 - Mongolia's new constitution gives first place to human rights and freedoms. In the first democratic elections the MPRP wins 71 of the 76 seats in the new single-chamber Great Hural.
- 1993 - The first direct presidential elections are won by Ochirbat, nominated by the National and Social Democrats.
- 1996 - The National and Social Democrats win 50 seats in the Great Hural elections, but the MPRP can deny a quorum, hindering passage of legislation.

4.2.2 Promoting theIntegrity of the Electoral Process

From 1951 onwards several elections of the State Great Hural or *Ulsyn Ikh Khural* were held in Mongolia. During this period, elections were often used by the Communist party MPRP as a way of strengthening their existing political monopoly and identifying the opposition. Since then, democratic progress has been sporadic and unpredictable. Although the opposition coalition has fared well in several elections since 1990, that time saw little electoral progress, no matter who was in government.[21]

Promote the integrity of the election process and highlight several essential steps to guarantee basic fair competition in the country's democratic elections, those are:[22]

1. *Promote access to a transparent voter registration process:* Ensuring a comprehensive and accurate voter-roll that is accessible to the public is imperative to make sure that only eligible voters are allowed to vote on Election Day. A clean and transparent voter-roll will increase public acceptance of the election result.

2. *Promote fair level playing field at any means;* The competition will never be able to be called fair as long as the playing field, both the campaign and electoral environment is seen as unfair or too tilted to favour one side or the other. Judgement of the level playing field includes not only the campaign period; rather it begins at the very beginning and includes an assessment of each of the electoral phases from

start to finish. This includes monitoring the use of state machinery and state facilities; they should never be used in a way that favours the ruling party.

3. *Promote the professionalism of the electoral officers to perform in a neutral manner:* Elections are usually only rigged with the participation of electoral officers at various levels. The notion of increasing the professionalism of electoral officers then should be promoted as a crucial factor to increase public trust in the electoral result as well as a means to avoid disputes and a repetition of the destructive civil unrest that occurred after the 2008 election.

4.2.3: Democratic role of political parties in elections

In 1989, students and other intellectuals formed several political circles, discussing current social and political problems. These groups did not meet regularly, nor did they have a clear organisational structure (Barkmann 2005). At the end of the year, he first opposition party was founded, the Mongolian Democratic Union. In early 1990, several other opposition parties, such as the Mongolian Democratic Party (MDP), the Mongolian Green Party (MGP), the Mongolian National Progress Party (MNPP), and the Mongolian Social-Democratic Party (MSDP) were established. The opposition parties organised several large demonstrations with some 40,000 people demanding free elections, referenda on important political issues and the implementation of a market economy. The MPRP leadership finally gave in, allowing political reforms.

The provisional parliament consisted of two chambers, with 430 members directly elected Lower House members, and fifty members indirectly elected members in the Upper House. The number of seats allocated to each party in the Upper House had to be proportional to the number of seats held by the party in the Lower House.

The first free multi-party election was held in July 1990. Even though the opposition won less than twenty per cent of seats, the election was a watershed in Mongolia's political development. Competition was fairly tough with more than two thousand candidates from six parties contesting 430 seats (Siemers 1995: 694). Apart from the fact that the ruling party mobilised the entire state apparatus in support of its candidates, the electoral power of the opposition was also weakened by the disunity within the opposition and the fact that the opposition had difficulties in finding promising candidates in all of the 430 districts. A new electoral system and a more united opposition seemed to be a solution.

In February 1992, Mongolia's new constitution came into force. According to Article 21, the parliament consists of one chamber and has 76 members. Citizens aged 25 or older are eligible to run for office and citizens aged 18 or older may exercise their right to vote. The term of office is four years. Moreover, a new election law was passed. The law stipulated that the 76 members of parliament be elected by plurality vote in 26 electoral districts with a district magnitude ranging from two to four.

The first election under the new law was held in June 1992. The new electoral system seemed promising and the opposition was certain to win more seats this time. Parts of the opposition learned from their failures in 1990 and formed coalitions. There were two broad coalitions. The first (known as the Democratic Alliance, DA) consisted of the Mongolian Democratic Party, Mongolian Green Party and the Mongolian National Party, and the second comprised the Democratic Party of Mongolian Believers and the Mongolian People's Party (Barkmann 2005). The opposition camp was, however, still too fragmented as to oust the ruling MPRP, lacked qualified candidates and could not enter strategic alliances. The ruling party nominated one candidate in each of the 76 constituencies, whereas the DA could only nominate 48 hopefuls and the MSDP only 28 candidates. Other opposition parties fielded a total of 141 hopefuls. The applied Block Vote worsened the chances of the opposition, leading to the landslide victory of the MPRP.[23] The MPRP captured 92.1 per cent of the 76 seats at stake with less than 60 per cent of the votes cast. The DA gained four seats, the MSDP one and one independent the remaining seat.[24] The result was widely considered to be not merely unfair but dangerous to the nation-state's political development (Brick, Gastil, and Kimberling 1992).

In January 1996, parliament finally amended the election law, such that all the 76 members of parliament are now elected by plurality vote in single seat constituencies. On 30th June 1996, the Democratic Alliance (DA) consisting of the Mongolian National Democratic Party (MNDP) and the Mongolian Social Democratic Party (MSDP) ended the seventy-five year parliamentary majority of the Mongolian People's Revolutionary Party (MPRP). The alliance captured 65.8 per cent of the 76 seats at stake in the Great State Hural, Mongolia's parliament. The MPRP lost 45 of the 70 seats the party had obtained in the previous election. The election was a watershed event in Mongolia's short history of democracy. The new government under Premier M. Enkhsaikhan carried out a number of highly unpopular measures that, for instance, led to a drastic rise in energy prices. Moreover, service fees and the prices for other daily necessities rose by about 40 per cent. Consequently, the DA lost popular support within a short time. The situation worsened when the new government had to admit that it lacked qualified personnel to replace the MPRP-loyal bureaucrats it had sacked at all levels of administration.

What was seen during the period of this study was that in the 1992 election, the MPRP won over 70 out of the 76 total seats in the Hural, making those periods of government much like other one-party dominant regimes such as the Institutional Revolutionary Party (PRI) in Mexico, the Kuomintang Party (KMT) in Taiwan, and the Liberal Democratic Party (LDP) in Japan. But unlike these countries, its dominance has not lasted long, since it lost to the Democratic Union Coalition in 1996 Parliamentary Elections. The MPRP comprises many of the political elements that dominated the Communist period, while the main opposition coalition was initially formed by Mongolian intellectuals influenced by political changes in the former Soviet Union (Lee 2002: 834).[25] At the time of the transition, the MPRP won 357 out of 430 total seats in the former Great Hural and until 1993 remained the only major political force (Fish 1998: 135).[26] Opposition groups thus had to start from scratch in building viable party organisations that would challenge the hegemony of the MPRP (Fritz 2002: 79).[27] Between 1993 and 1996, they established their presence throughout the 21 *aimags*, and amalgamated their organisations to build a small set of stronger parties, which came together in the Democratic Union Coalition and defeated the MPRP in the 1996 Parliamentary elections (Fish 1998: 135). Mongolia now has 'remarkably strong and representative' political parties that ranges across the ideological spectrum and have become deeply-rooted in Mongolian society, whose formation was due to 'resourceful leadership and dogged dedication to party-building by political entrepreneurs' (Fish 1998: 134).[28]

However, at the internal level the reforms carried out by democratic government that won 1996 elections, did not deliver the country into a better situation as Mongolia experienced political disability and economic crisis. Corruption at the time was seen as rampant and unemployment skyrocketed to 50 per cent. The dysfunctional political system and political rivalries reached their Nadir when a Cabinet Minister was murdered. The effectiveness of the Democratic Coalition was tempered and restrained by its own political inexperience as evidenced by the coalition installing four different governments within a four years period under the Motherland Democratic Coalition, which had governed Mongolia.[29] But at the external level, the democratic coalition government tried to ensure the implementation of foreign policy in Mongolia's favour. This was more so because in the post-1991 period, irrespective of any government Mongolia wanted to secure itself both for diplomatic and economic gains. The two neighbours—Russia and China began respecting Mongolia's sovereignty apart from supporting at various regional groupings. Due to the support of Russia and China, Mongolia achieved a success in the Shanghai Cooperation Organigation (SCO) by gaining an observer status. It also began taking active part in the affair of North East Asia and participated in the meeting of North East Asian Region. Relations with not only the US and EU countries but also with Australia and New Zealand started developing. In Asia, the major countries with Which Mongolia's foreign policy implementation worked for its benefit included Japan, South Korea and India. Mongolia not only benefitted from bilateral but also from multilateral relations to ensure its economic security.

In fact, Mongolia's foreign policy implementation was guided by a few serious objectives that included ensuring independence and sovereignty by following the trends of human society's advancement; maintaining friendly relations with all countries; strengthening its position in the international community; and forming a network of relationships with influential countries in the region and in the world based on the interdependence of political, economic and other interests. "While following a policy of creating realistic interest of the developed countries in Mongolia, it will seek to avoid becoming overly reliant or dependent on any particular country." Since Mongolia is 'sandwiched' between Russia and China, "All Mongolian governments since 1990 have therefore pursued pro-Western foreign policy since external support is regarded as essential to ensure continued independence" (Fritz 2002: 91).[30] Despite popular attachment to Russia and the Society experience, Mongolia has sought closer ties with the United States, Japan, and Germany, and economic relations have increased with China.[31]

During 1990s Mongolian diplomacy worked on filling the political vacuum created by the demise of the Soviet Union, Mongolia's sole creditor and overwhelming trading partner. By some estimates, the USSR provided economic assistance annually equal to about 30 per cent of Mongolia's GDP (Batbayar 2003:51).[32] Much needed help was sought by breaking the previous isolation, and establishing and maintaining all-round cooperation with the USA, Japan, and Western Europe. Mongolia's admission to the International Monetary Fund (IMF), the World Bank, and the Asian Development Bank (ADB) in February 1992 was an important step toward promoting ties with the international community and the country's further integration with the world economy.

In January 1991, on the request of President Bush (senior) the US Congress granted Mongolia most-favoured nation status and in March the Congress passed its first resolution for Mongolia's support of the movement for democracy. The US Secretary of State, James Baker, visited Mongolia twice (1990 and 1991) and urged other countries, including Japan, to join the broad-based world community support for Mongolia.

Toshiki Kaifu, Prime Minister of Japan visited Mongolia in 1991. It was the first visit to Mongolia by a leader of leading industrialised democracies, demonstrating the Japanese government's strong commitment to Mongolia's recently born democracy and its market transition (Batbayar 2003:51).[33] Japan co-chaired with the World Bank the first Mongolia support group meeting in Tokyo in September 1991, which brought together the IMF, World Bank, ADB, and 14 countries. The participating financial institutions and states allotted a total of about US $150 million, of which Japan's share alone equaled US$55 million.[34] At the end of October 1991, the Executive Director of the IMF, Michel Camdessus, went to Mongolia and committed the support of the IMF to Mongolia, its 155th member country, in the implementation of a joint set of measures directed at pulling

Mongolia out of its crisis. The IMF pledged about US$30 million, half of it devoted to stabilising Mongolia's balance of payments.[35] This measure allayed some concerns about the country's economic viability and quickly elicited the interest of other donor institutions and individual countries (Batbayar 2003:52).

Access to external resources was essential for economic recovery and sustained growth in Mongolia. With a large fiscal deficit and low saving rates and the need to build up adequate foreign exchange reserves, substantial net capital inflows were required throughout the 1990s.[36] The IMF, ADB and the World Bank have worked closely together to support the Mongolian Government's macro-economic stabilisation and reform program since 1991 (Batbayar 2003:55).

Mongolia's international partners met with the representatives of the MPRP Government in to discuss Mongolia have renewed efforts to strengthen the foundations for growth and poverty reduction. Donors commended the new government's commitment to move forward on a comprehensive agenda for further macro-economic stabilisation, deepening of structural and sectoral reforms, and strategies to reduce poverty. In this context, they emphasised the importance of private-sector led and broad-based growth for poverty reduction and the critical role of supporting infrastructure and social services. Donors indicated new aid-commitments of about US$330 million for the next year and stressed the importance of enhanced donor coordination[37].

Mongolia became a member of the Asian Development Bank (ADB) in February 1991. The ADB entered into a Poverty Partnership Agreement (PPA) with the Government of Mongolia. The ADB formulated its new Country Operational Strategy (COS). The new COS is aimed at fostering economic growth and combat poverty by switching the main mechanism for growth generation from public sector investments in infrastructure to employment-generating investments aimed at engaging the private sector. Accordingly, the ADB currently focusses its operations on the five core sectors, namely, finance, public sector, social sector, agriculture, and urban development[38].

Mongolia became a member of the World Bank Group in February 1991. Following severe external shocks in 1989–1990, after the withdrawal of Soviet assistance and the collapse of the

Table 2: ADB Lending to Mongolia

Sector	*Number of loans*	*Loan amount (US$) million*	*Per cent*
Transport and communications	5	134.5	28.7
Energy	4	93.8	20.0
Agriculture and natural resources	5	64.9	13.8
Industry and non-fuel minerals	2	60.0	12.8
Finance	3	53.0	11.3
Social infrastructure	5	38.2	8.1
Others	1	25.0	5.3
Total	**25**	**469.4**	**100.0**

(*Source*: A fact sheet: Mongolia and ADB http:// www.adb.org).

Council for Mutual Economic Assistance's trading system, the World Bank Group's International Development Association (IDA) offered a program of support that focussed on quick-disbursing balance of payments assistance and technical assistance for economic management (Batbayar 2003:53). The IDA's portfolio has since developed to comprise operations supporting poverty alleviation, rehabilitation of infrastructure, and structural reforms primarily in the financial and enterprise sectors. The IDA has committed a total of US$272 million to date for various projects. The annual lending program has averaged US$25–30 million equivalent[39].

The World Bank dispatched its Vice President for East Asia and the Pacific, Jemal-ud-din Kassum, to Mongolia for pledge its strong and continuing support for Mongolia in its transition to a market economy (Batbayar 2003:54).[40] On other issues, Jemal-ud-din Kassum encouraged the Government to continue reaching out to the civil society, including the media, non-governmental organisations, other donors to gather differing views and build consensus on important policy decisions[41]. The World Bank office in Mongolia in cooperation with the Parliament of Mongolia and IFC organised the first round table discussion on Private Sector Development in Ulaanbaatar. The purpose was to discuss ways to improve the environment for private sector development and growth in Mongolia, and to build a dialogue with government representatives on private sector issues. The Bank was to organise such a discussion with the government and private businesses twice a year. The Parliament of Mongolia has agreed to establish a Working group through the Standing Committee on Economic Policy to improve tax regulations (Batbayar 2003:54).

The above discussions indicate that the post-Soviet period in the history of Mongolia formed new loyalties and transformed the old ones. This transition helped the country to carry out changes through reforms in both the internal and external policies. While the country's think-tanks and leadership brought out changes in the existing foreign policy to make it a "multi-pillar" foreign policy, the democratically elected government after 1996 parliamentary elections ensured the implementation of this new foreign policy in that sense 1996 was the turning point to ensure Mongolia's presence on the international map through bilateral and multilateral relations.

Notes and References

1. Soni, Sharad K. (2006), India's New Role In East Asia: Implications For Mongolia, The Mongolian Journal of International Affairs, pp. 32-41
2. Kapolonski, C. (2005), "Truth, History and Politics in Mongolia", Critical Asian Studies, 37(2): pp. 323-337.
3. Soni, Sharad K. (2006), India's New Role In East Asia: Implications For Mongolia, The Mongolian Journal of International Affairs, pp. 32-41
4. Embassy of Mongoliya in the Ukhttp://www.embassyof mongolia .co.uk/index.php?option=com_ content&view= article&id =59&Itemid=76&lang=en.
5. http://www.mongolianembassy.us/eng_foreign_policy/ the_concept_of_foreign_policyhp?
6. http://www.mongolembassy.com/sub03_02_3.php.
7. *Ibid.*
8. http://www.mongolianembassy.us/eng_foreign_policy/the_ concept_ of_foreign_policy.php?
9. Ts. Batbayar and Sharad K. Soni (2007), Modern Mongolia: Aconcise history, New Delhi: Pentagon, pp.121-123.
10. *Ibid.*
11. *Ibid.*
12. *Ibid.*

13. Embassy of Mongoliya in the Uk, http://www.embassyof mongolia. co.uk/index.php? option=com_content&view=article&id=59&Itemid=76&lang=en.

14. *Ibid.*

15. *Ibid.*

16. Mongolia's Foreign policy objectives have been taken from 'Concept of Mongolia's Foreign Policy', Ulaanbaatar, 1999:36-46.

17. Mongolia's Foreign policy objectives have been taken from 'Concept of Mongolia's Foreign Policy', Ulaanbaatar, 1999: pp. 36-46.

18. Mongolia's Foreign policy objectives have been taken from 'Concept of Mongolia's Foreign Policy', Ulaanbaatar, 1999: pp. 36-46.

19. For detail see Embassy of Mongolia in the UK http://www. embassyofmongolia.co.uk/index.php?option=com_content& view=article&id=59&Itemid=76&lang=en.

20. See www.ipu.org/parline-e/reports/2219_e.htm.

21. Read: Parliament (State Great Hural) of Mongolia Election.

22. Read: Regulation of observation and reporting of Election.

23. See Table 1, TV Appearance of Parties and Balanced Information Mongolian Election 2004.

24. Brick, Andrew, Raymond Gastil, and William Kimberling (1992), An assessment of great people's Hural Mongolia,ww.ifes. org/reg-activities/report.htm.

25. Lee, J. (2002) 'Primary Causes of Asian Democratisation: Dispelling Conventional Myths,' Asian Survey, 42 (6): pp. 821-837.

26. Fish, S. (1998), 'Mongolia: Democracy without Prerequisites', Journal of Democracy, 9 (3): pp. 127-141.

27. Fritz, V. (2002), 'Mongolia: Dependent Democratisation', Journal of Communist Studies and Transition Politics, 18 (4): pp. 75-100.

28. Fish, S. (1998), 'Mongolia: Democracy without Prerequisites', Journal of Democracy, 9 (3): pp. 127-141.

29. Seehttp://www.duke.edu/web/diem/reports/IRI/Mongolia 2000.pdf.

30. Fritz, V. (2002), 'Mongolia: Dependent Democratisation', Journal of Communist Studies and Transition Politics, 18 (4): pp. 75-100.

31. Batbayar, T. (2003), "Foreign Policy and Domestic Reform in Mongolia." Central Asian Survey 22(1): pp. 45-59.

32. *Ibid.*

33. TS. Batbayar, 'Mongolia in 1991: the first year of the reform', Ts. Batbayar, Essays on Mongolia, China, and Japan (Ulaanbaatar:

Mongolian Center for Scientific and Technological Information, 1996), pp. 19–21.

34. Batbayar, T. (2003), "Foreign Policy and Domestic Reform in Mongolia." Central Asian Survey 22(1): pp. 45-59.

35. *Ibid.*

36. Mongolia Consultative Group Meeting, 'Development partners affirm support for poverty reduction', http://www. worldbank.org.

37. Mongolia and ADB: http://www.adb.org.

38. Brief Overview of the IDA funded Projects: http://www. world bank.org.

39. Batbayar, T. (2003), "Foreign Policy and Domestic Reform in Mongolia." Central Asian Survey 22(1): pp. 45-59.

40. World Bank promises strong support for Mongolia's transition: http://www.worldbank.org.

41. Joint Mongolian Parliament, WB and IFC discussions on Private Sector Development in Mongolia, 11th September 2001: http:/ /www.worldbank.org.

5

India–Mongolia Relations: Future Prospective

India and Mongolia have interacted through the medium of Buddhism over a period of 2600 years. Following the emergence of Mongolia as a modern nation state in the 20th century, the two countries have continued to build relations based on shared historical and cultural legacy.

Relations between Mongolia and India have entered into a new stage since the beginning of 1990s when Mongolia embarked the uneasy road of multi-party democracy and a market-oriented economy. India was the first country among the non-socialist world to establish diplomatic relations with Mongolia in 1995 and opened its Embassy in Ulaanbaatar in1970. The 1992 visit of India's Vice-President Dr Shankar Dayal Sharma to Mongolia can be considered as an Indian support of Mongolia's firm commitment to choose a democracy and a market-oriented economy. The Vice-President of India pledged to increase technical assistance to Mongolia, i.e., training Mongolian technicians through Indian programs (Batbayar 2001:77).

From 21-24 February 1994 the then President of Mongolia P. Ochirbat paid an official visit to India. The highlight of the visit was the signing of the Treaty on Friendly Relations and Cooperation between Mongolia and India. Besides, a number of agreement including an agreement on avoidance of double taxation and an inter-governmental agreement about the creation of the bilateral committee on cooperation were also concluded. More recently, the President of Mongolia

N. Bagabandi paid a state visit to India on 1-5 January 2001. During his visit both sides noted the relevance of the 1994 treaty of friendly relations and cooperation and also signed a number of agreements. The new agreements formed a solid basis for further development of bilateral relations between the two countries. (Nyamdava 2003:66-71).

Mongolia attaches great importance to trade and economic relations with India. The government of India in 2001 decided to render Mongolia for the first time a soft loan of 50 million Rupees (US $1.7 million) to be used for financing the construction of a factory of vegetable oil with a capacity of five to six thousand tons per year. (Soni 2001:4-5) A new loan from India was to be used to finance a small scale hydro-energy projects in the western part of Mongolia. Earlier, Indian Commerce Minister visited Mongolia in September 1994, and signed a number of Protocols to create inter-governmental sub-committee on Commerce and to establish working relations between two state planning organisations. In June 1995, more than 20-member delegation of Indo-Mongolian Chamber set up in Bombay came to Mongolia to meet Mongolian businessmen and to explore ways of developing trade and investment. The Mongolian side expressed interest in the import of Indian drugs, tea, coffee, and industrial equipment. Indian side was interested in cooking coal, fluorspar, copper, uranium, and other minerals. At this stage, transportation of goods becomes a major obstacle for trade promotion. One way to overcome this natural barrier is to establish regular flights between Mongolia and India (Foreign Policy Blue Book, 2000:31-32).

5.1 Historical Linkages

In 1526, Babur, a Timurid descendant of Timur and Genghis Khan from Fergana Valley (modern day Uzbekistan), swept across the Khyber Pass and established the Mughal Empire, covering modern day Afghanistan, Pakistan, India and Bangladesh. However, his son Humayun was defeated by the Afghan warrior Sher Shah Suri in the year 1540, and Humayun was forced to retreat to Kabul.[1] After Sher Shah's death, his son Islam Shah Suri and the Hindu king Samrat Hem Chandra Vikramaditya, who had won 22 battles against Afghan rebels and forces of Akbar, from Punjab to Bengal and had established a secular Hindu rule in North India from Delhi till 1556. Akbar's forces defeated and killed Hemu in the second battle of Panipat on November 6, 1556.[2]

The Mughal dynasty ruled most of the Indian sub-continent by 1600; it went into a slow decline after 1707. The Mughals suffered severe blow due to invasions from **Marathas** and **Afghans** due to which the Mughal dynasty were reduced to puppet rulers by 1757. The remnants of the Mughal dynasty were finally defeated during the **Indian Rebellion of 1857**, also called the 1857 War of Independence. This period marked a vast social change in the sub-continent as the Hindu majorities were ruled over by the Mughal emperors, most of who showed religious tolerance, liberally patronising Hindu culture. The famous emperor Akbar, who was the grandson of Babar, tried to establish a good relationship with the Hindus. However, later emperors such as Aurangazeb tried to establish complete Muslim dominance, and as a result several historical temples were destroyed during this period and taxes imposed on non-Muslims. During the decline of the Mughal Empire, several smaller states rose to fill the power vacuum and themselves were contributing factors to the decline. In 1739, **Nadir Shah**, emperor of Iran, defeated the Mughal army at the huge **Battle of Karnal**. After this victory, Nadir captured and sacked Delhi, carrying away many treasures, including the **Peacock Throne**.[3]

The Mughals were perhaps the richest single dynasty to have ever existed. During the Mughal era, the dominant political forces consisted of the Mughal Empire and its tributaries and, later on, the rising successor states - including the **Maratha Empire** - which fought an increasingly weak Mughal dynasty. The Mughals, while often employing brutal tactics to subjugate their empire, had a policy of integration with Indian culture, which is what made them successful where the short-lived Sultanates of Delhi had failed. Akbar the Great was particularly famed for this. Akbar declared "Amari" or non-killing of animals in the holy days of Jainism. He rolled back the *jizya* tax for non-Muslims. The Mughal emperors married local royalty, allied themselves with local ***maharajas***, and attempted to fuse their Turko-Persian culture with ancient Indian styles, creating a unique **Indo-Saracenic architecture**. It was the erosion of this tradition coupled with increased brutality and centralisation that played a large part in the dynasty's downfall after **Aurangzeb**, who unlike previous emperors, imposed relatively non-pluralistic policies on the general population, which often inflamed the majority Hindu population.[4]

5.2 Cultural Linkages

The doctrines of Buddhism that originated in India more than 2,500 years ago have once again become the hope of human survival in the current world scenario when we are witnessing both the threats and challenges to the very existence of human race.[5] It is more so because the universal relevance of Buddhism as an organised form of knowledge and spiritual force has the proven record of peaceful co-existence with all religions and the people around the world.[6] Buddhism is a religion which teaches people to 'live and let live'. In the history of the world, there is no evidence to show that Buddhists have interferred or done any damage to any other religion in any part of the world for the purpose of introducing their religion. Buddhists do not regard the existence of other religions as a hindrance to worldly progress and peace.[7] For quite some time now India, for that matter, has been witnessing several activities for not only reviving Buddhism on its land from where it was once routed out but also providing a common platform for a united voice of Buddhists worldwide.

For example, recently on 27-30 November, 2011, the first Global Buddhist Congregation took place in New Delhi in which more than 900 delegates including heads and representatives from Buddhist Sanghas, national Buddhist federations, organisations and institutions from 46 countries participated. The event was marked by a decision to set up a new international Buddhist organisation in India, which will be called the "International Buddhist Confederation".[8]

Buddhism forms an important factor in reformulating and rebuilding not only the national identity of the Mongolian people but also bringing them more close to the Indians. On the other side, due to its close historical links based on Buddhism India would always like to see Mongolia prosper through strengthening bilateral and multilateral relations in every area in the spirit of comprehensive partnership. It is more so because the Buddhist linkages between the two countries are fascinating, intense and inseparable; transcending all human activities from language, literature, religion, medicine, and folklore to culture and traditions. This really sets an example relevant to other regions of the world as to how Buddhism in today's scenario becomes a major factor in keeping the bond of trust between the two or more countries alive and what should further be done to uphold the same. The Austral Asian region too can be seen in that perspective. And herein comes the need for establishing close relationships between not only various Buddhist traditions and communities but also academics who could share and exchange knowledge and wisdom in order to contribute to further development of Buddhism in any region of the world. What is striking to note here is that Buddhism can also be employed as geopolitical tool in regional and international perspectives to meet the varied challenges facing the world in the 21st century.[9]

5.3 Political Linkages

Diplomatic relations between India and Mongolia were established on 24th December 1955. India was the first country outside the Soviet bloc to establish diplomatic relations with Mongolia. India supported Mongolia in having UN and NAM memberships. In 2010, Mongolia marked 55th Anniversary of the establishment of bilateral diplomatic relations. Exchange of High Level Visits: Mongolia was visited by Presidents Mrs. Pratibha Devisingh Patil (2011) and President R. Venkataraman (1988); Vice-Presidents Dr. S. Radhakrishnan (1957), Dr. Shankar Dayal Sharma (1992), Mr. KR Narayanan (1996), and Krishan Kant (1999) and Lok Sabha Speakers Dr. G.S. Dhillon (1974), Dr. Balram Jhakhar (1985), Mr. Shivraj Patil (1995), Mr. P.A. Sangma (1997) Mr. GMC Balayogi (2001) and Mrs. Meira Kumar (2010).[10] The important visits from Mongolia to India were the Chairmen of the Presidium U. Tsendenbal (1959) and Mr. Bathmunkh (1989); Presidents P. Ochirbaat (1994), President N. Bagabandi (2001) and President T. S. Elbegdorj (2009); Chairmen of the State Great Hural Mr. N. Bagabandi (1996), Mr. R. Gonchigdorj (1998), Mr. S. Tumur-Ochir (2003) and Mr. D. Demberel (2010); Prime Ministers Mr. Tsendenbal (1973 and earlier in 1959 as Chairman of the Presidium), N. Enkhbayar (2004 and earlier as the then Leader of Opposition in 1999).[11]

President of India Mrs Prathibha Patil paid a State Visit to Mongolia from 27-30 July, 2011. She was accompanied by an official delegation, including Cabinet Minister and Members of Parliament, and a composite business delegation. India confirmed providing a line of credit of US $ 20 million for India-Mongolia Joint Information Technology Education and

Outsourcing Centre to be established in Ulaanbaatar. India also agreed to upgrade and modernise Rajiv Gandhi Arts and Production School and the Atal Bihari Vajpayee Centre for Excellence in Information and Communication Technology Education and to work with Mongolian authorities on Joint India-Mongolia School to be set up at Ulaanbaatar. During the visit bilateral Defence cooperation agreement, an MOU on media exchanges and an MOU on cooperation between Planning Commission of India and National Development and Innovation Committee (NDIC) were signed. There were discussions on cooperation in peaceful uses of radioactive minerals and nuclear energy and improving air connectivity between the two countries. President of India felicitated President Elbegdorj on Mongolia assuming the Chair of 'Community of Democracies'. Mongolia reiterated its support to India in becoming a permanent member of a reform and expanded UNSC.[12]

An India-Mongolian Joint Declaration was issued following the visit of Premier Yu. Tsendenbal in February 1973. The Declaration includes general principles to guide bilateral relations. In February 1994, a Treaty of Friendly Relations and Co-operation was signed during the visit of President Ochirbat to India. During the state visit of Mongolian President Natsagiin Bagabandi in 2001, a Joint Declaration was issued outlining the future direction of bilateral relations. Six Agreements were also signed during the visit relating to Extradition, Defence cooperation, Co-operation in Information Technology, Investment Promotion and Protection, Mutual Legal Assistance in Criminal Matters and Mutual Legal Assistance concerning Civil and Commercial Matters.[13]

5.4 Trade Linkages

During the visit of the then Minister for Commerce Mr. Pranab Mukherjee, in 1994 two MOUs pertaining to the establishment of a Joint Trade Sub-committee and Cooperation between the Planning Commission of India and the National Development Board of Mongolia were signed. An agreement for co-operation in the field of geology and mineral resources was signed in September 1996. In 1996 during the visit of the then Vice President, Mr. K.R. Narayanan to Mongolia, an Agreement on Trade and Economic Cooperation between India and Mongolia was signed. The Agreement provides for MFN status to each other in respect of customs duties and all other taxes on imports and exports. During the visit of President Bagabandi in 2001, both sides signed an Investment Promotion and Protection Agreement. The main items of exports to Mongolia include medicines, mining machinery and auto parts, etc. Imports from Mongolia include raw wool.

India must look beyond its latest pre-occupation with uranium diplomacy. In terms of location, few countries are as strategic as Mongolia. And fewer share so much spiritual heritage with India. Above all Mongolia is critical for a rising India's Asian strategy. After its liberation from three-and-a-half decades of international isolation, the Department of Atomic Energy has embarked on an ambitious expansion of India's nuclear power programme. Given the limited Uranium resources at home, the DAE needs to have reliable agreements on importing the stuff. The Foreign Office is now on a mission mode to secure Uranium deals. Mongolia's Uranium reserves are estimated to be around some 62,000 tonnes, putting it in the list of the world's top 15 countries having Uranium. That figure could be at least twice as much, according to some reports. Mongolia with no nuclear power plants and a population of just over three million has every incentive to export uranium. Uranium is only one of the elements in Mongolia's vast mineral riches. Ulan Bator is setting up a sovereign wealth fund to manage its booming mining sector. In Mongolia's recent presidential elections, distribution of the mineral wealth was the main political question. As India's own demand for imported natural resources multiplies, Mongolia is a natural and long-term economic partner.[14] It is the geopolitical location; however, that makes Mongolia very special for India's Asian strategy. Since the end of the Cold War, Mongolia's innate strategic genius has reasserted itself in creating a dynamic foreign policy. Calling America its 'third neighbour', Mongolia has deftly played a balance of power game between Beijing, Moscow and Washington. With President Elbegdorj choosing India for his first foreign destination, Delhi has the rare opportunity to emerge as Mongolia's 'fourth neighbour'. All it needs is to match the strategic imagination of Ulan Bator and reciprocate the special warmth that Mongolia reserves for India.[15]

5.5: India's Role in Mongolia's Third Neighbour Policy

Mongolia's third neighbour policy is in the interest of both Mongolia and India. India as a country and collection of related cultures is attempting to spread its soft power throughout the region to counter China's role in most of Asia. Chinese influence in Central Asia is quickly catching up with the Russified history of the region, Southeast Asia appears to be in between India and China for the time being, and India's own South Asian dominance is also being encroached upon with the issue of Tibet, Pakistan-Chinese relations, and the vulnerability of such *de facto* protectorates as Nepal and Bhutan. For Mongolia the benefit is even clearer. Beyond the already expanded upon issue of China, Mongolia is already seeing benefits of relations with India from trade deals ranging from India's world-class IT sector to a budding nuclear deal. Energy independence may be the new trendy issue in international relations, but Mongolia is only too aware of its dependence on Russian gas as fuel as well the net-value of its energy trade with China in coal and other mineral resources. Mongolia's contribution to the world's copper supply is also an important factor in supplying the IT sector, potentially of India. Recent diplomatic gestures such as state visits and the celebration of 50 years of diplomatic relations have led to a cutting of visa requirements for diplomatic and official passport holders, culture development agreements, and even the naming of a street in Mongolia as Gandhi Street, and the street leading to New Delhi Airport in India as Ulaanbaatar Street (BBC 2005). [16]

India is also important for Mongolia it is one of the world's fastest growing economies as well as the largest democracy. Mongolia's complex relations with China as well as its unique foreign policy leave India and Mongolia in a situation where bilateral ties will be increasingly helpful and politically appropriate. Mongolian foreign policy is constructed with a firm eye on the security of the country. Mongolia's foreign policy takes into account all the factors of the nation's security policy. Much of the written policy is focussed on Mongolia's immediate neighbours. To this end the state will not interfere in conflicts between Russia and China unless such a conflict affects the nation directly and will avoid military alliances against either. The second direction is relations with highly developed countries from the East and West, such as the United States, Japan, and Germany. Also, the country will maintain friendly relations with India, South Korea, Thailand, Singapore, Turkey, Denmark, Netherlands, Finland, Austria, Sweden, and

Switzerland in an appropriate level according to economic and other considerations. The third direction: integration into regional regimes in the Asia-Pacific, Northeast and Central Asia, as well as with international organisations such as the UN, IMF, WB, and the Asian Development Bank (ADB). Mongolia will maintain friendly relations with former and currently communist/socialist states with which it enjoys a positive legacy; however, the nation will develop relations according to the new international political reality. The final direction of Mongolia's foreign policy is keeping up a continued dialogue with other developing countries through mediums such as the G-77, UN, and Non-Aligned Movement (MFA webpage). Mongolia essentially seeks to maintain good relations on a global scale, while continuing to develop its own culture, language, and tradition.[17]

India's foreign policy reflects India's status as a rising power and its need for regional and continental representation. Indian foreign policy is said to favour five principles: conventional security, economic growth, energy security, nuclear capability/ non-proliferation, and prestige security (Dormandy 1). Like Mongolia, India's colonialised past clearly drives some of the nation's diplomacy. There are also some other characteristics of Indian foreign policy like, third-largest provider of peacekeeping forces to the UN and India seeks more integration outside of its traditional role in South Asia, as China engages Pakistan, Myanmar, and even Sri Lanka.[18] India is keen to integrate itself into the larger Asian international regimes such as APEC and ASEAN/ARF. However, the lack of any comprehensive, wide-ranging security agreement, such as that provided to Europe by the EU, complicates relations between all Asian states and regional actors (Rapkin and Thompson 332).

Formal diplomatic relations were declared December 24, 1955. This communique became realised with the Mongolian Embassy in New Delhi in 1956, and the Indian Embassy in Ulaanbaatar in 1970. This beginning of formal diplomacy developed into something of a small scale Mongolian-Indian bloc, where India campaigned tirelessly for the inclusion of Mongolia into the United Nations, along with regular high-level visits between the two. The third phase in relational development is marked by the signing of the "Joint Indo-Mongol Declaration" during the second official visit of Prime Minister Yu. Tsendenbal of the Mongolian Peoples' Republic to India in 1973. This declaration established the eight guiding principles of Indo-Mongolian relations:[19]

(I) Development cooperation in the fields of politics, economics, culture, science, and technology.

(II) Peaceful co-existence (between states with different socio-political systems.

(III) Independence, sovereignty, and territorial integrity.

(IV) Equality and non-interference.

(V) Renunciation of the use of force in disputes.

(VI) Cooperation in the UN and other international organisations.

(VII) Peaceful and friendly relations between the Asian states and Mongolia and India.

(VIII) Regular mutual consultations.

Many of these same principles are backbones of Mongolian and Indian foreign policy to-date. In 1988 during the President of the Republic of India, Ramaswami Venkataraman's visit to Mongolia a two-year agreement on cooperation in scientific and technological spheres particularly as those fields apply to agriculture as well as general research and educational endeavours was signed. In 1989, the Mongolian Studies department was established in Jawaharlal Nehru University as a result of the earlier mentioned agreement. These agreements paved the way for the newly-democratic Mongolia and increasingly powerful India to establish their current relationships as part of (but also a continuation of, to some extent) Mongolia's "third neighbour policy". In any close state-to-state relations, treaties become the central pillars of determining the direction of development between the states in question. The first treaty between a democratic Mongolia and India was signed in 1994: the Treaty of Friendly Relations and Cooperation. This treaty contained a total of twelve articles that are a continuation of the principles set forward in the joint declaration of 1973, revised to fit the new realities of the global political sphere.[20] Article 1 continues the idea of territorial integrity, sovereignty, non-violence/interference, equality, and mutual benefit. The second defines the above-mentioned spheres of cooperation. Article 3 sets a precedent for networking among the governments and public institutions of both countries. The fourth articles define the settings and nature of the cooperation, which is in line with Mongolia's own foreign policy of bi/multi-lateral relations and work in institutions such as the UN, NAM, etc. Article 10 declares the treaty subject or ratification, while articles 11 and 12 set the timeframe of validity to the document and allow for amending, respectively (Nyamdavaa 140).[21]

The same year two other important documents were signed: the Agreement Between the Government of Mongolia and the Government of the Republic of India for the Establishment of a Joint Committee on Cooperation; Agreement Between the Government of Mongolia and the Government of the Republic of India for the Avoidance of Double Taxation and the Prevention of Fiscal Evasion with Respect to Taxes and Income and on Capital. While the titles of these agreements are rather drawn-out and exhausting, both serve a definite purpose. The first one establishes long-term relations between the nations encouraging fresh engagement and discussion on areas of cooperation. The second of them sets a foundation for the free, fair and uninterrupted development of economic ties between the two countries (Nyamdavaa 146-168).[22] Over the past 15 years, many other documents and treaties have developed out of Indo-Mongolian cooperation efforts, building on the well-formulated articles of the 1994 agreements.[23]

Mongolia has benefitted tremendously from cooperation with India in the field of defense and other military concerns. Mongolia has been restructuring their military into an effective peacekeeping force for UN missions worldwide. India as the third largest supplier of forces to the UN is an excellent partner for Mongolia in training for such missions (Soni 56). Mongolia and India have recently started conducting several joint military trainings and war-games. The first of these was Khaan Quest 2006, where seven nations jointly conducted exercises. These seven nations were India, Mongolia, Bangladesh, Fiji, Thailand, Tonga, and the USA).[24]

The next year Khaan Quest was held again this time with Russia, Malaysia, and Japan attending as observers. The third of such games was Nomadic Elephant, the most recent. In India itself, trainings are conducted at the Jungle Warfare School at Vairangte near the northeast border with Myanmar. China criticised the developments as a disguise for conducting counter-terrorism operations near or even beyond its border with India (Soni 57).[25] While this seems unlikely, Mongolia and India have taken a joint statement on terrorism. The two countries issued a joint statement in January 2001, condemning terrorism and religious fundamentalism irrespective of the socio-political considerations used in its justification (Soni 55).[26] Although, one has to wonder why China would be suspicious of such activities considering its own counter-terrorism role in the SCO. The India-Mongolia Joint Working Group commented on cooperation in the field of defence stating that the two ancient civilizations enjoy strong historical ties and that Mongolia stands to benefit from Indian experience in modernising its military. Also, India provides training in English language, a *de facto* requirement of internationally lead peacekeeping forces. For its part, India's traditional South Asian-centric security policies are being expanded into East Asia and the Pacific as well as a northward movement into Central Asia. With an ever increasing liberal interpretation of regional security it may well be the case that East Asia as a division could expand into South Asia and northward to include Russia and Mongolia, bringing into question the whole issue of geographical divisions in an increasingly transnational world.[27]

5.6 India-Mongolia Strategic Partnership

On May 29, 2006, a website story entitled "Mongolia to become Strategic Military Location?" highlighted growing Chinese concerns over setting up of a foreign military base in Mongolia, which pointed to India as a prospective country to do that.[28] The story quoted reports by the Chinese governmental papers as saying that "India is trying to expand its military resources to establish a potential base in Mongolia."[29] The issue came into forefront ever since Delhi disclosed its plans to join a multilateral peace keeping exercise in Mongolia called "Khaan Quest 2006".[30] Reports had even indicated that India's traditional security thrust in South East Asia is now being extended to East Asia and the Pacific and is being complemented by a "Push North" attempt in Central Asia.[31] Obviously, Mongolia figured prominently in so-called India's scheme of extending its influence in East Asia, particularly if it goes beyond to include North East Asia.[32]

Although China's geopolitical concerns make it imperative to voice against any countries setting up military operations in Mongolia, "Khaan Quest" was a totally different kind of affairs.

Hence, it would seem unfair on the part of China to remain suspicious of this planned peace keeping exercise. Especially, when the fact remains that it was not only India which was participating in that event but there were several others also including Bangladesh, Fiji, Mongolia, Thailand, Tonga and the USA whose platoons did such exercises in order to get certified to assist in UN peacekeeping missions around the world. For the first five years since 2001, only Mongolian and US troops participated but in 2006, when the Khaan Quest was held on 11-25 August at the Five Hills Training Center located about 60 kilometers. West of Ulaanbaatar, it expanded to include several other countries as well. China voiced its concerns that the event was to be a disguise for rehearsing counter-terrorism or even full-fledged combat operations near their border with Mongolia. Such Chinese concerns were raised in an article published on 25th March 2006 in the Chinese government-controlled newspaper Qingnian Cankao.[33] But quite surprisingly a year after, when the Khaan Quest 2007 took place on 1-16 August, China came forward along with Russia, Malaysia and Japan to participate as observer states in this annual military training exercise.[34] What conclusion can be drawn from this development, particularly about China's thinking, is difficult to predict at least at the moment. It is yet to be seen if Chinese suspicion has really come to an end in the light of another report appeared in the online edition of an Indian newspaper. The Tribune saying "India is quietly expanding its defence and security links with Mongolia in a bid to monitor China's space and military activities in the region."[35] Whatever analysis we have with regard to India-Mongolia defence and security links, it looks like a cooperative partnership that the two countries are trying to develop. Evidently, in December 2005, India and Mongolia agreed to upgrade their defence cooperation in training and explore collaboration in other areas of mutual concerns and benefit.[36] The two countries decided to establish an India-Mongolia Joint Working Group to work out details of cooperation in the field of defence, including holding of regular joint exercises. These commitments lie in to fact that India and Mongolia are two ancient civilizations whose spiritual and cultural bonds go back into history, and that Mongolia wants to learn from Indian expertise to modernise its defence.[37]

Since 2001, the defence ties between India and Mongolia have moved forward in the fields of training, bilateral visits and joint military exercises. India has been providing training facilities to Mongolian defence personnel in English language, peace keeping and military operations. As regards bilateral visits, Mongolian Defence Minister paid a visit to India in November 2003 and December 2005, while India's Minister of State for Defence M. M. Pallam Raju visited Mongolia in May 2006. The first joint military exercise was held in Mongolia in October 2004, while the second one took place in December 2005 at the Counter-Insurgency Jungle Warfare School (CIJWS) at Vairangte, in India's north eastern state of Mizoram bordering Myanmar.[38] And the third joint military exercise called "Nomadic Elephant" was to be held in the Mongolian territory after the Khaan Quest 2007.[39] It is also significant to note here that the first meeting of the India-Mongolia Joint Working Group on Defence Cooperation was held in Ulaanbaatar in March /April 2006.[40] Since then both sides have set off several initiatives including the regular dialogue between the National Security Councils of the two countries for exchanging ideas of bilateral and international concern.[41]

Nevertheless, India fully understands that Mongolia is a sensitive issue so far as outside world's strategic interest is concerned in this tiny populated (just 2.6 million) but strategically important country in the post-cold war geo-strategic set up. And India would not allow itself to involve in any controversy, especially at a time when it is being praised in whole Asia both by small as well as big nations, for its efforts towards establishment of regional peace and security.[42] What is relevant at this point is that India's participation in multilateral military exercises on the Mongolian soil must be viewed in a broad perspective of India's new role in East Asia that could give New Delhi a boost for its involvement in regional cooperation/integration process in which Mongolia could also be a participant.[43] Hence, India's strategic relations with Mongolia can always be viewed in terms of mutual partnership that the two distant neighbours can have, without jeopardising the relations with the third country. Just a few days back on 6th June 2008, while delivering a speech at Peking University, Beijing, even India's External Affairs Minister Pranab Mukherjee revealed that "Friendship between India and any one strategic partner is not at the expense of relations with any third country or another strategic partner."[44] He, however, stressed that "our ties are not a product of strategic expediency, but of a long-term vision."[45]

Recently (July 27, 2011) President *Pratibha Devisingh Patil* visited Mongolia; Ms. Patil was the first Indian President to visit Mongolia in 23 years and said "India will explore new avenues to impart more dynamism into its relations with mineral-rich Mongolia especially in coal, steel and infrastructure sectors. India will focus on the ways and means to impart more economic content to our relationship and to see how India can play a more dynamic role in the core strengths of the Mongolian economy for example in coal and steel. In a more contemporary context, we seek to connect with Mongolia through what I call the 3 E's i.e. Enterprise, Economics and Education. In today's milieu, I see a responsibility for all assembled here, as you are the people who interact on a regular basis and propel India-Mongolia relations. You are the vehicle, the via-media to take the relationship forward, to provide the relationship content, substance and meaning, My visit seeks to strengthen our relationship, building upon the momentum generated by the visit of President Elbegdorj to India in September 2009, when our ties were expanded to a comprehensive partnership. We have signed an agreement of cooperation between the Planning Commission of India and its Mongolian counterpart. There is considerable expertise on plan formulation and implementation in India. We look forward to sharing our experience in this area with Mongolia. A bilateral defence cooperation agreement was also signed, and India is willing and ready to expand collaboration in this sphere. New Delhi will extend a Line of Credit of $20 million for the 'India-Mongolia Joint Information Technology, Education and Outsourcing Centre' to be established here. We also agreed to explore the possibilities of improving air connectivity between our two countries so as to enhance contacts between our peoples, including through tourism. With an MoU on media exchanges signed between the two governments, we can now hope to see more media persons from Mongolia in India. We will also send more Indian journalists here; it is encouraging that we also share other values such as democracy, rule of law and upholding the rights of the individual. This forms the bedrock of our bilateral cooperation, My discussions with President Elbegdorj today were wide-ranging and covered the entire gamut of our bilateral relations as well regional and global issues of mutual interest, India will also upgrade and modernise the Rajiv Gandhi Art and Production School as well as the Atal Bihari Vajpayee Centre of Excellence in Information and Communication Technology here. We will complete this work soon. Further, we have agreed to work together on a joint India-Mongolia School, Mongolia is spread in an area of 1.565 million square kilometer and has a population of about 2.7 million. About 92 per cent of its population follows Buddhism and the country shares its border with China and Russia. India and Mongolia are good trading partners. India exports pharma products, veterinary medicines, automobiles and their parts to this country and the bilateral trade has touched $16.9 million. India has also decided to increase the number of slots available to Mongolia under the Indian Technical Education Cooperation (ITEC) Programme to 150. The number of Indian Council of Cultural Relations (ICCR) scholarships available to Mongolia will be increased to 50. India will assist in human resource development and capacity building efforts of Mongolia" (Ulaanbaatar, July 27, 2011).[46]

Despite the fact that India and Mongolia are geographically far apart, there is no stoppage in continuation of their civilizational links spanning over a period of 2,700 years. These links are fascinating, intense and inseparable; transcending all human activities from language, literature, religion, medicine, and folklore to culture and traditions. India is venerated in Mongolia not only as a homeland of Buddha but also as a country to which the Mongolian people attribute all that have been considered the highest attainments of wisdom and learning. The spiritual linkages between India and Mongolia, therefore, make it imperative for the two sides to cooperate each other not only for mutual benefits but also for regional integration process. India's Look East policy as well as its ongoing role in East Asia may have far-reaching consequences to the extent of benefitting Mongolia so far as issue of regional cooperation is concerned. Obviously, Mongolia could seek India's support and certainly in view of the recent developments in India-Mongolia ties it seems possible to a large extent.[47] It would certainly benefit Mongolia economically. Geographical apartness of the two countries would, therefore, no longer be viewed as a barrier in the smooth conduct of their bilateral economic and trade relations, besides engagements in various regional cooperative initiatives. In view of India occupying an important place in Mongolia's foreign and security policies to the extent of becoming the "fourth neighbour", one can hope to see the two sides gaining maximum benefits through their cooperative partnership in all areas of mutual interest.[48]

Notes and References

1. See more The Islamic World to 1600: Rise of the Great Islamic Empires (The Mughal Empire).
2. Essays on Ancient India by Raj Kumar p. 199.
3. The Princeton Encyclopaedia of Islamic Political Thought: page 340.
4. David Meyler (2011), Iran in the Age of the Raj, Avalanche Press, Irondale.
5. P. Stobdan, "Challenges before Buddhism: The Way Ahead", in Suchandana Chatterjee and Anita Sen Gupta (eds.), *Contemporary Buddhism: Comparative Studies on Eurasia and South Asia* (Delhi: Shipra Publications, 2011), pp. 11-12.
6. Soni Sharad K. (2012), Buddhist linkages between India and Mongolia: Implications for Australasian region in Chinese, *Buddhist Encyclopaedia Berkeley University*, USA.
7. Ven K. Sri Dhammananda, (2013), "The Buddist Attitude towards other Religions" http://www.knowbuddhism.info/2009/03/buddhist-attitude-towards-religions.html.
8. Soni Sharad K. (2012), Buddhist linkages between India and Mongolia: Implications for austral-Asian region in Chinese *Buddhist Encyclopaedia Berkeley University*, USA.
9. *Ibid.*
10. *Ibid.*
11. http://www.aseanindia.com/wp,content/uploads/2013/51/india_mongolila_brief_updated_in_ january_ 2013_ for_ xp_ division.pdf).
12. *Ibid.*
13. *Ibid.*
14. C. Raja Mohan, "India and Mongolia: Beyond uranium diplomacy": Mon Sept., 14 2009, 18:50. *The Indian Express*, New Delhi.
15. *Ibid.*
16. Miliate, Brandon Joseph, "India's Role in Mongolia's Third Neighbour Policy" (2009). Independent Study Project (ISP) Collection. Paper 802. http://digitalcollections.sit.edu/isp_collection/802.

17. *Ibid.*

18. Rapkin, David R., and William R. Thompson. *Strategic Asia 2007-07: Will Economic Interdependence Encourage China's and India's Peaceful Ascent?* Print.

19. Miliate, Brandon Joseph, "India's Role in Mongolia's Third Neighbour Policy" (2009). Independent Study Project (ISP) Collection.Paper 802. http://digitalcollections.sit.edu/isp_ collection/ 802.

20. Miliate, Brandon Joseph, "India's Role in Mongolia's Third Neighbour Policy" (2009). Independent Study Project (ISP) Collection.Paper 802. http://digitalcollections.sit.edu/isp_ collection/ 802

21. Nyamdavaa, Oidov. *Mongolia-India relations*. New Delhi: Bhavana Books and Prints, 2003. Print.

22. *Ibid.*

23. Miliate, Brandon Joseph, "India's Role in Mongolia's Third Neighbor Policy" (2009). Independent Study Project (ISP) Collection.Paper 802. http://digitalcollections.sit.edu/isp_ collection/ 802

24. Soni, Sharad K. "India-Mongolia Relations: Implications for Regional Cooperation in North East Asia." *Challenges and Opportunities*. Procedure. of India's Foreign Policy: Post -11th September, Dayal Singh College, Delhi University, Delhi (India). 50-65. Print.

25. *Ibid.*

26. *Ibid.*

27. Soni, Sharad K. *Towards Confidence Building: Sino-Mongolian Relations in the Post-Cold War Era*. Rep. Print.

28. "Mongolia to become Strategic Military location?," 29th May 2006 at http://mongolia.neweurasia.net/?p=226.

29. *Ibid.*

30. Khaan Quest is being organised in Mongolia since 2001 by the General Staff of the Mongolian armed Forces with the support of the US Pacific Command, see Lt. Col. G. Nyamdorj, "Canada goes to Khan Quest", The Maple Leaf, 17th May 2006, p. 15.

31. "Mongolia to become Strategic Military location?", 29th May 2006 at http://mongolia.neweurasia.net/?p=226.

32. Soni, Sharad K. (2009), India-Mongolia Relations: Implications for Regional Cooperation in North East Asia, *Mongolian and Tebetan Quarterly (Taipei,Taiwan)*, Vol.18, No. 2, June 2009, pp. 50-65.

33. "Mongolia to become Strategic Military location?", 29th May 2006 at http://mongolia.neweurasia.net/?p=226.

34. See "Khaan Quest 2007: Multi-national Military Exercise Starts in Mongolia," 30th July 2007, at http://ubpost.blogspot. com/ 2007/07/khan-quest-2007-multi-national-military.html.

35. Rahul Bedi, "Defence ties with Mongolia Expanded: Bid to Monitor China's Military Activities", 10th August 2007, at http:// www. tribuneindia.com/2007/20070810/main5.htm.

36. "India, Mongolia to set up Joint Working Group on Defence", 7th December 2005, at http://www.india-defence.com/ reports/986.

37. Soni, Sharad K. (2009), India-Mongolia Relations: Implications for Regional Cooperation in North East Asia, *Mongolian and Tebetan Quarterly (Taipei,Taiwan)*, Vol. 18, No. 2, June 2009, pp. 50-65.

38. *Ibid.*

39. "Khaan Quest 2007: Multi-national Military Exercise Starts in Mongolia", 30th July 2007, at http://ubpost.blogspot. com/2007/07/ khan-quest-2007-multi-national-military.html.

40. See Government of India, Ministry of Defence, Annual Report: 2006-2007, p.156.

41. Soni, Sharad K. (2009), India-Mongolia Relations: Implications for Regional Cooperation in North East Asia, *Mongolian and Tebetan Quarterly (Taipei,Taiwan)*, Vol. 18, No. 2, June 2009, pp 50-65.

42. Soni, Sharad K. (2009), India-Mongolia Relations: Implications for Regional Cooperation in North East Asia, *Mongolian and Tebetan Quarterly (Taipei,Taiwan)*, Vol.18, No. 2, June 2009, pp. 50-65.

43. For more on Mongolia's efforts for regional cooperation, see Ts. Munkh-Orgil, "Regional Integration Processes and Mongolia", The Mongolian Journal of International Affairs, No. 12, 2005, pp. 3-7.

44. See External Affairs Minister's Speech on "India's Foreign Policy Today" at Peking University in Beijing, China on 6th June 2008, at http://www.meaindia.nic.in.

45. *Ibid.*

46. President Pratibha Devisingh Patil address members of the Indian community based in Mongolia, during a reception hosted at the India Embassy in Ulaanbaatar on July 27.

47. Soni, Sharad K.(2009), "India-Mongolia Relations in Regional Perspective." Proc. of SIS, JNU, New Delhi.

48. *Ibid.*

Other References

Marga, Mongolia. "ISP." Personal interview. 18th November 2009.

Bayasgalan-NUM Professor. "ISP." Personal interview. 11th November 2009.

Bedi, Rahul. "Defence ties with Mongolia expanded bid to monitor China's military activities." *The Tribune*. 10th August 2007. Web. 21 November 2009.

Bedi, Rahul. "India Quietly Expands Ties with Mongolia." *Southern Mongolian Human Rights Information Center*. 9th Aug. 2007. Web. 27th November 2009. <http://www.smhric.org/SMW_36.htm>.

"Concept of Security/Foreign Policy." *MFA official web*. Web. 1st November 2009.

<http://www.mfat.gov.mn/>.

Dashpurev, D.-Director of Institute for International Studies "ISP." Personal interview. 24 Nov. 2009.

Dashpurev, D. *Mongolia: Revolution and Independence (1911-1992)*. New Delhi: JNU, 1993. Print.

Dashpurev, D. *Philosophy, Sociology, Political Science*. Ulaanbaatar: The Institute of International Studies, 2008. Print.

Dormandy, Xenia. "India's Foreign Policy." Proc. of Project on India and the Subcontinent, Harvard University. Belfer Center for Science and International Affairs, 5th Nov. 2007. Web. 8th Nov. 2009.

Dr. Bayasakh; NUM Professor. "ISP." Personal interview. 11 Nov. 2009.

Enkhsaikhan, J. "Mongolia's Nuclear-Weapon-Free Status: Concept and Practice."*Asian Survey* 40.2 (2000): 342-59. *JSTOR*. Web. 23 Nov. 2009.

"Foreign Relations." *Country Studies*. Library of Congress. Web. 8 Nov. 2009. Ginsburg, Tom. "Political Reform in Mongolia: Between Russia and China."*Asian Survey* 35.5 (1995): 459-71. *JSTOR*. Web. 6 Nov. 2009. <http://www.jstor.org/stable/2645748>.

"India, China hold dialogue on human rights issues." *BBC Monitoring Asia-Pacific* 31 Apr. 2005. *LexisScholar*. Web. 25 Oct. 2009.

"India, Mongolia mark ties anniversary with visa waiver for officials." *BBC Monitoring South Asia* 23 Dec. 2005. *Lexis Scholar*. Web. 25 Oct. 2009.

"India signs civil nuclear pact with Mongolia." *BBC Monitoring South Asia* 14 Sept. 2009. Print.

Indian Council for Cultural Relations: Annual Report 2003-2004. Rep. Web. 17 Nov. 2009. <http://www.iccrindia.org/annualreport03/report03.htm>.

"Indian minister of state for defence visits Mongolia." *BBC Monitoring Asia- Pacific* 11 May 2006. *LexisScholar*. Web. 25 Oct. 2009.

Indian Studies in Mongolia 4 (2008): 1-117. Print.

Indian Studies in Mongolia 6 (2009): 1-27. Print.

Joseph, Anil K. "Mongolia Keen to Deepen Bilateral Ties." *New India-Times* [New York] 7 July 2001, 31st ed., sec. 7: 8. *ProQuest*. Web. 25 October 2009.

Ministry of External Affairs: Annual Report 2004-2005. Rep. New Delhi: Joint Secretary, Policy Planning and Research, Ministry of External Affairs. Print. *Mongolia: India Mission in*. Rep. Web.

"Mongolia names road after India's Mahatma Gandhi." *BBC Monitoring South Asia* 23 Decemeber 2005. *Lexis Scholar*. Web. 25 October 2009.

"Mongolian president to pay state visit to India 13-16 Sep." *BBC Monitoring Asia-Pacific* 8 Sept. 2009. *LexisScholar*. Web. 25 October 2009.

Narangoa, Li. *Mongolia and Preventative Diplomacy: Haunted by History and Becoming Cosmopolitian*. March 2009. Web.

Negi, R.L.-Office of Affairs: Indian Embassy, Ulaanbaatar "ISP." Personal interview. 25 November 2009.

Noosgoi, Altantsetseg- NUM Doctorate Student. "ISP." E-mail interview. 19 November 2009.

Nyamdavaa, O.- Ambassador to India "ISP." Personal interview. 20 Nov. 2009.

Nyamdavaa, Oidov. *Mongolia-India relations*. New Delhi: Bhavana Books and Prints, 2003. Print.

Rapkin, David R., and William R. Thompson. *Strategic Asia 2007-07: Will Economic Interdependence Encourage China's and India's Peaceful Ascent?* Print.

Sharma, Ritu. "India shelves proposal to set up airbase in Mongolia?" *Jansmachar.net*. 18 Sept. 2009. Web. 17 November 2009.

Soni, Sharad K. "India-Mongolia Relations: Implications for Regional Cooperation in North East Asia." *Challenges and Opportunities*. Proc. of India's Foreign Policy: Post -11th September, Dayal Singh College, Delhi University, Delhi (India). 50-65. Print.

Soni, Sharad K. "India-Mongolia Relations in Regional Perspective." Proc. of SIS Monthly Faculty Meetings, Jawaharal Nehru University, New Delhi. 1-3. Print.

Soni, Sharad K. –JNU Professor "ISP." E-mail interview. 24 November 2009.

Soni, Sharad K. *Mongolia's Security Thinking and Outside World: A Reappraisal*. Rep. Print.

Soni, Sharad K. *Towards Confidence Building: Sino-Mongolian Relations in the Post-Cold War Era*. Rep. Print.

6

Conclusion

While concluding this work discussed in the last five chapters, first of all we find that when the theoretical framework of foreign policy is conceptualised in the Mongolian context, the theory of "realism" seems to be most appropriate. This is more so because Mongolia's foreign policy is based on pragmatism, i.e., Mongolia follows a pragmatic approach in the conduct of its foreign policy, which was adopted in 1994. This has been quite a different foreign policy from what was there in Mongolia in the pre-1986 period. However, major changes in the then existing foreign policy of Mongolia were seen between 1986 and 1991, first as a result of Gorbachev's reform policies and then due to the collapse of the Soviet Union. The diplomatic relations established with USA in 1987 was a very significant event in Mongolia's foreign policy changes. The other significant event in Mongolia's foreign affairs was that its relations with China started normalising that also indicated positive changes in Mongolia's foreign policy priorities.

In the light of the above-mentioned scenario, the main purpose of this book was to examine the dynamics of changes in Mongolia's foreign policy during the reform period beginning from 1986 until 1996. The year 1986 was chosen as the starting period of the study because it was in this year that Mongolia launched its reform policies of and *Iltod* (openness) and *Orchilan baigalalt* (restructuring) on the model of Gorbachev's policies of *Glasnost* and *Perestroika*. It was also in 1986 that Gorbachev delivered his seminal Vladivostok speech to change Soviet foreign policy particularly towards Asia. This has had tremendous influence on Mongolia which also began changing its own foreign policy priorities. The first significant change saw Mongolia opening itself to the outside world away from the Soviet orbit which is evident from the establishment of diplomatic relations with the United States in 1987. The year 1996 was chosen as cut off year because it was in this year that the Democrats gained a landslide victory in the parliamentary elections, thus ending for the first time the 75-year rule of the Communist party. The victory was assigned to their election campaign which focussed mainly on aggressive domestic and foreign policy reforms to attract more overseas partners who could be a reliable ally in international affairs besides helping to set right Mongolian economy.

In fact, the year 1986 was marked by the beginning of reforms under the influence of Soviet leader Mikhail Gorbachev's reform policies. Gorbachev became the General Secretary of the Communist Party of the Soviet Union (CPSU) on March 11, 1985. With the new leadership the conduct of Soviet foreign policy improved. A skilful public relations effort became an important component of Moscow's diplomacy, but the substance of the USSR's international behaviour also changed considerably. Gorbachev himself increasingly talked about the need for "a new approach" in addressing the problems of the world. At the 27th Congress of the CPSU held in February 1986 he said: "It is not only in internal affairs that the turning point has been reached. It characterises external affairs as well. The changes in contemporary world development are so profound and significant that they required a rethinking and comprehensive analysis of all factors involved. The situation of nuclear deterrence demands the development of new approaches, methods and forms of relations between different social systems, states and regions".

In a speech delivered in Vladivostok in July 1986, Gorbachev was even bolder, claiming that "the current stage in the development of civilisation is dictating the need for an urgent, radical break with many of the conventional approaches to foreign policy, a break with the traditions of political thinking." The Soviet foreign policy changes under Gorbachev went beyond words. He reshuffled the national security leadership, bringing younger and less doctrinaire officials to key positions and giving himself more personal control over decision-making. The new team quickly distinguished itself not only in launching Gorbachev's "charm offensive" but also by introducing a wide variety of foreign policy initiatives ranging from arms control proposals to overtures to China.[1] The atmosphere of reforms in the Soviet Union prompted similar reforms in Mongolia also both at the domestic as well as foreign affairs. At the domestic level, following mass demonstrations in the winter of 1990, the ruling Mongolian People's Republican Party (MPRP) began to loosen its controls of the political system. The Politburo of the MPRP resigned in March, and in May the constitution was amended, deleting reference to the MPRP's role as the guiding force in the country, legalising opposition parties, creating a standing legislative body, and establishing the office of President. On July 29, 1990, the first free, multiparty elections in Mongolia were held. The election results returned a majority for the MPRP, which won with 85 per cent of the vote. It was not until 1996 that the reformed MPRP was voted out of office by the democrats for the first time in the contemporary history of Mongolia.[2]

At the external level, for the first time Mongolia diversified itself to come closer to the United States and established, as already mentioned, their diplomatic relations in 1987. On the other side normalisation of relations with China also began to be witnessed at about the same time. These two events provided Mongolia a self-confidence to pursue its own independent foreign policy away from the one that was influenced by the Soviet Union. Though in terms of geography Mongolia's international position remained same, in terms of security its international position began to change that after the Soviet collapse in 1991 became even more pronounced. Developments on the international front in 1991 demonstrated Mongolia's commitment to integration as an active participant in the Asia-Pacific community and to strengthening ties with the European Community. These developments were consistent with Mongolia's foreign policy stance as a non-aligned nation. During early 1990s Mongolian diplomacy worked on filling the political vacuum created by the demise of the Soviet Union, Mongolia's sole creditor and overwhelming trading partner. By some estimates, the USSR provided economic assistance annually equal to about 30 per cent of Mongolia's GDP. [3]

Mongolia's much-needed help was sought by breaking the previous isolation, and establishing and maintaining not only the all-round cooperation with the major powers of the world like USA, Japan, and Western Europe but also Mongolia's admission to the International Monetary Fund (IMF), the World Bank, and the Asian Development Bank (ADB) in February 1992. It was indeed an important step toward promoting ties with the international community and the country's further integration with the world economy. The disintegration of the world socialist system dramatically changed the external situation of Mongolia which used to be aligned with them. The major changes taking place in Mongolia's two neighbouring countries had a direct impact on its external environment.[4] The restructuring and reforming of the country's political, social and economic systems provided it with favourable conditions for conducting a new foreign policy based on realism and its national interests.

Once having a distinction of being the second Communist state of the world after the erstwhile Soviet Union, the then political status of Mongolia as a "buffer" in the Sino-Soviet relations underwent a change. Emergence of a new geopolitical situation as well as impact of domestic political reforms and economic restructuring particularly during 1990-1992 compelled both the leadership and intellectuals in Mongolia to debate on national interests. Finally, they reached a consensus to consider Mongolia's future development and security issues in the framework of new realities. An extraordinary degree of foreign policy consensus that emerged in Mongolia in early 1990s reflected in such ideas as 'multi-pillar' foreign policy and a 'balanced' relationship with two neighbours. The President, a weak and symbolic post defined by the 1992 Constitution, emerged as a key foreign policy player in the Mongolian domestic political scene. What has been found during the period of this research study is that there have been interrelations between foreign policy and domestic reforms and that both the domestic as well as external influence on foreign policy changes in Mongolia has been very significant.

For centuries, Mongolia was a territorial buffer. When the Manchus conquered China and established the Qing Empire, they swept Mongolia into their realm. When the Qing collapsed, Moscow sucked Mongolia into its own expanding domain and, during the period of Sino-Soviet enmity from the mid-1960s to

1989, the Soviet Union stationed troops and military equipment in Mongolia to enhance its strategic advantage over the PRC.[5] However, the USSR withdrew its troops stationed in Mongolia, and its technical and financial assistance, between 1987 and 1992. The impact of Mongolia's internal and external policies changes was that the country declared: "Maintaining friendly relations with the Russian Federation and the People's Republic of China shall be a priority of Mongolia's foreign policy activity.[6] It shall not adopt the line of either country but shall maintain in principle a balanced relationship with both of them and shall promote all-round good neighbourly cooperation".

Influenced by the changes in the geopolitical situation in the immediate surroundings, Mongolia found its borders secured and relations with neighbours stable. The next step was to begin focussing on a number of pressing domestic socio-economic issues. Unemployment, poverty, rapid urbanisation and the ensuing social displacement posed potential threats to long-term stability and economic prosperity. And Mongolia had no option but to take such measures that could help the country progress both at the domestic as well as foreign affairs levels at a time when globalisation was becoming the order of the day. In that sense introduction of democracy and market economy brought about significant changes in Mongolia's domestic policy which ultimately influenced the country's foreign policy as well, though the issues concerning national security were always kept in mind while formulating any policy. The national security of Mongolia represents the status when favourable external and internal conditions are secured to ensure vital national interests. Such national interests lay in the existence of the Mongolian people and their civilization, in the country's independence, sovereignty, territorial integrity, inviolability of State frontiers, relative economic independence, sustainable ecological development and national unity.

Mongolia's main national interests during the period of this study focussed on sovereignty and economic independence. As a sovereign nation in her own right, due to membership of, and participation in multilateral organisations such as the UN, Mongolia has been able to make fully independent foreign policy decisions. Besides, relations with the Soviet Union/Russia, China and the US provided much-needed bulwarks to change the existing foreign policy and adopt a new one by taking into consideration the new geopolitical environment surrounding Mongolia and its national security interest. As such, a major review of its foreign and security policy was undertaken which, in June 1994, resulted in the formulation of three very important documents i.e., Concept of National Security, Concept of Foreign Policy and Military Doctrine. These three documents were interlinked in terms of their basic objectives, i.e., safeguarding the country's national interests both internal as well as external in order to ensure overall advancement of its people. The idea behind adopting such foreign policy was to make constructive relations with all nations, seek independence from its two giant neighbours, and avoid dependence on any single partner.

In fact, Mongolia's foreign policy implementation was guided by a few serious objectives that included ensuring independence and sovereignty by following the trends of human society's advancement; maintaining friendly relations with all countries; strengthening its position in the international community; and forming a network of relationships with influential countries in the region and in the world based on the interdependence of political, economic and other interests. While following a policy of creating realistic interest of the developed countries, Mongolia expressed its commitments to avoid becoming overly reliant or dependent on any particular country. Since Mongolia is 'sandwiched' between Russia and China, all Mongolian governments since 1990 have therefore pursued pro-Western foreign policy since external support is regarded as essential to ensure continued independence'. In that sense, despite popular attachment to Russia and the societal experience over the years, Mongolia has sought closer ties with the United States, Japan, and Germany, and economic and trade relations have increased with China.[7]

At the same time, it is also true that at the internal level the reforms carried out by democratic government that won 1996 elections, did not deliver the country into a better situation as Mongolia experienced political disability and economic crisis. The effectiveness of the Democratic Coalition was tempered and restrained by its own political inexperience. But at the external level, the democratic coalition government tried to ensure the implementation of new foreign policy in Mongolia's favour. This was more so because in the post-1991 period, irrespective of any government Mongolia wanted to secure itself both for diplomatic and economic gains. The two neighbours- Russia and China began respecting Mongolia's sovereignty apart from supporting it at various regional groupings. Due to the support of Russia and China, Mongolia achieved a success in the Shanghai Cooperation Organisation (SCO) by gaining an observer status. It also began taking active part in the affairs of North East Asia and participated in the meetings of North East Asian Region. Relations with not only the US and EU countries but also with Australia and New Zealand started developing. In Asia, the major countries with Which Mongolia's foreign policy implementation worked for its benefit included Japan, South Korea and India. Mongolia not only benefitted from bilateral but also from multilateral relations to ensure its economic security.

In sum, Mongolia's foreign policy during the period of this study has been based on mutual respect for sovereignty, territorial integrity and inviolability of frontiers, right to self-determination, non-interference in internal affairs, non-use of force, settlement of disputes by peaceful means, respect for human rights and freedoms, and equal and mutually beneficial cooperation with other countries. While pursuing its "multi-pillar" foreign policy, Mongolia upholds peace and tries to avoid confrontation with other countries keeping in mind its national interests first and foremost. At the same time, it is committed to respect the legitimate interests of other countries and its partners. Besides, as per the directions of its reformed foreign policy, it also ensures itself not to interfere in the disputes between its two neighbouring countries unless the disputes affect Mongolia's national interests.

All the arguments highlighted in this book, thus, point to the fact that the post-Soviet period in the history of Mongolia formed new loyalties and transformed the old ones. This transition helped the country to carry out changes through reforms in both the internal and external policies. While the country's think-tanks and leadership brought out changes in the existing foreign policy to make it a "multi-pillar" foreign policy, the democratically elected government after 1996 parliamentary elections ensured the implementation of this new foreign policy. In that sense, 1996 was the turning point to ensure Mongolia's presence on the international map through bilateral and multilateral relations. So, finally it can articulate that Mongolia's foreign policy aims to securing its sovereignty and economic independence rather than remaining dependent on an external power as was the case during Soviet days, and also Mongolia pursues a multi-pillar foreign policy with democratic countries to consolidate its national interest.

References

1. http://www.foreignaffairs.com/articles/41714/dimitri-k-simes/gorbachev-a-new-foreign-policy.
2. http://india.smashits.com/wikipedia/Mongolian_ People's_ Republic.
3. Tsedendamba Batbayar. "Foreign policy and domestic reform in Mongolia", Central Asian Survey, 3/1/2003.
4. *Ibid.*
5. http://www.eai.or.kr/data/bbs/eng_report/20090520 17262087.pdf.
6. *Ibid.*
7. http://www.icnrd5-mongolia.mn/pdf/desk_study.pdf.

APPENDIX I

THE CONSTITUTION OF MONGOLIA

13 January, 1992

We, the people of Mongolia:

- Strengthening the independence and sovereignty of the state,
- Cherishing human rights and freedoms, justice and national unity,
- Inheriting the traditions of national statehood, history and culture,
- Respecting the accomplishments of human civilization,
- And aspiring toward the supreme objective of building a human, civil and democratic society in our homeland,

Hereby proclaim the Constitution of Mongolia.

CHAPTER ONE

Sovereignty of the Mongolian State

Article One

1. Mongolia is an independent, sovereign republic.

2. The fundamental principles of the activities of the State shall be securing democracy, justice, freedom, equality, national unity and rule of law.

Article Two

1. By its state organisation, Mongolia shall be a unitary State.

2. The territory of Mongolia shall be divided into administrative units only.

Article Three

1. In Mongolia state power shall be vested in the people of Mongolia. The Mongolian people shall exercise it through their direct participation in state affairs as well as through the representative bodies of the State authority elected by them.

2. Illegal seizure of State power or any attempt to do so shall be prohibited.

Article Four

1. The territorial integrity and frontiers of Mongolia shall be inviolable.

2. The frontiers of Mongolia shall be fixed by law.

3. Stationing of foreign troops in the territory of Mongolia, allowing them to cross the state frontier for the purpose of passing through the country's territory shall be prohibited unless an appropriate law is adopted.

Article Five

1. Mongolia shall have an economy based on different forms of property consistent to universal trends of world economic development and own country's specifics.

2. The State recognises all forms of public and private property and shall protect the rights of the owner by law.

3. The owner's rights shall be limited exclusively by grounds specified in the law.

4. The State shall regulate the economy with a view to ensure the nation's economic security, the development of all forms of property and social development of the population.

5. Livestock are national wealth and shall be protected by the State.

Article Six

1. In Mongolia the land, its sub-soil, forests, water, fauna and flora and other natural resources shall be subject to people's power and State protection.

2. The land, except that given to the citizens of Mongolia for private ownership, as well as the sub-soil with its mineral resources, forests, water resources and wildfowl shall be the property of the State.

3. The State may give for private ownership plots of land, except pasturage and land under public utilisation and special use, only to the citizens of Mongolia. This provision shall not apply to the ownership of the sub-soil thereof. Citizens shall be prohibited to transfer the land in their ownership to foreign citizens and stateless persons by way of selling, bartering, donating or pledging as well as from transferring it to others for their possession and use without permission from competent State authorities.

4. The State shall have the right to hold landowners responsible for the land, to exchange or take it over with compensation on the grounds of special public need, or confiscate the land if it is used in a manner adverse to the health of the population, the interests of environmental protection or national security.

5. The State may allow foreign citizens, legal persons and stateless persons to lease land for a specified period of time under conditions and procedures as provided for by law.

Article Seven

1. The historical, cultural, scientific and intellectual heritage of the Mongolian people shall be under State protection.

2. Intellectual values produced by citizens are the property of their authors and the national wealth of Mongolia.

Article Eight

1. The Mongolian language is the official language of the State.

2. Paragraph 1 of this Article shall not affect the right of national minorities of other tongues to use their native languages

in education and communication and in the pursuit of cultural, artistic and scientific activities.

Article Nine

1. The State shall respect the religions and the religions shall honour the State.

2. State institutions shall not engage in religious activities and the Church shall not carry out political activities.

3. The relationship between the State and the Church shall be regulated by law.

Article Ten

1. Mongolia shall adhere to the universally recognised norms and principles of international law and pursue a peaceful foreign policy.

2. Mongolia shall fulfill in good faith its obligations under international treaties to which it is a Party.

3. The international treaties to which Mongolia is a Party shall become effective as domestic legislation upon the entry into force of the laws on their ratification or accession.

4. Mongolia shall not abide by any international treaty or other instruments incompatible with its Constitution.

Article Eleven

1. The duty of the State is to secure the country's independence, ensure national security and public order.

2. Mongolia shall have armed forces for self-defence. The structure and organization of the armed forces and rules of military service shall be determined by law.

Article Twelve

1. The symbols of the independence and sovereignty of Mongolia are the State Emblem, Banner, Flag, Seal and Anthem.

2. The State Emblem, Banner, Flag and Anthem shall express the historical tradition, aspiration, unity, justice and the spirit of the people of Mongolia.

3. The State Emblem shall be of circular shape with the white lotus serving as its base and the "Never-ending Tumen

Nasan" pattern forming its outer frame. The main background is of blue colour signifying the eternal blue sky, the Mongols' traditional sanctity. In the centre of the Emblem a combination of the Precious Steed and the Golden Soyombo sign is depicted as an expression of the independence, sovereignty and spirit of Mongolia. In the upper part of the Emblem the Chandmani (Wish-granting Jewel) sign symbolises the past, the present and the future. In the lower part of the Emblem the sign of the Wheel entwined with the silk scarf Khadag in an expression of reverence and respect, symbolising continued prosperity. It is placed against the background of a "hill" pattern conveying the notion of "Mother Earth".

4. The traditional Great White Banner of the unified Mongolian State is a state ceremonial attribute.

5. The State Flag shall be a rectangle divided vertically into three equal parts coloured red, blue and red. The blue colour of the center of the flag, symbolises "the eternal blue sky" and the red colour on both sides symbolizes progress and prosperity. The Golden Soyombo sign shall be depicted on the red stripe nearest to the flag pole. The ratio of the width and length of the Flag shall be 1:2.

6. The State Seal having a lion-shaped handle shall be of a square form with the state Emblem in the center and the words "Mongol Uls" (Mongolia) inscribed on both sides. The President shall be the holder of the State Seal.

7. The procedure for the ceremonial use of the State symbols and the text and melody of the State Anthem shall be fixed by law.

Article Thirteen

1. The capital of the State shall be the city in which the State Supreme bodies permanently sit. The capital city of Mongolia is the city of Ulaanbaatar.

2. The legal status of the capital city shall be determined by law.

CHAPTER TWO

Human Rights and Freedoms

Article Fourteen

1. All persons lawfully residing within Mongolia are equal before the law and the Court.

2. No person shall be discriminated against on the basis of ethnic origin, language, race, age, sex, social origin and status, property, occupation and position, religion, opinion and education. Every one shall be a person before the law.

Article Fifteen

1. The grounds and procedure for Mongolian nationality, acquisition or loss of citizenship shall be determined only by law.

2. Deprivation of Mongolian citizenship, exile and extradition of citizens of Mongolia shall be prohibited.

Article Sixteen

The citizens of Mongolia are guaranteed to enjoy the following rights and freedoms:

1. *The right to life.* Deprivation of human life shall be strictly prohibited unless capital punishment is imposed by due judgment of the Court for the most serious crimes, pursuant to Mongolian Criminal law.

2. The right to a healthy and safe environment, and to be protected against environmental pollution and ecological imbalance.

3. The right to fair acquisition, possession, ownership and inheritance of moveable and immoveable property. Illegal confiscation and requisitioning of the private property of citizens shall be prohibited. If the State and its bodies appropriate private property on the basis of exclusive public need, they shall do so with due compensation and payment.

4. The right to free choice of employment, favourable conditions of work, remuneration, rest and private farming. No one shall be subjected to forced labour.

5. The right to material and financial assistance in old age, disability, child-birth and child-care and in other circumstances as provided by law.

6. The right to the protection of health and medical care. The procedure and conditions of free medical aid shall be determined by law.

7. The right to education. The state shall provide basic general education free of charge; Citizens may establish and operate private schools if these meet the requirements of the State.

8. The right to engage in creative work in cultural, artistic and scientific fields and to benefit thereof. Copyrights and patents shall be protected by law.

9. The right to take part in the conduct of State affairs directly or through representative bodies. The right to elect and to be elected to State bodies. The right to elect shall be enjoyed from the age of eighteen years and the age of eligibility for being elected shall be determined by law according to the requirements in respect of the bodies or positions concerned.

10. The right to form a party or other mass organisation and freedom of association to these organisations on the basis of social and personal interests and opinion. All political parties and other mass organisations shall uphold public order and state security, and abide by law. Discrimination and persecution of a person for joining a political party or other mass organisation or for being their member shall be prohibited. Party membership of some categories of state employees may be suspended.

11. Men and women shall enjoy equal rights in political, economic, social, cultural fields and in family relationship. Marriage shall be based on the equality and mutual consent of the spouses who have reached the age determined by law. The State shall protect the interests of the family, motherhood and the child.

12. The right to submit a petition or a complaint to State bodies and officials. The State bodies and officials shall be obliged to respond to the petitions or complaints of citizens in conformity with law.

13. The right to personal liberty and safety. No one shall be searched, arrested, detained, persecuted or restricted of liberty except in accordance with procedures and grounds determined by law. No person shall be subjected to torture, inhumane, cruel or degrading treatment. Where a person is arrested his/her family and counsel shall be notified within a

period of time established by law of the reasons for and grounds of the arrest. The privacy of citizens, their families, correspondence and homes shall be protected by law.

14. The right to appeal to the court to protect his/her rights if he/she considers that the rights or freedoms as spelt out by the Mongolian law or an international treaty have been violated; to be compensated for the damage illegally caused by others; not to testify against himself/herself, his/her family, or parents and children; to self-defence; to receive legal assistance; to have evidence examined; to fair trial; to be tried in his/her presence; to appeal against a court decision, to seek pardon. Compelling to testify against himself/herself shall be prohibited. Every person shall be presumed innocent until proved guilty by a court by due process of law. The penalties imposed on the convicted shall not be applicable to his/her family members and relatives.

15. Freedom of conscience and religion.

16. Freedom of thought, opinion and expression, speech, press, peaceful assembly. Procedures for organising demonstrations and other assemblies shall be determined by law.

17. The right to seek and receive information except that which the state and its bodies are legally bound to protect as secret. In order to protect human rights, dignity and reputation of persons and to ensure State defence, national security and public order secrets of the State, organisation or individuals, which are not subject to disclosure shall be determined and protected by law.

18. The right to freedom of movement and residence within the country, right to travel and reside abroad and to return to their home country. The right to travel and reside abroad may be limited exclusively by law in order to ensure national security and the security of the population and protect public order.

Article Seventeen

1. Citizens of Mongolia, while upholding justice and humanity, shall fulfill in good faith the following basic duties:

(1) To respect and abide by the Constitution and other laws;

(2) To respect dignity, reputation, rights and legitimate interests of others;

(3) To pay taxes levied by law;

(4) To defend the motherland and to perform military service according to law.

2. It is a sacred duty for every citizen to work, protect his/her health, bring up and educate his/her children and to protect nature and the environment.

Article Eighteen

1. The rights and duties of foreign citizens residing in Mongolia shall be regulated by Mongolian law and by the treaties concluded with the State of the person concerned.

2. Mongolia shall adhere to the principle of reciprocity in determining the rights and duties of foreign citizens in an international treaty being concluded with the country concerned.

3. The rights and duties of stateless persons within the territory of Mongolia shall be determined by Mongolian law.

4. Foreign citizens or stateless persons persecuted for their beliefs, political or other activities pursuing justice may be granted asylum in Mongolia on the basis of their well-founded requests.

5. In allowing foreign citizens and stateless persons under the jurisdiction of Mongolia to exercise the basic rights and freedoms provided for in Article 16 of this Constitution, the State may establish by law relevant restrictions upon the rights other than the inalienable rights spelt out in international instruments to which Mongolia is a Party, out of the consideration of ensuring national security, the security of the population and public order.

Article Nineteen

1. The State shall be responsible to the citizens for the creation of economic, social, legal and other guarantees ensuring human rights and freedoms, to fight against violations of human rights and freedoms and to restore infringed rights.

2. In case of announcement of a state of emergency or martial law, the human rights and freedoms as determined by

the Constitution and other laws shall be subject to limitation only by a law. Such a law shall not affect the right to life, the freedom of thought, conscience and religion, as well as the right not to be subjected to torture, inhuman and cruel treatment.

3. In exercising his/her rights and freedoms one shall not infringe the national security, rights and freedoms of others or violate public order.

CHAPTER THREE

State System of Mongolia

One. The State Ikh Khural

Article Twenty

The State Ikh Khural of Mongolia is the highest organ of State power and the legislative power shall be vested solely in the State Ikh Khural.

Article Twenty one

1. The State Ikh Khural shall have one chamber and consist of 76 members.

2. The members of the State Ikh Khural shall be elected by citizens eligible for election, on the basis of universal, free, direct suffrage by secret ballot for a term of four years.

3. Citizens of Mongolia who have reached the age of twenty-five years and are eligible for elections shall be elected to the State Ikh Khural.

4. The procedure of the election of members of the State Ikh Khural shall be determined by law.

Article Twenty two

1. If extraordinary circumstances arising from sudden calamities occur in the whole or a part of the country, the imposition of martial law or the outbreak of public disorder prevent the holding of regular election the State Ikh Khural shall retain its mandate until the extraordinary circumstances cease to exist and the newly-elected members of the State Ikh Khural are sworn in.

2. The State Ikh Khural may decide on its dissolution if not less than two thirds of its members consider that the State

Ikh Khural is unable to carry out its mandate, or if the President, in consultation with the Chairman of the State Ikh Khural, proposes to do so for the same reason. In case of such a decision, the State Ikh Khural shall exercise its mandate till the newly elected members of the State Ikh Khural are sworn in. Unless otherwise specified in the Constitution, the State Ikh Khural shall decide on its dissolution or the President shall issue a decree on the dissolution of the State Ikh Khural if the State Ikh Khural fails to appoint a Prime Minister within 45 days from the submission of the proposal of his/her appointment to the Ikh Khural /*amendments from 24th December 1999 and 14th December 2000.*

Article Twenty three

1. A member of the State Ikh Khural shall be an envoy of the people and shall represent and uphold the interests of all the citizens and the State.

2. The mandate of a member of the State Ikh Khural shall begin with an oath taken before the State Emblem and expire when newly-elected members of the State Ikh Khural are sworn in.

Article Twenty four

1. Chairman and Vice-chairman of the State Ikh Khural shall be nominated and elected from among the members of the State Ikh Khural by open ballot. Each party and coalition group formed as a result of election shall elect the Vice-Chairman of the State Ikh Khural. /*amendments from 24th December 1999 and 14th December 2000.*

2. The term of office of the Chairman and Vice-Chairman of the State Ikh Khural shall be four years. They can be relieved of or removed from their posts before the expiry of their terms on grounds specified by law.

Article Twenty five

1. The State Ikh Khural may consider on its initiative any issue pertaining to domestic and foreign policies of the State, and shall keep within its exclusive power the following issues and decide thereon:

(1) To enact laws, make amendments to them;

(2) To define the basis of the domestic and foreign policies of the State;

(3) To set and announce the date of elections of the President and the State Ikh Khural and its members;

(4) To determine and change the structure and composition of the Standing Committees of the State Ikh Khural, the Government and other bodies directly accountable to it according to the law;

(5) To pass a law recognising the full mandate of the President after his/her election and to relieve or remove the President;

(6) To appoint, replace or remove the Prime Minister, members of the Government and other bodies responsible and accountable to the State Ikh Khural as provided for by law;

(7) To define the State's financial, credit, tax and monetary policies; to lay down the guidelines for the country's economic and social development; to approve the Government's program of action, the State budget and the report on its execution;

(8) To supervise the implementation of laws and other decisions of the State Ikh Khural;

(9) To fix the State frontier;

(10) To set the structure, composition and power of the National Security Council;

(11) To approve and change the administrative and territorial division of Mongolia on the Government submission;

(12) To determine the legal basis of the system, organisation and activities of local self-governing and administrative bodies;

(13) To institute State titles, orders, medals and higher military ranks, to determine the table of ranks in some special fields of State service;

(14) To issue acts of amnesty;

(15) To ratify and denounce international treaties to which Mongolia is a Party, to establish and sever diplomatic relations with foreign States on the Government submission;

(16) To hold national referenda. To verify the validity of a referendum in which the majority of citizens eligible for election has taken parts, and to abide by and give effect to the decision which has obtained a majority of votes;

(17) To declare a martial law in case the sovereignty and independence of the State are threatened by armed actions on the part of a foreign State, and to rescind it;

(18) To declare a state of emergency or martial law in the whole or part of the country in special circumstances described in Paragraph 2 and 3 of this Article and to approve or nullify the President's decree to that effect.

2. Under the following extraordinary circumstances the State Ikh Khural may declare a state of emergency to eliminate the consequences thereof and to restore the life of the population and society to normalcy:

(1) Natural disasters or other unforeseen dangers which threaten or may threaten directly the life, health, well-being and security of the population in the whole or a part of the country's territory;

(2) If State authorities are not able within legal limits to cope with public disorders caused by organised, violent, illegal actions of an organisation or a group of people threatening the Constitutional order and the existence of the legitimate social system.

(3) The State Ikh Khural may declare martial law if public disorder in the whole or a part of the country's territory result in armed conflict or create a real threat of armed conflict, or if there is armed aggression or a real threat of such aggression from a foreign state.

(4) The other power, organisation and the procedures of the State Ikh Khural shall be determined by law.

Article Twenty six

1. The President, members of the State Ikh Khural and the Government shall exercise the right to initiative laws.

2. Citizens and other organisations shall forward their suggestions on draft laws to those entitled to initiate a law.

3. National laws shall be subject to official promulgation by the State Ikh Khural through publication and, unless law provides otherwise, shall enter into force 10 days after the date of publication.

Article Twenty seven

1. The State Ikh Khural shall exercise its power through its sessions and other organisational forms.

2. Regular sessions of the State Ikh Khural shall be convened once every half year and last but not less than 50 working days. ***amendments from 24th December 1999 and 14th December 2000.***

3. Extraordinary sessions may be convened at the demand of more than one-third of the members of the State Ikh Khural or at the initiative of the President and the Chairman of the State Ikh Khural.

4. The President shall convoke the first sessions of the State Ikh Khural within 30 days of an election. Other sessions shall be convoked by the Chairman of the State Ikh Khural.

5. In case of the proclamation by the President of a state of emergency or martial law, the State Ikh Khural shall be convened for an extraordinary session within 72 hours without prior announcement.

6. The presence of a majority of members shall be required to consider a session of the State Ikh Khural and Standing Committee valid, and decisions shall be taken by the majority voting of all members present. The Prime Minister's and Government members' appointment and other issues shall be decided by open ballot unless other laws provide otherwise. ***amendments from 24th December 1999 and 14th December 2000.***

Article Twenty eight

1. The State Ikh Khural shall have Standing Committees dealing with specific fields of its activity.

2. The State Ikh Khural shall determine the power, organisation and procedures of the work of Standing Committees.

Article Twenty nine

1. Members of the State Ikh Khural shall be remunerated from the State budget during their term and shall not hold concurrently any posts and employment other than those assigned by law except for the post of Prime Minister and member of Government. */amendments from 24th December 1999 and 14th December 2000.*

2. The legal immunity of members of the State Ikh Khural shall be protected by law.

3. Questions concerning the involvement of a member of the State Ikh Khural in a crime shall be considered by the session of the State Ikh Khural, which shall decide whether to suspend his/her mandate. If a court rules the member in question to be guilty of crime, the State Ikh Khural shall terminate his/her membership in Legislature.

Two. The President

Article Thirty

1. The President shall be the Head of State and embodiment of the unity of the Mongolian people.

2. An indigenous citizen of Mongolia, who has attained the age of forty-five years and has permanently resided as a minimum for the last five years in Mongolia, shall be eligible for election to the post of President for a term of four years.

Article Thirty one

1. Presidential elections shall be conducted in two stages.

2. Political parties which have obtained seats in the State Ikh Khural shall nominate individually or collectively Presidential candidates, one candidate per party or coalition of parties.

3. At the primary stage of the elections citizens eligible for election shall participate in electing the President on the basis of universal, free and direct suffrage by secret ballot.

4. The State Ikh Khural shall consider the candidate who has obtained a majority of all votes cast in the first voting round as elected President and shall pass a law recognising his/her mandate.

5. If none of the candidates obtains a majority vote in the first round, a second round of voting shall take place involving the two candidates who have obtained the largest number of votes in the first round. The candidate who wins a majority of all votes cast in the second ballot shall be considered as elected President and a law recognising his/her mandate shall be passed by the State Ikh Khural.

6. If neither of the candidates wins a majority of votes in the second ballot, Presidential elections shall be held anew.

7. The President can be re-elected only once.

8. The President shall not be Prime Minister, a member of the State Ikh Khural or a member of the Government and shall not concurrently hold any other posts and pursue any occupation not relating to his duties assigned by law. If the President holds another office or a post he/she shall be relieved of it from the date on which he/she takes his/her oath.

Article Thirty two

1. The mandate of the President shall become effective with an oath taken by him/her and shall expire with an oath taken by the newly-elected President.

2. Within thirty days of the election, the President shall take the following oath before the State Ikh Khural: "I swear that I shall guard and defend the independence and sovereignty of Mongolia, the freedom of the people and national unity and I shall uphold and observe the Constitution and faithfully perform the duties of the President".

Article Thirty three

1. The President shall exercise the following power:

(1) to exercise a right to veto against all or part of laws and other decisions adopted by the State Ikh Khural. The laws or decisions shall remain in force if two thirds of the members of the State Ikh Khural present in the session do not accept the President's veto;

(2) to propose to the State Ikh Khural the candidature for the appointment to the post of Prime Minister nominated from the majority party or coalition in the State Ikh Khural; if none

of them has a majority a candidate nominated from the party/coalition which has the largest number of seats in consultation with other parties; if such party fails to propose a candidate on consultation with other parties, the candidate who has received the majority of votes from parties and the coalition which sits in the State Ikh Khural within five days / *amendments from 24th December 1999 and 14th December 2000*.

(3) to instruct the Government on issues within his/her power. If the President issues a relevant decree it shall become effective upon signature by the Prime Minister;

(4) to represent the State with full power in foreign relations and, in consultation with the State Ikh Khural, to conclude international treaties on behalf of Mongolia;

(5) to appoint and recall heads of plenipotentiary missions to foreign countries in consultation with the State Ikh Khural;

(6) to receive the Letters of Credence or Recall of Heads of diplomatic missions of foreign states to Mongolia;

(7) to confer state titles and higher military ranks and award orders and medals;

(8) to grant pardons;

(9) to decide matters related to granting and withdrawing Mongolian citizenship and granting asylum;

(10) to head the National Security Council of Mongolia;

(11) to declare general or partial conscription;

(12) to declare a state of emergency or martial law on the whole or a part of the national territory and order the deployment of armed forces when emergency circumstances described in Paragraphs 2 and 3 of the Article 25 of the Constitution arise and the State Ikh Khural concurrently is in recess. The State Ikh Khural within seven days shall consider the Presidential decree declaring a state of emergency or martial law and shall approve or disapprove it. If the State Ikh Khural does not make a decision on the matter, the Presidential decree shall be void.

2. The President shall be the Commander-in-Chief of the armed forces of Mongolia.

3. The President may address messages to the State Ikh Khural and/or to the people, he/she may at his/her own discretion attend sessions of the State Ikh Khural, report on and submit proposals concerning vital issues of domestic and foreign policies of the country.

4. Other specific power may be vested in the President only by law.

Article Thirty four

1. The President within his/her power shall issue decrees in conformity with law.

2. If a Presidential decree is incompatible with law, the President himself/herself or the State Ikh Khural shall invalidate it.

Article Thirty five

1. The President shall be responsible to the State Ikh Khural.

2. In case of a violation of the Constitution and/or abuse of power in breach of his oath, the President may be removed from his post on the basis of the findings of the Constitutional Court by an overwhelming majority of members of the State Ikh Khural present and voting.

Article Thirty six

1. The person, residence and transport of the President shall be inviolable.

2. Dignity and immunity of the President shall be protected by law.

Article Thirty seven

1. In the temporary absence of the President his/her full power shall be exercised by the Chairman of the State Ikh Khural.

2. In the event of the resignation, death or voluntary retirement of the President his/her full power shall be exercised by the Chairman of the State Ikh Khural pending the inauguration of the newly-elected President. In such a case, the State Ikh Khural shall announce and hold Presidential elections within four months.

3. The procedure of exercising the duties of President by the Chairman of the State Ikh Khural shall be determined by law.

Three. The Government

Article Thirty eight

1. The Government is the highest executive body of the State.

2. The Government shall implement the State laws, in accordance with duties to direct economic, social and cultural development, shall exercise the following power:

(1) to organise and ensure nationwide implementation of the Constitution and other laws;

(2) to work out a comprehensive policy on science and technology, guidelines for economic and social development, the State budget, credit and fiscal plans and to submit these to the State Ikh Khural and to execute decisions taken thereon;

(3) to elaborate and implement comprehensive measures on sector, inter-sector and regional development;

(4) to undertake measures on the protection of the environment and on the rational use and restoration of natural resources;

(5) to provide efficient leadership of central state administrative bodies and to direct the activities of local administrations;

(6) to strengthen the country's defense capabilities and to ensure national security;

(7) to take measures for the protection of human rights and freedoms, strengthening public order and the prevention of crime;

(8) to implement State foreign policy;

(9) to conclude and implement international treaties in consultation with and, subsequent ratification by the State Ikh Khural, as well as to conclude and abrogate inter-governmental treaties.

3. The specific competences, organisation and procedure of the Government shall be determined by law.

Article Thirty nine

1. The Government shall comprise the Prime Minister and members.

2. The Prime Minister, in consultation with President, shall submit his/her proposals on the structure and composition of the Government and on the changes in these to the State Ikh Khural. If the Prime Minister has not reached consensus with the President within seven days he/she shall submit proposals to the State Ikh Khural by himself/herself. */amendments from 24th December 1999 and 14th December 2000.*

3. The State Ikh Khural shall consider the candidates proposed by the Prime Minister one by one and take decisions on their appointment.

Article Forty

1. The term of the mandate of the Government shall be four years.

2. The terms of office of the Government shall start from the date of the appointment of the Prime Minister by the State Ikh Khural and terminate upon the appointment of a new Prime Minister.

Article Forty one

1. The Prime Minister shall lead the Government and shall be responsible to the State Ikh Khural for the implementation of state laws.

2. The Government shall be accountable for its work to the State Ikh Khural.

Article Forty two

Personal immunity of the Prime Minister and members of the Government shall be protected by law.

Article Forty three

1. The Prime Minister may tender his/her resignation to the State Ikh Khural before the expiry of his/her terms of office if he/she considers that the Government is unable to exercise its power.

2. The Government shall step down in its entirety upon the resignation of the Prime Minister or if half of the members of the Government resign at the same time.

3. The State Ikh Khural shall consider the matter and make a final decision within 15 days after taking the initiative to dissolve the Government or receiving the President's proposal or the Prime Minister's statement on resignation.

4. The State Ikh Khural shall consider and take a decision on the dissolution of the Government if not less than one quarter of the members of the State Ikh Khural formally propose the dissolution of the Government.

Article Forty four

If the Government submits a draft resolution requesting a vote of confidence, the State Ikh Khural shall proceed with the matter in accordance with paragraph 3 of Article 43.

Article Forty five

1. The Government in conformity with legislation and within its power shall issue resolutions and ordinances which shall be signed by the Prime Minister and the Minister responsible for its application.

2. If these resolutions and ordinances are incompatible with legislation, the Government itself or the State Ikh Khural shall invalidate them.

Article Forty six

1. Ministries and other government offices shall be constituted in accordance with law.

2. Genuine civil servants shall be Mongolian citizens. They shall strictly abide by the Constitution and other laws and work for the benefit of the people and in the interests of the State.

3. The working conditions and social guarantees of civil servants shall be determined by law.

Four. The Judiciary

Article Forty seven

1. In Mongolia the judicial power shall be vested exclusively in courts.

2. The unlawful establishment of a court under any circumstances and exercise of judicial power by any organisation other than court shall be prohibited.

3. Courts shall be established solely under the Constitution and other laws.

Article Forty eight

1. The judicial system shall consist of the Supreme Court, Aimag and capital city courts, Soum, inter-soum and District courts. Specialised courts such as criminal, civil and administrative courts may be formed. The activities and decisions of these specialised courts shall not but be outside the supervision of the Supreme Court.

2. The organisation of courts and the legal basis of their activities shall be determined by law.

3. The courts shall be financed from the State budget. The State shall ensure economic guarantee of the court's activities.

Article Forty nine

1. Judges shall be independent and subject only to law.

2. Neither a private person nor any official including the President, Prime Minister, members of the State Ikh Khural and the Government, officials of political parties or other mass organisations shall interfere with the exercise by the judges of their duties.

3. The General Council of Courts shall function for the purpose of ensuring the independence of the judiciary.

4. The General Council of Courts, without interfering in the activities of courts and judges, shall deal exclusively with the selection of judges from among legal professionals, protection of their rights and other matters pertaining to the ensuring of conditions for guaranteeing the independence of the judiciary.

5. The organisation and procedures of the General Council of Courts shall be determined by law.

Article Fifty

1. The Supreme Court shall be the highest judicial organ and shall exercise the following power:

(1) To try at first instance criminal cases and legal disputes under its jurisdiction;

(2) To examine decisions of lower-instance courts through appeal and supervision;

(3) to examine and take decisions on matters related to the protection of law and human rights and freedoms therein and transferred to it by the Constitutional court and the Prosecutor General;

(4) To provide official interpretations for correct application of all other laws except for the Constitution;

(5) To make judgments on all other matters assigned to it by law.

2. The decision made by the Supreme Court shall be a final judiciary decision and shall be binding upon all courts and other persons. If a decision made by the Supreme Court is incompatible with law, the Supreme Court itself shall have to repeal it. If an interpretation made by the Supreme Court is incompatible with a law, the latter shall prevail.

3. The Supreme Court and other courts shall have no right to apply laws that are unconstitutional or have not been promulgated officially.

Article Fifty one

1. The Supreme Court shall comprise the Chief Justice and judges.

2. The President shall appoint the judges of the Supreme Court upon their presentation to the State Ikh Khural by the General Council of Courts, and appoint judges of other courts on the proposal of the General Council of Courts. The President shall appoint the Chief Justice of the Supreme Court for a term of six years on proposal of the Supreme Court from among its members.

3. A Mongolian citizen who has reached thirty-five years of age with a higher education in law and a professional career of not less than 10 years may be appointed as a judge of the Supreme Court. A Mongolian citizen who has reached twenty-five years of age with a higher education in law and a professional

career of not less than three years may be appointed as a judge of the other courts.

4. Removal of a judge from a court of any instance shall be prohibited except in cases where he/she is relieved at his/her own request or removed on the grounds provided for in the Constitution and/or the Law on the judiciary and by a valid court decision.

Article Fifty two

1. Courts of all instances shall consider and make judgment on cases and disputes on the basis of collective decision-making.

2. In passing a collective decision on cases and disputes, the courts of first instance shall allow representatives of citizens to participate in the proceedings in accordance with the procedures prescribed by law.

3. A judge alone may decide those cases, which are specifically singled out for such trial by law.

Article Fifty three

1. Court trials shall be conducted in the Mongolian language.

2. A person who does not know Mongolian shall be acquainted with all the facts of the case through translation and shall have the right to presentation in his/her native language at the trial.

Article Fifty four

Court trials shall be open to the public except in cases specified by law.

Article Fifty five

1. The accused shall have a right to defend him/her.

2. The accused shall be accorded legal assistance according to law or at his/her request.

Article Fifty six

1. The Prosecutor shall exercise supervision over the inquiry into an investigation of cases and the execution of punishment, and participate in the court trial on behalf of the State.

2. The President shall appoint the Prosecutor General and his/her deputies in consultation with the State Ikh Khural for a term of six years.

3. The system, organisation and legal basis of the activities of the Prosecutor's organization shall be determined by law.

CHAPTER FOUR

Administrative and Territorial Units of Mongolia and their Governing Bodies

Article Fifty seven

1. The territory of Mongolia shall be divided administratively into Aimags and a capital city; Aimags shall be sub-divided into Soums; Soums into Baghs; the capital city shall be sub-divided into District and Districts into Khoroos.

2. The legal status of towns and villages within the administrative and territorial units shall be determined by law.

3. Revision of an administrative and territorial unit shall be considered and decided by the State Ikh Khural on the basis of a proposal by a respective local Khural and local citizens, and with account taken of the country's economic structure and the distribution of the population.

Article Fifty eight

1. Aimag, the capital city, Soum and District are administrative, territorial and socio-economic complexes with their functions and administrations provided for by law.

2. Borders of Aimags, the capital city, Soums and Districts shall be approved by the State Ikh Khural on the Government submission.

Article Fifty nine

1. Governance of administrative and territorial units of Mongolia shall be organised on the basis of a combination of the principles of both self-governance and Central government.

2. The self-governing bodies in Aimag, capital city, Soum and District shall be Khurals of Representatives of the citizens of respective territories; in Bagh and Khoroo they shall be Public Meetings of citizens. In between the sessions of the Khurals and Public Meetings their Presidiums shall assume administrative functions.

3. Khurals of Aimags and the capital city shall be elected for a term of four years. The membership of these Khurals as well as those of Soums and Districts and the procedure of their election shall be determined by law.

Article Sixty

1. State authority shall be exercised on the territories of Aimags, the capital city, Soums, Districts, Baghs and Khoroos by their respective Governors.

2. Candidates for Governors are nominated by the Khurals of respective Aimags, the capital city, Soums, Districts, Baghs and Khoroos. Governors of Aimags and the capital city are appointed by the Prime Minister; Governors Soum and District by the Governors of Aimags and the capital city; Governors of Baghs and Khoroos by the Governors of Soums and Districts respectively for a term of four years.

3. In case the Prime Minister and Governors of higher levels refuse to appoint the gubernatorial candidates, new nominations shall be held in the manner prescribed in Paragraph 2 of this Article. Pending the appointment of a new Governor the previously appointed Governor shall exercise his/her mandate.

Article Sixty one

1. While working for the implementation of the decisions of a respective Khural, a Governor, as a representative of State authority, shall be responsible to the Government and the Governor of higher instance for proper observance of national laws and fulfillment of the decisions of the Government and the respective superior body in his/her territory.

2. The Governor shall have a right to veto decisions of respective Aimag, capital city, Soum, District, Bagh and Khoroo Khurals.

3. If a Khural by a majority vote overrides the veto, the Governor may tender his/her resignation to the respective Khural, Prime Minister or to the Governor of higher instance if he/she considers that he/she is not able to implement the decision concerned.

4. Governors of Aimag, the capital city, Soum and District shall have secretariats (Offices of the Seal). The Government

shall determine the structure and staff limit of these offices individually or by a uniform standard.

Article Sixty two

1. Local self-governing bodies besides making independent decisions on matters of socio-economic life of the respective Aimag, the capital city, Soum, District, Bagh and Khoroo shall organise the participation of the population in solving problems of national scale and that of higher territorial units.

2. Authorities of higher instance shall not take decision on matters coming under the jurisdiction of local self-governing bodies. If law and decisions of respective superior state organs do not specifically deal with definite local matters, local self-governing bodies can decide upon them independently in conformity with the Constitution.

3. If the State Ikh Khural and the Government deem it necessary they may delegate some matters within their power to the Aimag and capital city Khurals and Governors for their resolution.

Article Sixty three

1. Khurals of Aimag, the capital city, Soum, District, Bagh and Khoroo shall adopt resolutions and Governors shall issue ordinances within their power.

2. Resolutions of the Khurals and ordinances of the Governors shall be in conformity with law, Presidential decrees and decisions of the Government and other superior bodies, and shall be binding within their respective territories.

3. Administrative and territorial units, and the power, organization and procedure of their governing bodies shall be determined by law.

CHAPTER FIVE

The Constitutional Court of Mongolia

Article Sixty four

1. The Constitutional Court shall be an organ exercising supreme supervision over the implementation of the Constitution, making judgment on the violation of its provisions and resolving constitutional disputes. It shall be the guarantee for the strict observance of the Constitution.

2. The Constitutional court and its members in the execution of their duties shall be subject to the Constitution only and shall be independent of any organisations, officials or any other person.

3. The independence of the members of the Constitutional court shall be ensured by the guarantees set out in the Constitution and other laws.

Article Sixty five

1. The Constitutional court shall consist of 9 members. Members of the Constitutional court shall be appointed by the State Ikh Khural for a term of six years upon the nomination of three of them by the State Ikh Khural, three by the President and the remaining three by the Supreme Court.

2. A member of the Constitutional court shall be a Mongolian citizen who has reached forty years of age and has a high political and legal qualification.

3. The Chairman of the Constitutional court shall be elected from among 9 members for a term of three years by a majority vote among the members of the Constitutional court. He/she can be re-elected once.

4. If the Chairman or a member of the Constitutional court violates the law, he/she may be withdrawn by the State Ikh Khural based on the decision of the Constitutional court and on the suggestion of the institution that nominated him/her.

5. The President, members of the State Ikh Khural, the Prime Minister, members of the Government and the Supreme Court shall not be members of the Constitutional court.

Article Sixty six

1. The Constitutional court shall examine and settle constitutional disputes on its own initiative on the basis of petitions and information received from citizens or at the request of the State Ikh Khural, the President, the Prime Minister, the Supreme Court and the Prosecutor General.

2. The Constitutional court, in accordance with Paragraph 1 of this Article, shall make and submit conclusions to the State Ikh Khural on:

(1) The conformity of laws, decrees and other decisions of the State Ikh Khural and the President, as well as Government decisions and international treaties to which Mongolia is a party with the Constitution;

(2) The conformity of national referenda and decisions of the Central election authority on the elections of the State Ikh Khural and its members as well as on Presidential elections with the Constitution;

(3) Whether the President, Chairman and members of the State Ikh Khural, the Prime Minister, members of the Government, the Chief Justice of the Supreme Court and the Prosecutor General have breached the law;

(4) Whether the grounds for the removal of the President, Chairman of the State Ikh Khural and the Prime Minister and for the recall of members of the State Ikh Khural existed.

3. If a conclusion submitted in accordance with sub-paragraph 1 and 2 of Paragraph 2 of this Article is not accepted by the State Ikh Khural, the Constitutional court shall reexamine it and make a final judgment.

4. If the Constitutional court decides that the laws, decrees and other decisions of the State Ikh Khural and the President as well as Government decisions and international treaties to which Mongolia is a party are inconsistent with the Constitution, the laws, decrees, instruments of ratification and decisions in question shall be considered invalid.

Article Sixty seven

Decisions of the Constitutional court shall enter into force immediately.

CHAPTER SIX

Amendment to the Constitution of Mongolia

Article Sixty eight

1. Amendments to the Constitution shall be initiated by organisation and officials enjoying the right to legislative initiative and could be submitted by the Constitutional court to the State Ikh Khural.

2. A national referendum on constitutional amendment may be held on the concurrence of not less than two thirds of the members of the State Ikh Khural. The referendum shall be held in accordance with the provisions of sub-paragraph 16 of Paragraph 1, Article 25 of the Constitution.

Article Sixty nine

1. An amendment to the Constitution shall be adopted by not less than three-quarters of votes of all members of the State Ikh Khural.

2. A draft amendment to the Constitution which has twice failed to win a three-quarters majority of votes of all members of the State Ikh Khural shall not be subject to consideration until the State Ikh Khural sits in a new composition following general elections.

3. The State Ikh Khural shall not undertake amendment of the Constitution within six months prior to general elections.

4. Amendments that have been adopted shall carry the same force as the Constitution.

Article Seventy

1. Laws, decrees and other decisions of state bodies, and activities of all other organisations and citizens should be in full conformity with the Constitution.

2. The Constitution of Mongolia shall enter into force at 12.00 hours on the 12th of February of 1992, or at the hour of Horse on the prime and benevolent ninth day of Yellow Horse of the first spring month of Black Tiger of the year of water Monkey of the Seventeenth 60-year Cycle.

Learn and Abide

THE STATE IKH KHURAL OF THE MONGOLIAN PEOPLE'S REPUBLIC

11.35 a.m.

13th January 1992, Ulaanbaatar.

APPENDIX II

TREATY ON FRIENDLY RELATIONS AND COOPERATION BETWEEN MONGOLIA AND THE RUSSIAN FEDERATION

Date February 12, 1991

Mongolia and the Russian Federation (hereinafter referred to as the "Contracting ties"):

Proceeding from their traditions of friendly relations, trust, and all-round cooperation,

Wishing to develop and reinforce an equal and mutually advantageous cooperation between Mongolia and the Russian Federation and, for that purpose, striving to strengthen the legal basis thereof in accordance with the existing situation and development in international relations,

Confirming their commitment to the objectives and principles of the Charter of the United Nations Organisations,

Aspiring to contribute to the ensurance of peace and security in the Asia-Pacific region, and to create an atmosphere of mutual understanding and cooperation therein,

Noting that the Treaty concluded between the People's Government of Mongolia and the Government of the Union of Soviet Socialist Republics in November 5, 1921 played a significant role in the development of good-neighbourly relations and cooperation between the two countries,

And proceeding from the provisions of the Declaration on friendship and good neighbourly cooperation concluded between the MPR and the USSR in February 12, 1991.

Have agreed as follows:

ARTICLE 1

The Contracting Parties will consider themselves as friendly nations and, in their relationship, will be guided by the principle of respect for each other's state sovereignty and independence, of being equally sovereign, of non-use of force, of not threatening with force, of inviolability of state frontiers, of territorial integrity, of non-interference in internal affairs; respect for fundamental human rights and liberties, for equality of rights, for the right to decide destiny on their own; and by the principle of fulfilling in good faith their obligations and cooperating as good neighbors and partners.

ARTICLE 2

The Contracting Parties will develop an equal and mutually advantageous cooperation on a sustainable and long-term basis in the political, cultural, arts, educational, scientific and technological, health, defense, ecological, road and transport, telecommunications, information,

Humanitarian and other fields.

ARTICLE 3

The Contracting Parties will consult regularly on deepening their bilateral relations and cooperation, as well as on international issues of mutual interest at various levels. The Contracting Parties will contribute towards developing cooperation between the parliaments and other state bodies of the two countries.

ARTICLE 4

The Contracting Parties will not take part in a military and political alliance directed against each other and are obligated not to conclude any treaty or agreement incompatible with the ensurance of the sovereignty and independence of the other Party with a third country. Neither of the Party shall allow a third country to use its territory for an aggression or violence against the other Party. The Russian Federation will respect Mongolia's policy aimed at not allowing stationing and transit passing of foreign troops, nuclear and other weapons of mass destruction on and through its territory.

ARTICLE 5

The Contracting Parties will inform each other on possible ways and means of remedying situations that one of the Parties perceives as posing threats to international peace and security and that may bring about disasters of international nature. Following the perception of one of the Parties that its security interests have come under threat, the Contracting Parties will, at the request of the above Party, consult each other.

ARTICLE 6

The Contracting Parties will, for the purpose of resolving global- and regional-scale international issues pertaining to the ensurance of peace, security, sustained economic development and environmental protection, strengthen their cooperation within the UN and international organisations.

ARTICLE 7

The Contracting Parties will cooperate on a bilateral and multilateral basis so as to render all-round support to the maintenance of stability, the creation of an atmosphere of confidence and trust, and the promotion of collaboration in the Asia-Pacific region, as well as to the facilitation of contacts among the regional nations in the economic, cultural, humanitarian and other fields.

ARTICLE 8

The Contracting Parties will pursue a policy of open economy with each other and develop an equal and mutually advantageous cooperation. For this purpose, they are obligated to mutually provide pleasant conditions for state property and non-state property manufactories, individuals and other legal entities taking part in the commercial, industrial, and financial activities. The Contracting Parties will promote investment cooperation between themselves or involving a third country partner. The Contracting Parties will provide an all-round support to developing border area trade and cooperation.

ARTICLE 9

The Contracting Parties will promote the development of cooperation in the railroad, air transport, authored, and other fields of transportation. The Contracting Parties will also take measures towards enhancing an access capacity of their roadways and improving an organisation of transports passing in transit through their territories. Taking into account the fact that Mongolia is landlocked, the Russian Federation will, in accordance with the norms of international law, assist the former in exercising its right to have access to the sea.

ARTICLE 10

The Contracting Parties will develop cooperation concerning environmental protection, the ensurance of ecological security, collective prevention from ecological crisis and elimination of the consequences of ecological crisis. For this purpose, the Contracting Parties will, aside from exchanging information on a regular basis, consult on issues directly related to the interests of one of the Parties or either Parties.

ARTICLE 11

The Contracting Parties will provide an all-round support to expanding contacts between their citizens. For this purpose, the Contracting Parties will take measures to put in order administrative rules and practices related to mutual transit of their citizens.

ARTICLE 12

The Contracting Parties will cooperate on a bilateral and multilateral basis in their combat against organised crime, terrorism, and illegal activities directed at adversely affecting the security of civil air transportation; and against smuggling of arms, drugs, and artworks of cultural and historical value. The Contracting Parties will create conditions necessary for mutual provision of legal assistance in civil, family, and penal proceedings.

ARTICLE 13

The Contracting Parties will pay special attention to utilizing achievements of modern technology; cooperating in the field of base and supplementary researches; and creating conditions for implementation of joint programmes and projects for the purpose of introducing the results of the above researches to the economy and production.

ARTICLE 14

The Contracting Parties will expand and deepen their ties in the fields of culture, arts, science, historical heritage, education, and information. Apart from assisting in the establishment of direct contacts between universities, scientific institutions, and cultural organisations and facilitating an exchange of books, periodicals, cinematographic and theatrical works, and tele- and radio-programs, the Contracting Parties will also encourage mutual study of the languages thereof.

ARTICLE 15

So as to implement this Treaty in accordance with the tenets thereof, the Contracting Parties will cooperate towards facilitating direct contacts between Aimags of Mongolia and Republics of the Russian Federation, and other administrative and territorial units at all levels, as well as between state, private, and composite property manufactories, offices and organisations.

ARTICLE 16

As per the principles of this Treaty, special agreements will be concluded between the Governments of the two Parties and other authorities on herein mentioned and other issues.

ARTICLE 17

The Contracting Parties will settle disputed questions that may arise in their relationship by means of goodwill. In case of the impossibility of settling a disputed question by the means as provided for herein, the Contracting Parties will, in accordance with the UN Charter, choose other means of peaceful settling of the disputed question.

ARTICLE 18

This Treaty does not affect the Contracting Parties' obligations under effective bilateral and multilateral treaties and agreements concluded by them with other States.

ARTICLE 19

This Treaty will remain in force for 20 years and thereafter will be extended every five years unless one of the Contracting Parties notifies the other of its intention to terminate the Treaty, in a written form and 12 months before the expiration date of the Treaty's validity.

ARTICLE 20

This Treaty requires a process of ratification and enters into force at the time of exchange of ratification documents. This Treaty was done in Moscow on January 20, 1993 in duplicate in the Mongolian and Russian languages, all texts being equally authentic.

For Mongolia and for The Russian
Federation,
P. Ochirbat,
B. Yeltsin.

APPENDIX III

TREATY ON FRIENDLY RELATIONS AND COOPERATION BETWEEN MONGOLIA AND THE PEOPLE'S REPUBLIC OF CHINA

April 29, 1994

Mongolia and the People's Republic of China (hereinafter referred to as the "Contracting Parties"):

Noting that the Treaty on Friendship and Mutual Assistance concluded between the Mongolian People's Republic and the People's Republic of China on May 31, 1960 has played an important role in developing the relations between the states.

Wishing to strengthen the traditional friendship of the peoples of Mongolia and China,

expressing their conviction that further development of good neighbourly relations and cooperation between Mongolia and China accords 'with the vital interests of the peoples of both states and serves the cause of peace, stability, and prosperity in the Asia-Pacific region, reconfirming their commitment to the objectives and principles of the UN Charter, and, in view of the above, making a decision to renew the Treaty on Friendship and Mutual Assistance concluded between the Mongolian People's Republic and the People's Republic of China, have agreed as follows:

ARTICLE 1

The Contracting Parties will develop their good neighbourly relations and cooperation on a basis of mutual respect for each other's independence, sovereignty, and territorial integrity, for the principle of mutual non-attack, non-interference in internal affairs, for equality of rights, for mutual advantages, and for peaceful co-existence.

ARTICLE 2

1. The Contracting Parties will consult regularly for the purpose of developing the relations between the parliaments and government bodies, as well as public organisations and local areas of the two states.

2. The Contracting Parties will sustainably develop an equal and mutually advantageous cooperation on a long-term basis in the political, economic, trade, cultural, educational, scientific-technological, health, environmental protection, road and transport, and \ telecommunications fields.

ARTICLE 3

1. The Contracting Parties will, if there is such a need, consult on the Asia-Pacific region and other international issues of mutual interest.

2. The Contracting Parties will cooperate within the UN and other international organisations for the purpose of developing relations and cooperation between nations and of settling global, and Regional issues.

ARTICLE 4

The Contracting Parties will not take part in any military political alliance directed against each other and will not conclude any treaty and agreement with a third country that may adversely affect the state sovereignty and security of the other Party. Neither Party will allow a third country to use its territory which may adversely affect the state sovereignty and security of the other Party.

ARTICLE 5

This Treaty does not affect the Contracting Parties' obligations under bilateral and multilateral treaties concluded by them with other states.

ARTICLE 6

This Treaty will remain in force for a long period of time and amendments will be made thereto upon the agreement of the two Parties to that effect. One of the Contracting Parties may notify the other, in a written form and a Year in advance, of its decision to terminate this Treaty. This Treaty requires a process of ratification and enters into force at the time of exchange of ratification documents. This Treaty was done in Ulaanbaatar on April 29, 1994 in duplicate in the Mongolian and Chinese languages, all texts being equally authentic.

For Mongolia	For The People's
P. Jasrai	Republic of China
	Li Pen

APPENDIX IV

LAW OF MONGOLIA ON ITS NUCLEAR-WEAPON-FREE STATUS, 3 FEBRUARY, 2000

CHAPTER ONE
General Provisions

Article 1. Purpose of the Law

The purpose of the present Law is to regulate relations pertaining to the preservation of the territory of Mongolia in its entirety, including its air space, land, waters and the sub-soil free from nuclear weapons, which constitutes an important factor for ensuring Mongolia's security.

Article 2. Legislation on Mongolia's Nuclear-weapon-free Status

2.1 The legislation on Mongolia's nuclear-weapon-free status shall consist of the Constitution of Mongolia, the present Law and other legislative acts adopted in conformity with them.

2.2 In case an international treaty to which Mongolia is a party contains provisions different from those provided for in the present Law, the provisions of the international treaty shall prevail.

Article 3. Definitions

3.1. The definitions contained in the present Law shall have the following meaning:

3.1.1. "Nuclear weapon" means any explosive device that is capable of releasing nuclear energy in an uncontrollable manner and that can be used for hostile purposes;

3.1.2. "Nuclear-weapon-free status" means a legal status of being free from nuclear weapons.

Article 4. Prohibitions Resulting from the Nuclear Weapon Free Status

4.1 An individual, legal person or any foreign State shall be prohibited on the territory of Mongolia from committing, initiating or participating in the following acts or activities relating to nuclear weapons:

4.1.1 Develop, manufacture or otherwise acquire, possess or have control over nuclear weapons;

4.1.2 Station or transport nuclear weapons by any means;

4.1.3 Test or use nuclear weapons;

4.1.4 Dump or dispose nuclear weapons grade radioactive material or nuclear waste.

4.2 Transportation through the territory of Mongolia of nuclear weapons, parts or components thereof, as well as of nuclear waste or any other nuclear material designed or produced for weapons purposes shall be prohibited.

Article 5. Uses of Nuclear Energy and Technology

5.1 The use of nuclear energy and technology shall be permitted only by the State administrative authority in charge of nuclear energy and solely for peaceful purposes such as health care, mining, energy production and scientific research in accordance with the provisions of the international treaties to which Mongolia is a party as well as in conformity with the norms and principles of international law.

5.2 For the purpose of implementing Article 5.1 of the present Law and banning the dumping or storage in the vicinity of the borders of Mongolia of nuclear material or waste that might directly or in the long run indirectly adversely affect the safety of the population and the environment. Mongolia shall cooperate with the International Atomic Energy Agency (IAEA), other appropriate international organisations and the States that have nuclear programs.

CHAPTER TWO
Verification

Article 6. National Verification of the implementation of the legislation on the nuclear-weapon-free status

6.1 On the basis of the proposals of the central administrative authority in charge of foreign relations and of other organisations, the National Security Council of Mongolia shall, within its functions and competence, coordinate the following activities:

6.1.1 Implementing of a single State policy concerning the prohibited and permitted activities pertaining to the nuclear-weapon-free status in Mongolia;

6.1.2 Institutionalising internationally Mongolia's nuclear-weapon-free status;

6.1.3 Taking an active part in the activities of the appropriate international organisations, exchanging information on the prohibited and permitted activities in Mongolia and providing information to national organizations.

6.2 The competent authority of Mongolia shall have the right to gather information, stop, detain and search any suspected aircraft, train, vehicle, individual or group of persons.

6.3 The central administrative authority in charge of foreign relations shall be entrusted with monitoring the compliance with the present Law and the international commitments assumed by Mongolia in connection with the nuclear-weapon-free status.

6.4 Non-governmental organisations or individuals may, within the mandate provided for by the legislation, exercise public oversight of the implementation of the legislation on the nuclear-weapon-free status and submit proposals thereon to the relevant State authority.

Article 7. International verification on the implementation of the legislation on the nuclear-weapon-free status

7.1 Mongolia shall conduct international verification over the implementation of the present Law in cooperation with the relevant international organisations or by concluding special international agreements thereon.

CHAPTER THREE
Liability

Article 8. Liability for violation of the legislation on the nuclear-weapon-free status

8.1 An individual or legal person that violates Article 4 of the present Law shall be held liable in accordance with the Criminal Code.

8.2 The facility, equipment, material, raw material or means of transportation used for the activities prohibited by Article 4.1 of the present Law shall be expropriated by the State.

8.3 An individual or legal person that violates the present Law shall pay compensation for the damage caused to the interests of Mongolia as well as to the population, the environment and the properties in accordance with the relevant legislation of Mongolia or in conformity with the appropriate international treaty, the principles and norms of international law.

8.4 In case of violation or suspected violation of the present Law by a foreign State, Mongolia shall, within its international treaty obligations or norms and principles of international law, officially notify the State concerned of the violation or suspected violation, request explanation and peacefully resolve any question that may arise therefrom. If deemed necessary, the International Atomic Energy Agency (IAEA) and other relevant bodies could be asked for assistance. In case of a dispute of a legal nature, measures could be taken up to referring the matter to the relevant international court or arbitration.

Article 9. Amendment and termination of the Law

9.1 If the vital interests of Mongolia are affected, the present Law may be amended or terminated.

Resolution 19 of the State Great Hural of Mongolia on measures to be taken in connection with the adoption of the law on its nuclear-weapon-free status, adopted on 3 February 2000.

In its foreign policy, Mongolia sets the goal of pursuing its national interests, developing friendly cooperation with all the countries of the world as well as actively contributing, to the extent possible, to the efforts of the international community to strengthen peace and security. It is also pursuing a policy of refraining from joining any military alliance or grouping, or allowing the use of its territory against any other State as well as banning the stationing on its territory of foreign troops and weapons, including nuclear and other weapons of mass destruction. With respect to its two neighboring States, Mongolia is pursuing the policy of maintaining balanced and friendly relations and developing broad cooperation.

Mongolia consistently advocates disarmament and, on its part, is taking concrete steps to promote the goal of non-proliferation of nuclear weapons. Within the framework of this policy, in 1992 Mongolia declared its territory a nuclear-weapon-free zone and has since been pursuing the policy of and taking the measures aimed at institutionalising and guaranteeing it. One of the results of such a policy has been the adoption by the United Nations General Assembly at it 53rd regular session on 4th December, 1998 of the resolution 53/77D entitled "Mongolia's international security and nuclear-weapon-free status".

Keeping Mongolia's territory free of nuclear weapons is fully in line with its policy aimed at strengthening its national security by political and diplomatic means.

Strengthening Mongolia's nuclear-weapon-free status at the State policy level, further clearer defining of the status and its observance would be important in strengthening mutual confidence and Mongolia's external security environment as well as in linking the country's national security to regional security and stability.

Mongolia's nuclear-weapon-free status represents a novel approach in the practice of international relations, which in its wider context could be considered as our country's concrete contribution to the policy and efforts of the international community aimed at strengthening the regime of non-proliferation of nuclear weapons. Based on the all above and in connection with the adoption of the Law of Mongolia on nuclear-weapon-free status, the State Great Hural of Mongolia resolves:

1. To mandate the Government /R. Amarjargal/ to take the following measures: 1/ to actively cooperate with and acquire assistance from the relevant States, international organisations, including the International Atomic Energy Agency, in implementing the Law of Mongolia on the nuclear-weapon-free status and the United Nations General Assembly resolution entitled "Mongolia's international security and nuclear-weapon-free status"; 2/ to take the necessary measures to ensure normal functioning of the stations designed to monitor nuclear weapons tests, that are situated on the territory of Mongolia; 3/ to report, as the case may be, to the Standing Committee on Security and Foreign Policy Affairs of the State Great Hural of Mongolia on the implementation of the Law of Mongolia on the nuclear-weapon-free status, of the present Resolution and other legislative acts adopted in conformity with them.

2. The present Resolution shall be implemented from the day of the entry into force of the Law of Mongolia on the nuclear-weapon-free status.

Chairman of The State Great Hural of Mongolia
R. Gonchigdorj.

APPENDIX- V

LIST OF SOME AGREEMENTS AND TREATIES ON SECURITY ISSUES CONCLUDED BY MONGOLIA WITH ITS NEIGHBOUR COUNTRIES

Mongolia-Russia

1. Agreement between the Government of Mongolian People's Republic and the Government of the Union of Soviet Socialist Republics on simplified regime of crossing border by citizens of the MPR and the USSR inhabiting in frontier areas. (1986.01.25, Ulaanbaatar).

2. Treaty between Mongolian People's Republic and the Union of Soviet Socialist Republics on Mongolian-Soviet borderline in western part from N° 41040 height in Tavan Bogd mountain to top of Asgat mountain and in eastern part from NQ 2855.8 height in Great Sayan range to Tarbagan Dakh hill. (1976.10.19, Moscow).

3. Declaration of Mongolia People's Republic and the Union of Soviet Socialist Republics on friendship and good-neighbourly cooperation. (1991.02.12, Moscow).

4. Agreement between the Government of Mongolia and the Government of the Russian Federation on border port and simplified regime of crossing Mongolian-Russian border. (1993.01.20, Ulaanbaatar).

5. Treaty between Mongolia and the Russian Federation on friendly relations and cooperation. (1993.01.20, Moscow).

6. Joint statement of the President of Mongolia and the President of the Russian Federation. (1993.01.20, Moscow).

7. Agreement between the Government of Mongolia and the Government of the Russian Federation on cooperation in customs issues. (1993.01.20, Moscow).

8. Agreement on military and technical cooperation between the Governments of the Russian Federation and Mongolia. (1993.04.07, Ulaanbaatar).

9. Agreement on military cooperation between the Ministry of Defence of Mongolia and the Ministry of Defence of the Russian Federation (1993.06.28, Ulaanbaatar).

10. Agreement between the Government of Mongolia and the Government of the Russian Federation on cooperation in border issues. (1994.11.15, Moscow).

Mongolia-China

1. Agreement between the Government of Mongolia and the Government of the People's Republic of China on cooperation in customs issues.(1993.09.07, Ulaanbaatar).

2. Treaty between Mongolia and the People's Republic of China on friendly relations and cooperation. (1994.04.29, Ulaanbaatar).

3. Agreement on granting permission for temporary location of cattle breeders from Inner Mongolian Autonomous Region of the People's Republic of China in the territory of Choibalsan aimag, the Mongolian People's Republic. (1957.01.06).

4. Protocol of the first inter-governmental negotiations on solution of border issues between the Mongolian People's Republic and the People's Republic of China. (1962.11.17).

5. Treaty on border between the Mongolian People's Republic and the People's Republic of China. (1962.12.26, Beijing).

6. First protocol of joint commission on demarcation of Mongolian- Chinese borderline. (1963.05.20).

7. Protocol on border concluded between the Government of the Mongolian People's Republic and the Government of the People's Republic of China. (1964.06.30).

8. Treaty between the Governments of the Mongolian People's Republic and the Government of the People's Republic of China on Mongolian-Chinese border regime and regulation of border issues. (1988.11.28, Beijing).

9. Agreement between the Governments of Mongolia and the People's Republic of China on border ports and the regimes thereon. (1992.06.24, Beijing).

10. Agreement between the Governments of Mongolia and the People's Republic of China on protection and utilisation of water resources in border areas. (1994.04.29, Ulaanbaatar).

11. Protocol on cooperation and exchanges between the Ministry of Defense of Mongolia and the Ministry of Defence of the People's Republic of China (1997.11.03, Beijing).

APPENDIX- VI

MONGOLIA BILATERAL INVESTMENT TREATY

Signed October 6, 1994; Entered into Force January 1, 1997

104TH CONGRESS 1st Session

SENATE TREATY DOC. 104-10

INVESTMENT TREATY WITH MONGOLIA
MESSAGE
FROM
THE PRESIDENT OF THE UNITED STATES
TRANSMITTING

THE TREATY BETWEEN THE UNITED STATES OF AMERICA AND MONGOLIA CONCERNING THE ENCOURAGEMENT AND RECIPROCAL PROTECTION OF INVESTMENT, WITH ANNEX AND PROTOCOL, SIGNED AT WASHINGTON ON OCTOBER 6,1994

JUNE 26, 1995.—Treaty was read the first time and, together with the accompanying papers, referred to the Committee on Foreign Relations and ordered to be printed for the use of the Senate.

US GOVERNMENT PRINTING OFFICE
99-118 WASHINGTON: 1995
LETTER OF TRANSMITTAL

THE WHITE HOUSE, *June 26, 1995.*

To the Senate of the United States:

With a view to receiving the advice and consent of the Senate to ratification, I transmit herewith the Treaty Between the United States of America and Mongolia Concerning the Encouragement and Reciprocal Protection of Investment, with Annex and Protocol, signed at Washington on October 6, 1994. Also transmitted for the information of the Senate is the report of the Department of State with respect to the Treaty, with Annex and Protocol.

The Bilateral Investment Treaty (BIT) with Mongolia will protect US investors and assist Mongolia in its efforts to develop its economy by creating conditions more favourable for US private investment and thus strengthening the development of the private sector.

The Treaty is fully consistent with US policy toward international and domestic investment. A specific tenet of US Policy, reflected in this Treaty, is that US investment abroad and foreign investment in the United States should receive national treatment. Under this Treaty, the Parties also agree to international law standards for expropriation and compensation for expropriation; free transfer of funds associated with investments; freedom of investments from performance requirements; fair, equitable, and most-favoured-nation status; and the investor's or investment's freedom to choose to resolve disputes with the host government through international arbitration.

I recommend that the Senate consider this Treaty as soon as possible, and give its advice and consent to ratification of the Treaty, with Annex and Protocol, at an early date.

WILLIAM J. CLINTON.

LETTER OF SUBMITTAL

DEPARTMENT OF STATE,

Washington, June 16, 1995.

The PRESIDENT,

The White House.

I have the honour to submit to you the Treaty Between the United States of America and Mongolia Concerning the

Encouragement and Reciprocal Protection of Investment, with Annex and Protocol, signed at Washington on October 6, 1994. I recommend that this Treaty, with Annex and Protocol, be transmitted to the Senate for its advice and consent to ratification.

The bilateral investment treaty (BIT) with Mongolia is based on the view that an open investment policy contributes to economic growth. This Treaty will assist Mongolia in its efforts to develop its economy by creating conditions more favourable for US private investment and thus strengthening the development of the private sector. It is US policy, however, to advise potential treaty partners during BIT negotiations that conclusion of a BIT does not necessarily result in immediate increases in private US investment flows.

To date, twenty-one BITs are in force for the United States—with Argentina, Bangladesh, Bulgaria, Cameroon, the Congo, the Czech Republic, Egypt, Grenada, Kazakhstan, Kyrgystan, Moldova, Morocco, Panama, Poland, Romania, Senegal, Slovakia, Sri Lanka, Tunisia, Turkey, and Zaire. In addition to the Treaty with Mongolia, the United States has signed, but not yet brought into force, BITs with Albania, Armenia, Belarus, Ecuador, Estonia, Georgia, Haiti, Jamaica, Latvia, Russia, Trinidad and Tobago, Ukraine, and Uzbekistan.

The Office of the United States Trade Representative and the Department of State jointly led this BIT negotiation, with assistance from the Departments of Commerce and Treasury, and the Overseas Private Investment Corporation.

THE US-MONGOLIA TREATY

The Treaty with Mongolia is based on the 1992 US prototype BIT, and achieves all of the prototype's objectives, which are:

- All forms of US investment in the territory of Mongolia are covered.

- Investments receive the better of national treatment or most-favoured-nation (MFN) treatment both on establishment and subject to certain specified exceptions.

- Performance requirements may not be imposed upon or enforced against investments.

• Exploration can occur only in accordance with international law standards, that is, for a public purpose; in a non-discriminatory manner; in accordance with due process of law; and upon payment of prompt, adequate, and effective compensation.

• The unrestricted transfer, in a freely usable currency, of funds related to an investment is guaranteed.

• Investment disputes with the host government may be brought by investors, or by their subsidiaries, to binding international arbitration as an alternative to domestic courts.

The US-Mongolia Treaty adds to the provisions of the 1992 U.S. prototype text definitions for "investment agreement" and "investment authorisation" as well as a Protocol clarifying that the national and MFN treatment obligations specified in Article II, Paragraph 1, apply to the establishment and acquisition, as well as to the expansion, management, conduct, operation and sale or other disposition of investments.

The following is an article-by-article analysis of the provisions of the Treaty:

Preamble

The Preamble states the goals of the Treaty. The Treaty is premised on the view that an open investment policy leads to economic growth. These goals include economic cooperation, increased flow of capital, a stable framework for investment, development of respect for international-recognised worker rights, and maximum efficiency in the use of economic resources. While the Preamble does not impose binding obligations, its statement of goals may serve to assist in the interpretation of the Treaty.

Article I (Definitions)

Article I sets out definitions for terms used throughout the Treaty. As a general matter, they are designed to be broad and inclusive in nature.

Investment

The Treaty's definition of investment is broad, recognising that investment can take a wide variety of forms. It covers investments that are owned or controlled by nationals or companies of one of the Treaty partners in the territory of the other. Investments can be made either directly or indirectly through one or more subsidiaries, including those of third countries. Control is not specifically defined in the Treaty. Ownership of over 50 per cent of the voting stock of a company would normally convey control, but in many cases the requirement could be satisfied by less than that proportion.

The definition provides a non-exclusive list of assets, claims and rights that constitute investment. These include both tangible and intangible property, interests in a company or its assets, "a claim to money or a claim to performance having economic value, and associated with an investment," intellectual property rights, and any right conferred by law or contract (such as government-issued licenses and permits). The requirement that a "claim to money" be associated with an investment excludes claims arising solely from trade transactions, such as a transaction involving only a cross-border sale of goods, from being considered investments covered by the Treaty.

Under Paragraph 2 of Article I, either country may deny the benefits of the Treaty to investments by companies established in the other that are owned or controlled by nationals of a third country if (1) the company is a mere shell, without substantial business activities in the home country, or (2) the third country is one with which the denying Party does not maintain normal economic relations. For example, at this time the United States does not maintain normal economic relations with, among other countries, Cuba or Libya.

Paragraph 3 confirms that any alteration in the form in which an asset is invested or reinvested shall not affect its character as investment. For example, a change in the corporate form of an investment will not deprive it of protection under the Treaty.

Company

The definition of "company" is broad in order to cover virtually any type of legal entity, including any corporation, company, association, or other entity that is organised under the laws and regulations of a Party. Coupled with the definition of investment, this definition also ensures that companies of a Party that establish investments in the territory of the other

Party have their investments covered by the Treaty, even if the parent company is ultimately owned by non-Party nationals, although the other Party may deny the benefits of the Treaty in the limited circumstances set forth in Article I, Paragraph 2. Likewise, a company of a third country that is owned or controlled by nationals or companies of a Party will also be covered. The definition also covers charitable and non-profit entities, as well as entities that are owned or controlled by the state.

National

The Treaty defines "national" as a natural person who is a national of a Party under its own laws. Under US law, the term "national" is broader than the term "citizen"; for example, a native of American Samoa is a national of the United States, but not a citizen.

Return

"Return" is defined as "an amount derived from or associated with an investment." The Treaty provides a non-exclusive list of examples, including: profits; dividends; interest; capital gains; royalty payments; management, technical assistance or other fees; and returns in kind. The scope of this definition provides breadth to the Treaty's transfer provisions in Article IV.

Associated activities

The Treaty recognises that the operation of an investment requires protections extending beyond the investment to numerous related activities. This definition provides an illustrative list of such investor activities, including operating a business facility, borrowing money, disposing of property, issuing stock and purchasing foreign exchange for imports. These activities are covered by Article II, Paragraph 1, which guarantees the better of national or MFN treatment for investments and associated activities.

Investment authorisation

The Treaty defines an "investment authorisation" as an authorisation granted by the foreign investment authority of a Party to an investment or a national or company of the other Party.

Investment agreement

The Treaty defines an "investment agreement" as a written agreement between the national authorities of a Party and an investment or a national or company of the other Party that (1) grants rights with respect to natural resources or other assets controlled by the national authorities, and (2) the investment, national, or company relies upon in establishing or acquiring a covered investment. This definition thus excludes agreements with subnational authorities (including US States) as well as agreements arising from various types of regulatory activities of the national government, including, in the tax area, closing agreements, advance pricing agreements, and agreements which arise out of judicial or administrative rulings, such as consent decrees.

Article II (Treatment)

Article II contains the Treaty's major obligations with respect to the treatment of investment.

Paragraph I generally ensures the better of MFN or national treatment in both the entry and post-entry phases of investment. It thus prohibits both the screening of proposed foreign investment on the basis of nationality and discriminatory measures once the investment has been made, subject to specific exceptions provided for in a separate Annex. The United States and Mongolia have both reserved certain exceptions in the Annex to the Treaty, the provisions of which are discussed in the section entitled "Annex." Paragraph 2 guarantees that investment shall be granted "fair and equitable" treatment. It also prohibits Parties from impairing, through unreasonable or discriminatory means, the management, operation, maintenance, use, enjoyment, acquisition, expansion or disposal of investments. This paragraph sets out a minimum standard of treatment based on customary international law.

In Paragraph 2 (c), each Party pledges to respect any obligations it may have entered into with respect to investments. Thus, in dispute settlement under Articles VI or VII, a Party would be foreclosed from arguing, on the basis of sovereignty, that it may unilaterally ignore its obligations to such investments.

Paragraph 3 allows, subject to each Party's immigration laws and regulations, the entry of each Party's nationals into the territory of the other for purposes linked to investment and involving the commitment of a "substantial amount of capital or other resources." This paragraph serves to render nationals of a BIT partner eligible for treaty-investor visas under US immigration law and guarantees similar treatment for US investors.

Paragraph 4 guarantees companies the right to engage top managerial personnel of their choice, regardless of nationality.

Under Paragraph 5, neither Party may impose performance requirements such as those conditioning investment on the export of goods produced or the local purchase of goods or services. Such requirements are major burdens on investors.

Paragraph 6 provides that each Party must provide effective means of asserting rights and claims with respect to investment, investment agreements and any investment authorisations.

Under Paragraph 7, each Party must make publicly available all laws, regulations, administrative practices and adjudicatory procedures pertaining to or affecting investments.

Paragraph 8 recognises that under the US federal system, States of the United States may, in some instance, treat out-of State residents and corporations in a different manner then they treat in-State residents and corporations. The Treaty provides that the national treatment commitment, with respect to the States, means treatment no less favourable than that provided to US out-of-State residents and corporations.

Paragraph 9 limits the Article's MFN obligation by providing that it will not apply to advantages accorded by either Party to third countries by virtue of a Party's membership in a free trade area or customs union or a future multilateral agreement under the auspices of the General Agreement on Tariffs and Trade (GATT). The free trade area exception in this Treaty is analogous to the exception provided for with respect to trade in the GATT.

Article III (Expropriation)

Article III incorporates into the Treaty the international law standards for expropriation and compensation.

Paragraph 1 describes the general rights of investors and obligations of the Parties with respect to expropriation and nationalisation. These rights also apply to direct or indirect state measures "tantamount to expropriation or nationalisation," and thus apply to "creeping expropriations" that result in a substantial deprivation of the benefit of an investment without a taking of the title to the investment.

Paragraph I further bars all expropriations or nationalisations except those that are for a public purpose; carried out in a non-discriminatory manner; subject to "prompt, adequate, and effective compensation"; subject to due process; and accorded the treatment provided in the standards of Article II, Paragraph 2. (These standards guarantee fair and equitable treatment and prohibit the arbitrary and discriminatory impairment of investment in its broadest sense).

The second sentence of Paragraph 1 clarifies the meaning of "prompt, adequate, and effective compensation." Compensation must be equivalent to the fair market value of the expropriated investment immediately before the expropriatory action was taken or became known (whichever is earlier); be paid without delay; include interest at a commercially reasonable rate from the date of expropriation; be fully realisable; be freely transferable; and be calculated in a freely usable currency on the basis of the prevailing market rate of exchange.

Paragraph 2 entitles an investor claiming that an expropriation has occurred to prompt judicial or administrative review of the claim in the host country, including a determination of whether the expropriation and any compensation conform to international law.

Paragraph 3 entitles investors to the better of national or MFN treatment with respect to losses related to war or civil disturbances, but, unlike Paragraph 1, does not specify an absolute obligation to pay compensation for such losses.

Article IV (Transfers)

Article IV protects investors from certain government exchange controls limiting current account and capital account transfers.

In Paragraph 1, the Parties agree to permit "transfers related to an investment to be made freely and without delay into and out of its territory." Paragraph 1 also provides a non-exclusive list of transfers that must be allowed, including returns (as defined in Article I); payments made in compensation for expropriation (as defined in Article III); payments arising out of an investment dispute; payments made under a contract, including the amortisation of principal and interest payments on a loan; proceeds from the liquidation or sale of all or part of an investment; and additional contributions to capital for the maintenance or development of an investment.

Paragraph 2 provides that transfers are to be made in a "freely usable currency at the prevailing market rate of exchange on the date of transfer with respect to spot transactions in the currency to be transferred. "Freely usable" is a standardof the International Monetary Fund; at present there are five such "freely usable" currencies: the US dollar, Japanese yen, German mark, French franc and British pound sterling.

Paragraph 3 recognises that notwithstanding these guarantees, Parties may maintain certain laws or obligations that could affect transfers with respect to investments. It provides that the Parties may require reports of currency transfers and impose income taxes by such means as a withholding tax on dividends. It also recognises that Parties may protect the rights of creditors and ensure the satisfaction of judgments in adjudicatory proceedings through their laws, even if such measures interfere with transfers. Such laws must be applied in an equitable, non-discriminatory and good faith manner.

Paragraph 4 adds to the prototype a provision that the Parties permit returns in kind be made as specified in an investment authorisation, investment agreement or other written agreement between the Party and an investment or a national or company of the other Party.

Article V (State-State consultations)

Article V provides for prompt consultation between the Parties, at either Party's request, on any matter relating to the interpretation or application of the Treaty.

Article VI (State-investor dispute resolution).

Article VI sets forth several means by which disputes between an investor and the host country may be settled.

Article VI Procedures apply to an "investment dispute," a term which covers any dispute arising out of or relating to an investment authorisation, an investment agreement, or to rights granted by the Treaty with respect to an investment.

When a dispute arises, Article VI, Paragraph 2, provides that the disputants should initially seek to resolve the dispute by consultation and negotiation, which may include non-binding third party procedures. Should such consultations fail,

Paragraphs 2 and 3 set forth the investors range of choices of dispute settlement.

Paragraph 2 permits the investor to: (1) employ one of the several arbitration procedures outlined in the Treaty; (2) submit the dispute to procedures previously agreed upon by the investor and the host country government in an investment agreement or otherwise; or (3) submit the dispute to the local courts or administrative tribunals of the host country.

Under paragraph 3, if the investor has not submitted the dispute under the procedures in Paragraph 2 and six months have elapsed from the date the dispute arose, the investor may choose among the International Center for the Settlement of Investment Disputes (ICSID) Convention arbitration, or the ICSID Additional Facility (if Convention arbitration is not available), or ad hoc arbitration using the Arbitration Rules of the United Nations Commission on International.

Trade Law (UNCITRAL). Paragraph 3 also recognises that, by mutual agreement, the Parties to the dispute may choose another arbitral institution or set of arbitral rules.

Paragraph 4 contains the consent of the United States and Mongolia to the submission of investment disputes to binding arbitration in accordance with the choice of the investor.

Paragraph 5 provides that a non-ICSID arbitration shall take place in a country that is a party to the United Nations Convention on the Recognition and Enforcement of Foreign Arbitral Awards. This requirement expands the ability of investors to obtain enforcement of their arbitral awards abroad. In addition,

Paragraph 6 includes a separate commitment by each Party to enforce arbitral awards rendered pursuant to Article VI procedures.

Paragraph 7 provides that in any dispute settlement procedure, a Party may not invoke as a defence, counter-claim, set-off or in any other manner the fact that the company or national has received or will be reimbursed for the same damages under an insurance or guarantee contract.

Paragraph 8 is included in the Treaty to ensure that ICSID arbitration will be available for investors making investments in the form of companies created under the laws of the Party with which there is a dispute.

Article VII (State-State arbitration)

Article VII provides for binding arbitration of disputes between the United States and Mongolia that are not resolved through consultations or other diplomatic channels. The article constitutes each Party's prior consent to arbitration. It provides for the selection of arbitrators, establishes time limits for submissions, and requires the Parties to bear the costs equally, unless otherwise directed by the Tribunal.

Article VIII (Exclusion from dispute settlement procedures)

Article VIII provides that the provisions of Articles VI and VII concerning dispute resolution do not apply to disputes arising under the export credit, guarantee or insurance programs of the Export-Import Bank of the United States or under other official credit, guarantee or insurance programs for which the Parties have agreed to other means of dispute settlement.

Article IX (Preservation of rights)

Article IX clarifies that the Treaty is meant only to establish a floor for the treatment of foreign investment. An investor may be entitled to more favourable treatment through domestic legislation, other international legal obligations, or a specific obligation assumed by a Party with respect to that investor. This provision ensures that the Treaty will not be interpreted to derogate from any entitlement to such more favourable treatment.

Article X (Measures not precluded)

Paragraph 1 of Article X reserves the right of a Party to take measures for the maintenance of public order and the fulfillment of its obligations with respect to international peace and security, as well as those measures it regards as necessary for the protection of its own essential security interests. These provisions are common in international investment agreements.

The maintenance of public order would include measures taken pursuant to a Party's police powers to ensure public health and safety. International obligations with respect to peace and security would include, for example, obligations arising out of Chapter VII of the United Nations Charter. Measures permitted by the provision on the protection of a Party's essential security interests would include security-related actions taken in time of war or national emergency; actions not arising from a state of war or national emergency must have a clear and direct relationship to the essential security interest of the Party involved.

The second paragraph allows a Party to promulgate special formalities in connection with the establishment of investment, provided that the formalities do not impair the substance of any Treaty rights. Such formalities would include, for example, US reporting requirements for certain inward investment.

Article XI (Tax policies)

Paragraph 1 exhorts both countries to provide fair and equitable treatment to investors with respect to tax policies. However, tax matters are generally excluded from the coverage of the Treaty, based on the assumption that tax matters are properly covered in bilateral tax treaties.

The Treaty, and particularly the dispute settlement provisions, do apply to tax matters in three areas, to the extent they are not subject to the dispute settlement provisions of a tax treaty, or, if so subject, have been raised under a tax treaty's dispute settlement process and are not resolved in a reasonable period of time.

Pursuant to Paragraph 2, the three areas where the Treaty could apply to tax matters are expropriation (Article III), transfers (Article IV) and the observance and enforcement of terms of an investment agreement or authorisation (Article VI(1) (a) or (b)). These three areas are important for investors, and two of the three—expropriatory taxation and tax provisions contained in an investment agreement or authorisation—are not typically addressed in tax treaties.

Article XII (Application to political subdivisions)

Article XII makes clear that the obligations of the Treaty are applicable to all political sub-divisions of the Parties, such as provincial, State and local governments.

Article XIII (Entry into force, duration and termination)

The Treaty enters into force thirty days after exchange of instruments of ratification and continues in force for a period of ten years. From the date of its entry into force, the Treaty applies to existing and future investments. After the ten-year term, the Treaty will continue in force unless terminated by either Party upon one year's notice. If the Treaty is terminated, all existing investments would continue to be protected under the Treaty for ten years thereafter.

Annex

US bilateral investment treaties allow for sectoral exceptions to national and MFN treatment. The US exceptions are designed to protect governmental regulatory interests and to accommodate the derogations from national treatment and, in some cases, MFN treatment in existing federal law.

The US portion of the Annex contains a list of sectors and matters in which, for various legal and historical reasons, the federal government or the States may not necessarily treat investments of nationals or companies of the other Party as they do US investments or investments from a third country. The US exceptions from national treatment are: air transportation; ocean and coastal shipping; banking, insurance, securities and other financial services; government grants; government insurance and loan programs; energy and power production; customhouse brokers; ownership of real property; ownership and operation of broadcast or common carrier radio and television stations; ownership of shares in the Communications Satellite Corporation; the provision of common carrier telephone and telegraph services; the provision of submarine cable services; use of land and natural resources;

mining on the public domain; and maritime and maritime-related services.

Ownership of real property, mining on the public domain, maritime and maritime related services' and primary dealership in US government securities are excluded from MFN as well as national treatment commitments. The last three sectors are exempted by the United States from MFN treatment obligations because of US laws that require reciprocity. Enforcement of reciprocity provisions could deny both national and MFN treatment.

The listing of a sector does not necessarily signify that domestic laws have entirely reserved it for nationals. Future restrictions or limitations on foreign investment are only permitted in the sectors listed; must made on an MFN basis, unless otherwise specified in the Annex; and must be appropriately notified. Any additional restrictions or limitations which a Party may adopt with respect to listed sectors may not affect existing investments.

Because the US exceptions to national treatment and MFN treatment are based on existing US law, they are not altered during negotiations.

Mongolia's exceptions to national treatment are: land ownership and banking. These exceptions were based on provisions of investment measures currently in force or under active consideration by the Government of Mongolia. Mongolia has not reserved any sectoral exceptions to MFN treatment in the Annex.

Protocol

In a Protocol to the Treaty, the two sides clarify their understanding that the obligation to accord the better of national or most favoured nation treatment extends to all phases of investment—both to establishment and acquisition as well as to the expansion, management, conduct, operation and sale or any other disposition of investments.

The other US Government agencies which negotiated the Treaty join me in recommending that it be transmitted to the Senate at an early date.

Respectfully submitted,
Strobe Talbott.

TREATY BETWEEN THE UNITED STATES OF AMERICA AND MONGOLIA CONCERNING THE ENCOURAGEMENT AND RECIPROCAL PROTECTION OF INVESTMENT

The United States Of America and Mongolia (hereinafter the "Parties");

Desiring to promote greater economic cooperation between them, with respect to investment by nationals and companies of one Party in the territory of the other Party;

Recognising that agreement upon the treatment to be accorded in such investment will stimulate the flow of private capital and the economic development of the Parties;

Agreeing that fair and equitable treatment of investment is desirable in order to maintain a stable framework for investment and maximum effective utilisation of economic resources;

Recognising that the development of economic and business ties can contribute to the well-being of workers in both Parties and promote respect for internationally recognised worker rights; and

Having resolved to conclude a Treaty concerning the encouragement and reciprocal protection of investment;

Have agreed as follows:

ARTICLE I

1. For the purposes of this Treaty,

(a) "investment" means every kind of investment in the territory of one Party owned or controlled directly or indirectly by nationals or companies of the other Party, such as equity, debt, and service and investment contracts; and includes:

(i) tangible and intangible property, including rights, such as mortgages, liens and pledges;

(ii) a company or shares of stock or other interests in a company or interests in the assets thereof;

(iii) a claim to money or a claim to performance having economic value, and associated with an investment;

(iv) intellectual property which includes, *inter alia*, rights relating to:

literary and artistic works,

including sound recordings,

inventions in all fields of human

endeavour,

industrial designs,

semi-conductor mask works,

trade secrets, know-how, and

confidential business information, and

trademarks, service marks, and trade

names; and

(v) any right conferred by law or contract, and any licenses and permits pursuant to law;

(b) "company" of a Party means any kind of corporation, company, association, partnership, or other organisation, legally constituted under the laws and regulations of a Party or a political sub-division thereof whether or not organised for pecuniary gain, or privately or governmentally owned or controlled;

(c) "national" of a Party means a natural person who is national of a Party under its applicable law;

(d) "return" means an amount derived from or associated with an investment, including profit; dividend; interest; capital gain; royalty payment; management, technical assistance or other fee; or returns in kind;

(e) "associated activities" include the organisation, control, operation, maintenance and disposition of companies, branches, agencies, offices, factories or other facilities for the conduct of business; the making, performance and enforcement of contracts; the acquisition, use, protection and disposition of property of all kinds including intellectual property rights; the borrowing of funds; the purchase, issuance, and sale of equity shares and other securities; and the purchase of foreign exchange for imports;

(f) "investment authorisation" means an authorisation granted by the foreign investment authority of a Party to an investment or a national or company of the other Party;

(g) "investment agreement" means a written agreement between the national authorities of a Party and an investment or a national or company of the other Party that (i) grants rights with respect to natural resources or other assets controlled by the national authorities and (ii) the investment, national or company relies upon in establishing or acquiring an investment.

2. Each Party reserves the right to deny to any company the advantages of this Treaty if nationals of any third country control such company and, in the case of a company of the other Party, that company has no substantial business activities in the territory of the other Party or is controlled by nationals of a third country with which the denying Party does not maintain normal economic relations.

3. Any alteration of the form in which assets are invested or reinvested shall not affect their character as investment.

ARTICLE II

1. Each Party shall permit and treat investment, and activities associated therewith, on a basis no less favourable than that accorded in like situations to investment or associated activities of its own nationals or companies, or of nationals or companies of any third country, whichever is the most favourable, subject to the right of each Party to make or maintain exceptions falling within one of the sectors or matters listed in the Annex to this Treaty. Each Party agrees to notify the other Party before or on the date of entry into force of this Treaty of all such laws and regulations of which it is aware concerning the sectors or matters listed in the Annex. Moreover, each Party agrees to notify the other of any future exception with respect to the sectors or matters listed in the Annex, and to limit such exceptions to a minimum. Any future exception by either Party shall not apply to investment existing in that sector or matter at the time the exception becomes effective. The

treatment accorded pursuant to any exceptions shall, unless specified otherwise in the Annex, be not less favourable than that accorded in like situations to investments and associated activities of nationals or companies of any third country.

2. (a) Investment shall at all times be accorded fair and equitable treatment, shall enjoy full protection and security and shall in no case be accorded treatment less than that required by international law.

(b) Neither Party shall in any way impair by unreasonable and discriminatory measures the management, operation, maintenance, use, enjoyment, acquisition, expansion, or disposal of investments.

(c) Each Party shall observe any obligation it may have entered into with regard to investments.

3. Subject to the laws relating to the entry and sojourn of aliens, nationals of either Party shall be permitted to enter and remain in the territory of the other Party for the purpose of establishing, developing, administering or advising company on the operation of an investment to which they, or a company of the first Party that employs them, have committed or are in the process of committing a substantial amount of capital or other resources.

4. Companies which are legally constituted under the applicable laws or regulations of one Party, and which are investments, shall be permitted to engage top managerial personnel of their choice, regardless of nationality.

5. Neither Party shall impose performance requirements as condition of establishment, expansion or maintenance of investments, which require or enforce commitments to export goods produced, or which specify that goods or services must be purchased locally, or which impose any other similar requirements.

6. Each Party shall provide effective means of asserting claims and enforcing rights with respect to investment, investment agreements, and investment authorisations.

7. Each Party shall make Public all laws, regulations, administrative practices and procedures, and adjudicatory decisions that pertain to or affect investments.

8. The treatment accorded by the United States of America to investments and associated activities of nationals and companies of Mongolia under the provisions of this Article shall in any State, Territory or possession of the United States of America be no less favourable than the treatment accorded therein to investments and associated activities of nationals of the United States of America resident in, and companies legally constituted under the laws and regulations of other States, Territories or possessions of the United States of America.

9. The most favoured nation provisions of this Article shall not apply to advantages accorded by either to nationals or companies of any third country by virtue of:

(a) that Party's binding obligations that derive from full membership in a free trade area or customs union; or

(b) that Party's binding obligations under any multilateral international agreement under the framework of the General Agreement on Tariffs and Trade that enters into force subsequent to the signature of this Treaty.

ARTICLE III

1. Investments shall not be expropriated or nationalised either directly or indirectly through measures tantamount to expropriation or nationalisation ("expropriation") except: for a public purpose; in a non-discriminatory manner; upon payment of prompt, adequate and effective compensation; and in accordance with due process of law and the general principles of treatment provided for in Article II(2). Compensation shall be equivalent to the fair market value of the expropriated investment immediately before the expropriatory action was taken or became known, whichever is earlier; be calculated on the basis of the prevailing market rate of exchange at that time; be paid without delay; include interest at a commercially reasonable rate from the date of expropriation; be fully realisable; and be freely transferable.

2. A national or company of either Party that asserts that all or part of its investment has been expropriated shall have a

right to prompt review by the appropriate judicial or administrative authorities of the other Party to determine whether any such expropriation has occurred and, if so, whether such expropriation, and any associated compensation, conforms, to the principles of international law.

3. Nationals or companies of either Party whose investments suffer losses in the territory of the other Party owing to war or other armed conflict, revolution, state of national emergency, insurrection, civil disturbance or other similar events shall be accorded treatment by such other Party no less favourable than that accorded to its own nationals or companies or to nationals or companies of any third country, whichever is the most favourable treatment, as regards any measures it adopts in relation to such losses.

ARTICLE IV

1. Each Party shall permit all transfers related to an investment to be made freely and without delay into and out of its territory. Such transfers include: (a) returns; (b) compensation pursuant to Article III; (c) payments arising out of an investment dispute; (d) payments made under a contract, including amortisation of principal and accrued interest payments made pursuant to a loan agreement; (e) proceeds from the sale or liquidation of all or any part of an investment; and (f) additional contributions to capital for the maintenance or development of an investment.

2. Transfers shall be made in a freely usable currency, as defined in Article 30 of the Articles of Agreement of the International Monetary Fund, at the prevailing market rate of exchange on the date of transfer with respect to spot transactions in the currency to be transferred.

3. Notwithstanding the provisions of paragraphs 1 and 2, either Party may maintain laws and regulations (a) requiring reports of currency transfer; and (b) imposing income taxes by such means as a withholding tax applicable to dividends or other transfers. Furthermore, either Party may protect the rights of creditors, or ensure the satisfaction of judgments in adjudicatory proceedings, through the equitable, non-discriminatory and good faith application of its law.

4. Each Party shall permit returns in kind to be made as authorised or specified in an investment authorisation, investment agreement, or other written agreement between the Party and an investment or a national or company of the other Party.

ARTICLE V

The Parties agree to consult promptly, on the request of either, to resolve any disputes in connection with the Treaty, or to discuss any matter relating to the interpretation or application of the Treaty.

ARTICLE VI

1. For purposes of this Article, an investment dispute is a dispute between a Party and a national or company of the other Party arising out of or relating to (a) an investment agreement between that Party and such national or company; (b) an investment authorisation granted by that Party's foreign investment authority to such national or company; or (c) an alleged breach of any right conferred or created by this Treaty with respect to an investment.

2. In the event of an investment dispute, the parties to the dispute should initially seek a resolution through consultation and negotiation. If the dispute cannot be settled amicably, the national or company concerned may choose to submit the dispute for resolution:

(a) to the courts or administrative tribunals of the Party that is party to the dispute;

(b) in accordance with any applicable, previously agreed dispute-settlement procedures; or

(c) in accordance with the terms of Paragraph 3.

3. (a) Provided that the national or company concerned has not submitted the dispute for resolution under Paragraph 2 (a) or (b) and that six months have elapsed from the date on which the dispute arose, the national or company concerned may choose to consent in writing to the submission of the dispute for settlement by binding arbitration:

(i) to the International Centre for the Settlement of Investment Disputes ("Centre") established by the convention on the Settlement of Investment Disputes between States and Nationals of Other.

States, done at Washington, March 18, 1965 ("ICSID Convention"), provided that the Party is a party to such Convention; or

(ii) to the Additional Facility of the Centre, if the Centre is not available; or

(iii) in accordance with the Arbitration Rules of the United Nations Commission on International.

Trade Law (UNICTRAL); or

(iv) to any other arbitration institution rules, or in accordance with any other arbitration rules, as may be mutually agreed between the parties to the dispute.

(b) Once the national or company concerned has so consented, either party to the dispute may initiate arbitration in accordance with the choice so specified in the consent.

4. Each Party hereby consents to the submission of any investment dispute for settlement by binding arbitration in accordance with the choice specified in the written consent of the national or company under Paragraph 3. Such consent, together with the written consent of the national or company when given under Paragraph 3 shall satisfy the requirement for:

(a) written consent of the parties to the dispute for purposes of Chapter II of the ICSID Convention (Jurisdiction of the Centre) and for purposes of the Additional Facility Rules; and

(b) an "agreement in writing" for purposes of Article II of the United Nations Convention on the.

Recognition and enforcement of Foreign Arbitral Awards, done at New York, June 10, 1958 ("New York Convention").

5. Any arbitration under Paragraph 3(a) (ii), (iii) or (iv) of this Article shall be held in a state that is a party to the New York Convention.

6. Any arbitral award rendered pursuant to this Article shall be final and binding on the parties to the dispute. Each Party

undertakes to carry out without delay the provisions of any such award and to provide in its territory for its enforcement.

7. In any proceeding involving an investment dispute, a Party shall not assert, as a defence, counter-claim, right of set-off or otherwise, that the national or company concerned has received or will receive, pursuant to an insurance or guarantee contract, indemnification or other compensation for all or part of its alleged damages

8. For purposes of an arbitration held under paragraph 3 of this Article, any company legally constituted under the applicable laws and regulations of a Party or a political sub-division thereof but that, immediately before the occurrence of the event or events giving rise to the dispute, was an investment of nationals or companies of the other Party, shall be treated as a national or company of such other Party in accordance with Article 25 (2) (b) of the ICSID Convention.

ARTICLE VII

1. Any dispute between the Parties concerning the interpretation or application of the Treaty which is not resolved through consultations or other diplomatic channels, shall be submitted, upon the request of either Party, to an arbitral tribunal for binding decision in accordance with the applicable rules of international law. In the absence of an agreement by the Parties to the contrary, the arbitration rules of the United Nations Commission on International Trade Law (UNCITRAL), except to the extent modified by the Parties or by the arbitrators, shall govern.

2. Within two months of receipt of a request, each Party shall appoint an arbitrator. The two arbitrators shall select a third arbitrator as Chairman, who is a national of a third State. The UNCITRAL Rules for appointing members of three member panels shall apply *mutatis mutandis* to the appointment of the arbitral panel except that the appointing authority referenced in those rules shall be the Secretary General of the Centre.

3. Unless otherwise agreed, all submissions shall be made and all hearings shall be completed within six months of the date of selection of the third arbitrator, and the Tribunal shall render its decisions within two months of the date of the final

submissions or the date of the closing of the hearings, whichever is later.

4. Expenses incurred by the Chairman, the other arbitrators, and other costs of the proceedings shall be paid for equally by the Parties. The Tribunal may, however, at its discretion, direct that a higher proportion of the costs be paid by one of the Parties.

ARTICLE VIII

The provisions of Articles VI and VII shall not apply to a dispute arising (a) under the export credit, guarantee or insurance programs of the Export-Import Bank of the United States, or (b) under other official credit, guarantee or insurance arrangements pursuant to which the Parties have agreed to other means of settling disputes.

ARTICLE IX

This Treaty shall not derogate from:

(a) laws and regulations, administrative practices or procedures, or administrative or adjudicatory decisions of either Party;

(b) international legal obligations; or

(c) obligations assumed by either Party, including those contained in an investment agreement or an investment authorisation, that entitle investments or associated activities to treatment more favourable than that accorded by this Treaty in like situations.

ARTICLE X

1. This Treaty shall not preclude the application by either Party of measures necessary for the maintenance of public order, the fulfillment of its obligations with respect to the maintenance or restoration of international peace or security, or the protection of its own essential security interests.

2. This Treaty shall not preclude either Party from prescribing special formalities in connection with the establishment of investments, but such formalities shall not impair the substance of any of the rights set forth in this Treaty.

ARTICLE XI

1. With respect to its tax policies, each Party should strive to accord fairness and equity in the treatment of investment of nationals and companies of the other Party.

2. Nevertheless, the provisions of this Treaty, and in particular Article VI and VII, shall apply to matters of taxation only with respect to the following:

(a) expropriation, pursuant to Article III;

(b) transfers, pursuant to Article IV; or

(c) the observance and enforcement of terms of an investment agreement or authorisation as referred to in Article VI (1) (a) or (b), to the extent they are not subject to the dispute settlement provisions of a Convention for the avoidance of double taxation between the two Parties, or have been raised under such settlement provisions and are not resolved within a reasonable period of time.

ARTICLE XII

This Treaty shall apply to the political subdivisions of the Parties.

ARTICLE XIII

1. This Treaty shall enter into force thirty days after the date of exchange of instruments of ratification. It shall remain in force for a period of ten years and shall continue in force unless terminated in accordance with paragraph 2 of this Article. It shall apply to investments existing at the time of entry into force as well as to investments made or acquired thereafter.

2. Either Party may, by giving one year's written notice to the other Party, terminate this Treaty at the end of the initial ten years period or at any time thereafter.

3. With respect to investments made or acquired prior to the date of termination of this Treaty and to which this Treaty otherwise applies, the provisions of all of the other Articles of this Treaty shall thereafter continue to be effective for a further period of ten years from such date of termination.

4. The Annex and Protocol shall form an integral part of the Treaty.

IN WITNESS WHEREOF, the respective plenipotentiaries have signed this Treaty.

DONE in duplicate at Washington on the sixth of October, 1994, in the English and Mongolian languages, both texts being equally authentic.

FOR THE UNITED STATES OF AMERICA: [signature]

FOR MONGOLIA: [signature]

ANNEX

1. The United States reserves the right to make or maintain limited exceptions to national treatment, as provided in Article II, paragraph 1, in the sectors or matters it has indicated below: air transportation; ocean and coastal-shipping; banking, insurance, securities and other financial services; government grants; government insurance and loan programs; energy and power production; custom-house brokers; ownership of real property; ownership and operation ofbroadcast or common carrier radio and television stations; ownership of shares in the,

Communications Satellite Corporation; the provision of common carrier telephone and telegraph services; the provision of submarine cable services; use of land and natural resources; mining on the public domain; and maritime services and maritime-related services.

2. The United States reserves the right to make or maintain limited exceptions to most favoured nation treatment, as provided in Article II, paragraph 1, in the sectors or matters it has indicated below: ownership of real property; mining on the public domain; maritime services and maritime-related services; and primary dealership in United States government securities.

3. Mongolia reserves the right to make or maintain limited exceptions to national treatment, as provided in Article II, paragraph 1, in the sectors or matters it has indicated below: land ownership and banking.

PROTOCOL

With respect to Article 11, Paragraph 1, the Parties confirm their mutual understanding that the national and most favoured nation treatment obligations specified therein apply to the establishment and acquisition as well as to the expansion, management, conduct, operation and sale or other disposition of investments.

APPENDIX- VII

TRADE AGREEMENT BETWEEN THE GOVERNMENT OF INDIA, AND THE GOVERNMENT OF THE MONGOLIAN PEOPLE'S REPUBLIC

New Delhi, 13th February 1968.

The Government of India and The Government of the Mongolian People's Republic BEING desirous of developing trade relations between the two countries,

HAVE agreed upon the following:

HAVE agreed as follows:

ARTICLE I

The Contracting Parties will, in every possible way, support development of mutually beneficial trade between the two countries on the basis of mutual respect and equally and will consider with goodwill the suggestions which either party may present for consideration of the other.

ARTICLE II

The Contracting Parties will in the course of trade between the two countries accord facilities allowed by their respective laws relating to import and export and foreign exchange rules and regulations. Mutual deliveries of goods between the two countries will be carried out in accordance with Annexures "A" and "B" as may be needed by either of the two Contracting Parties.

ARTICLE III

The competent foreign trade organisations of both Contracting Parties and the persons authorised by them will conclude contracts about deliveries of goods covered by the present Agreement.

ARTICLE IV

(a) Both contracting Parties will accord each other most favoured treatment in respect of customs duties and charges of any kind imposed on imports or exports, or in connection herewith, in respect of the methods of levying such duties and charges and in respect of rules formalities and charges in connection with customs clearing operations.

(b) The Contracting Parties will grant each other in respect of the import and export licences or permissions where such licences/permissions are prescribed under their regulations, treatment no less favourable than that granted to any other country.

ARTICLE V

Any advantages, favour, privilege or immunity granted by either of the Contracting Parties to any product originating in the territory of a third country or destined for its territory shall be granted immediately and unconditionally to the like product originating in the territory of either of the Contracting Parties or designated to be imported into its territory.

ARTICLE VI

The provisions of Articles IV and V above shall not, however apply to the grant, or continuance of any:

(a) advantages accorded by either party to contiguous countries for the purpose of facilitating frontier traffic;

(b) preferences, or advantages, accorded by either party to any country, as existing on the date of the conclusion of the present Agreement or in replacement of such preferences or advantages that existed prior to the 15th August 1947.

ARTICLE VII

The export of goods from India to Mongolia and from Mongolia to India during the period of validity of the present Agreement will be carried out in accordance the the Annexure

"A" and "B" the details of which will be agreed upon from time to time between the two Contracting Parties.

The Annexures "A" and "B" can be extended, altered, or renewed by letters exchanged between the two Contracting Parties with mutual consent.

ARTICLE VIII

All payments for current transactions between the two countries shall be effected in convertible currency unless otherwise agreed to between the two Parties.

In case the two Parties agreed to payment for goods imported by either country to be settled through a clearing account, such goods shall not be re-exported to any third country, but would be consumed in the importing country unless otherwise agreed to by the two Contracting Parties.

ARTICLE IX

Both Parties will take all possible steps to facilitate speedy transportation of their goods sold and purchased under this Agreement.

ARTICLE X

Any contract concluded under this Agreement but not carried out before the date of the expiry of this Agreement will continue to be implemented in accordance with the provisions of this Agreement.

ARTICLE XI

The physical and juridical persons in India and the physical and juridical persons in Mongolia may agree that legal dispute arising from contract concluded in commercial or other economic matters shall be referred to arbitration.

ARTICLE XII

The two Contracting Parties agree to consult each other on questions that may arise in the course of the implementation of the present Agreement.

ARTICLE XIII

The present Agreement will come into force from the date of its signing and will remain valid for a period of three years.

The present Agreement has been drawn up and signed in New Delhi on the 13th February 1968 in two original copies in

Mongolian and in English, the Mongolian and English texts being equally authentic.

Dinesh Singh and D Dorzhgotov

By authority of the Government of India and Mongolian People's Republic

LIST "A"

GOODS FOR EXPORT FROM INDIA TO MONGOLIA

Food-Stuffs

1. Fruits, fruit juices and canned products,
2. Nuts,
3. Pepper and other spices,
4. Canned fish,
5. Tobacco and tobacco goods,
6. Tea.

Raw Materials

7. Shellac and goods based on shellac,
8. Gum and Rubber,
9. Vegetable oil.

Industrial Goods

10. Ferrous and non-ferrous rolled metals,
11. Ferrous and non-ferrous metal ware,
12. Light industry machinery,
13. Electro-technical goods,
14. Lifting-handling (transport equipment),
15. Other measuring instruments,
16. Chemical goods,
17. Medical equipment and pharmaceuticals,
18. Consumer goods,
19. Other goods, including films,
20. Textiles including woolen, cotton and silk,
21. Jute manufactures,
22. Tarpaulins.

LIST "B"

GOODS FOR EXPORT FROM MONGOLIA TO INDIA

Wool

1. Camel mane unwashed

2. Sheep wool, fleece, washed,
3. Sheep wool, autumn, unwashed,
4. Lamb's wool felt, unwashed,
5. Horse-hair,
6. Got-hair.

Skin of Animals

7. Horse and camel skins, raw,
8. Sheep and goat skins, worked up,
9. Baby camel skin, lambskin, raw fur,
10. Marmot,
11. Fox,
12. Wolf skin,
13. Squirrel and other furs.

Other Goods

14. Tungsten and other metals which do not contain,
15. Woollen knitwear,
16. Woollen cloth,
17. Woollen blankets,
18. Tanned skins, leather goods, leather coats, jackets,
19. Cattle horns,
20. Medicinal herbs,
21. Films.

Ministry of External Affairs, India

APPENDIX- VIII

Joint Declaration on the Comprehensive Partnership between India and Mongolia.

September 14, 2009

1. The President of Mongolia, His Excellency Mr. Tsakhiagiin Elbegdorj is presently on a State Visit to India from September 13 to 16, 2009 at the invitation of the President of the Republic of India, Her Excellency Shrimati Pratibha Patil.

2. The President of Mongolia was accorded a ceremonial welcome at the Rashtrapati Bhawan on 14th September 2009, and also had a meeting with the President of India. The Presidents of India and Mongolia reviewed bilateral relations and exchanged views on recent regional and international developments of mutual interest.

3. The Vice President of India and the Minister of External Affairs called on the President of Mongolia.

4. The President of Mongolia held delegation-level discussions with the Prime Minister of India. Both sides agreed that the Treaty of Friendly Relations and Cooperation between the Republic of India and Mongolia signed in 1994 constitutes the firm foundation for bilateral relations. They noted with satisfaction the all-round progress in the bilateral relationship since the visit of the Prime Minister of Mongolia to India in January 2004. They were in complete agreement that the decision to elevate bilateral relations to a new level of

partnership, which was decided during that visit, has strengthened bilateral relations.

5 The two sides acknowledged the excellent state of political relations based on historical and cultural ties, common democratic traditions and a shared desire for regional peace and stability.

6. Both parties agreed to upgrade the level of bilateral relations to a Comprehensive Partnership and shared a broad consensus on the future direction of India-Mongolia relations. They have reached the following understandings:

I. Regular exchange of high-level visits between the two countries.

II. Regular consultations between the Foreign Ministries of the two countries. The Foreign Affairs and Trade Minister of Mongolia will visit India at a mutually convenient time in 2010. The two sides will also hold the next meeting of the Joint Committee on Cooperation in New Delhi at an early date.

III. Development of defence exchanges and cooperation on the basis of the Agreement on Cooperation in Defence Matters signed in 2001. The 5th joint military exercise will be held in Mongolia later this month. The 3rd meeting of the Joint Working Group on Defence Cooperation will be held in Ulaanbaatar at a mutually convenient time in 2010.

IV. Regular consultations between the National Security Councils of India and Mongolia on issues of mutual interest in regional and multilateral affairs, including on the subject of cooperation against terrorism.

V. Promotion of greater trade and economic activity between the two countries.

VI. Participation of Indian companies through joint venture and investment in the mining sector in Mongolia. A delegation from India has been invited to Mongolia to discuss the prospects for such cooperation.

VII. Exploring cooperation in the area of agriculture, including through the deputation of Indian experts to assist Mongolia in enhancing output through high yield crops.

VIII. To double the number of slots to 120 in recognition of the importance that the Government of Mongolia attaches to the training of their students in India under the Indian Technical and Economic Cooperation (ITEC) Programme. The Ministry of External Affairs will also provide three slots annually to the Foreign Ministry of Mongolia in the Professional Courses for Foreign Diplomats at the Foreign Service Institute of India.

7. The Government of Mongolia has requested the Government of India for economic assistance to mitigate the adverse impact of the global financial crisis. The Government of India has agreed to the request of the Government of Mongolia for a soft loan of US$ 25 million to assist in the stabilisation of the economy.

8. The two sides attach importance to cooperation with Mongolia in the field of education on the basis of the Memorandum of Understanding signed in 2003. They agree that the teaching assistance provided by India has contributed to the development of cooperation in this area. In pursuance of this cooperation, the Government of India has agreed to consider the request of the Mongolian side for financial assistance for the construction of a school building in Ulaanbaatar for the India-Mongolia Joint School after the Mongolian side makes a specific proposal. The Government of India also agrees to give positive consideration to the request of the Mongolian side for the provision of additional teaching staff by India when the necessary infrastructure has been established.

9. The two parties have agreed to cooperate in information and communications technology sector through exchanges between businesses, research and educational institutions, government agencies and other organisations. The Mongolian side requested India to assist in launching an IT education and outsourcing centre and a national monitoring centre for detection and prevention of intrusion. The Indian side expressed its willingness to consider these proposals, including assistance through a Line of Credit, at the next meeting of the India-Mongolia Joint Committee.

10. The two sides also agreed that the historical, cultural and spiritual links between India and Mongolia are important and need to be nurtured through the promotion of tourism and

culture. They welcomed the signing of a new Cultural Exchange Programme for the years 2009 to 2012. They welcomed the establishment of a Mongolian Monastery in Bodhgaya, and decided to strengthen exchanges in the field of Buddhism, including Buddhist studies, in order to preserve this common heritage. The Indian side welcomed the growing number of Mongolian students who are coming to India for educational purposes.

11. The two sides share a complete identity of views on regional and multilateral matters. Both sides reiterated their readiness to enhance their cooperation on issues related to peace and stability in the Asia-Pacific region, including through enhanced interaction at multilateral forums such as the ASEAN Regional Forum (ARF) and the Asia Europe Meeting (ASEM).

12. The Government of Mongolia reiterated its complete support to India's candidature for permanent membership of the UN Security Council when the expansion takes place. The Government of India expressed its appreciation to the Government of Mongolia for this expression of support and for the expression of support to India's candidature for election to the non-permanent seat for 2011-2012.

13. Both India and Mongolia strongly condemn the menace of international terrorism and its devastating effect on democratic societies and on human civilization itself. They affirmed that there can be no justification for terrorism, and reiterated their resolve to work towards strengthening of the global consensus and legal regimes against terrorism, including early finalisation of a Comprehensive Convention on International Terrorism.

14. The following agreements were signed during the visit:

Agreement on Cooperation in the Field of Health

(I) Agreement on Stabilisation Loan Assistance.

(II) MoU on Cooperation in the Field of Statistics.

(III) MoU on Cooperation in the Field of Peaceful Use of adio active Minerals and Nuclear Energy.

(IV) Cultural Exchange Programme for 2009-2012.

15. The two sides agreed that the State Visit of the President of Mongolia has strengthened the traditionally friendly and cooperative relations between the two countries, and will provide impetus for the further development of the bilateral partnership. The President of Mongolia has invited the President, Vice-President and Prime Minister of the Republic of India to visit Mongolia at a mutually convenient time. The invitations were accepted with appreciation. The timing of these visits will be decided through diplomatic channels.

New Delhi,
September 14, 2009

Bibliography

(*Indicates a primary source)

Alexei V. Mikhalev (2011), "Soviet-Mongolian Commonwealth: Dynamics of Collective Memory in Post-Soviet Discourse, *Journal of Siberian Federal University. Humanities and Social Sciences* 4(4): pp. 521-527.

Alicia, Campi (2005), "Sino-Mongolian Relations from Beijing's Viewpoint", *China Brief (The Jamestown Foundation,* 5(10): pp. 8-9.

Almond. G. and Sidney V. (1963), *The Civic Culture: Political Attitudes and* Democracy *in Five Nations,* Princeton: Princeton University Press.

Alan M. Wachman (2009), *Mongolia's Geopolitical Gambit: Preserving a Precarious Independence While Resisting "Soft Colonialism"*, The East Asia Institute (EAI) working Paper series no 18 , Korea.

Baabar, B (1995), "The Central Asian Security Zone", *The Mongolian Journal of International Affairs*, 2 (18): pp. 19-32.

______(1999) . *History of Mongolia*. Cambridge, UK: The White Horse Press.

Batbayar, Tsedendamba (2003), "Foreign Policy and Domestic Reform in Mongolia, *Central Asian Survey*, 22 (1): pp. 45-59.

Batbayar, T. (1994), "Mongolia in 1993: A Fragile Democracy." *Asian Survey* 34 (1): 41-45.

Batbayar, T. (1998), "*Open Mongolia and Mongol-Russian Relations*", *The Mongolian Journal of International Affairs*, 5 (1): pp. 7-14.

__________ (2002), "Mongolia's New Identity and Security Dilemmas", *The Mongolian Journal of International Affairs*, 8 (9): pp. 3-11.

__________ (2003), "Foreign Policy and Domestic Reform in Mongolia." *Central Asian Survey* 22 (1): pp. 45-59.

__________ (2003), "Foreign Policy and Domestic Reform in Mongolia", *Central Asian Survey*, 22 (1): pp. 172-204.

Batbayar, T. and Soni, Sharad K. (2007), *Modern Mongolia: A Concise History* New Delhi: Pentagon Press.

Bayarkhuu, D. (2000), "Mongolian Foreign Policy in the Changing World", *China Report*, 36 (1): pp. 83-88.

__________ (1999), "New World Order in the Asia-Pacific Region: A Mongolian perspective", *World Affairs*, 3 (4): pp. 98-109.

__________ (2001), "Mongolia and its Third Neighbours", *Himalayan and Central Asian Studies*, 5 (1): pp. 80-90.

Bayasakh, K. (2000), "Mongolia, Russia and China on the eve of new millennium", *China Report*, 36 (1): pp. 73-81.

Baylis and S. Smith (eds). *The Globalization of World Politics: An introduction to international relations,* (2nd ed.) Oxford: Oxford University Press.

Bedi, Rahul (2007), "Defence ties with Mongolia expanded: Bid to monitor China's military activities," *The Tribune* (India), accessed 10/03/2012, http://www.tribuneindia.com/2007/20070810/main5.htm.

Beetham, D. (1999), *Democracy and Human Rights*, Cambridge: Polity Press.

__________ (2005), 'The State of Democracy Project' in International IDEA, *Ten Years of Supporting Democracy Worldwide*, Stockholm: International IDEA, pp. 145-155.

Boix, C. (2003), *Democracy and Redistribution*, Cambridge: Cambridge University Press.

Boone, P. (1994), "Grassroots Macro-economic Reform in Mongolia," *Journal of Comparative Economics* 18 (3): pp. 329-356.

Brooks, D. H. (1998), "The Kyrgyz Republic and Mongolia." In Brooks, Douglas and Myo Thand eds. *Social Sector Issues in Transitional Economies of Asia*. Pp. 337-366.

Bruun, O and Odgaard, O. (1997b), "Consolidating Independence", in Bruun, O. and Odgaard, O. eds. *Mongolia in Transition: Old Patterns, New Challenges,* Curzon: Routledge.

__________ and Odgaard, O. (1997a), "A Society and Economy in Transition", in Bruun, O. and Odgaard, O. eds. *Mongolia in Transition: Old Patterns,* New Challenges, Curzon: Routledge .

Campi, A. (2003a), Review of *Mongolia's Foreign Policy in the 1990s: New Identity and New Challenges* by Tsedendamba Batbayar. US; Mongolia Advisory Group.

__________ (2003b), "Mongolia as a Bridge to Central Asia", in *The Geopolitical Relations between Contemporary Mongolia and Neighbouring Asian Countries: Democracy*, Economy and Security, Taipei: Mongolian and Tibetan Affairs.

__________ (2004), *Modern Mongolian-Chinese Strategic Relations: Challenges for the New Century*. US: Mongolia Advisory Group.

Carothers, Thomas. (2002), "The End of the Transition Paradigm," *Journal of Democracy* (January), pp. 5-21.

Cheng, Kevin C. (2003). Growth and Recovery in Mongolia During Transition. Working Paper 03/217, *International Monetary Fund*.

China daily, (27th May 2012), *China-Mongolia Relations*, Accessed 29 may 2012.

Cooter, Robert. (1997), "*The Role of State Law* vs *the Rule of Law*: Economic Analysis of the Legal foundations of Development." *Macro-economics and* Growth 5(4): 92-97.

Dahl, R. (1971), *Polyarchy*, New Haven: Yale University Press.

Diamond, L. (1999), *Developing Democracy: Toward Consolidation*, Baltimore: Johns Hopkins University Press.

Donnelly, J. (2005), "Realism", in S. Burchill, *et.al. Theories of International Relations* (3rd ed.). Houndsmills: Palgrave Macmillan.

Doorenspleet, R. (2000), 'Reassessing the Three Waves of Democratisation', *World Politics*, 52 (3): pp. 384-406.

__________ (2001), *The Fourth Wave of Democratisation: Identification and Explanation*, PhD. Thesis Manuscript, University of Leiden.

Drakulic, Slavenka. (1990), *How We Survived Communism and Even Laughed* New York: Harper Perennial.

Dunne, T. and Schmidt, B. C. (2001), "Liberalism" in John Baylis and Steve Smith (eds.) *The Globalisation of World Politics: Introduction to international relations.* (2nd eds.) Oxford: Oxford University Press.

Evan, G. and Newnham, J. (1992), *The Dictionary of World Politics: Reference Guide to Concepts, Ideas and Institutions.* New York: Harvester Wheat Sheaf Press.

__________and Newham, J. (1998), *the Penguin Dictionary of International Relations.* London: Penguin Group.

Finch, C. (2002), 'Mongolia in 2001: Political Consolidation and Continued Economic Reform', *Asian Survey*, 42 (1): pp. 39-45.

Finch, Christopher. (2002), "Mongolia in 2001: Political Consolidation and Continued Economic Reform." *Asian Survey* 42 (1): pp. 39-45.

Finnemore, M. and Sikkink, K. (1998), "International Norms Dynamic and Political Change" in International Organisation, 52(4): pp. 887-917.

Fish S. and Steven M. (1998), "Mongolia: Democracy without Prerequisites." *Journal of Democracy* 9(3): pp. 127-141.

__________(1998), 'Mongolia: Democracy without Prerequisites', *Journal of Democracy*, 9 (3): pp. 127-141.

__________(2001), "The Inner Asian Anomaly: Mongolia's Democratisation in Comparative Perspective," *Communist and Post Communist Studies* 34(3): pp. 323-38.

Foweraker J. and Krznaric, R. (2000), 'Measuring Liberal Democratic Performance: A Conceptual and Empirical Critique', *Political Studies*, 45 (3): pp. 759-787.

Fritz, V. (2002), 'Mongolia: Dependent Democratisation', *Journal of Communist Studies and Transition Politics*, 18 (4): pp. 75-100.

Fritz, Verna. (2002), "Mongolia: Dependent Democratisation," *Journal of Communist Studies and Transition Politics* 18 (4): pp. 75-100.

Fukuyama, Francis. (1996), *Trust: The Social Virtues and the Creation of Prosperity*. New York: Simon and Schuster.

Fujiko Isono (1976), The Mongolian Revolution of 1921, *Modern Asian Studies*, 10(3): pp. 375-394 .

G. Tumerchuluun, (1999), "Mongolia's Foreign Policy Revisited: Relations with Russia and the PRC into the 1990s", in Kotkin, S. and Elleman, B. eds. *Mongolia in the Twentieth Century, Landlocked Cosmopolitan,* New York: M.E. Sharpe.

Galina Yaskina, (1998), "Russian-Mongolian Relations: Reality and Outlook", *Far Eastern Affairs*, No. 5, p. 37.

Garver, J. (1988), *Sino-Soviet Relations, 1937–1945: The Diplomacy of Chinese Nationalism.* Oxford: Oxford University Press.

Galsandorj, D. and H. Bud (2001), *Brief History of Mongolia's Foreign Economic Relations (1921-2000)*, Ulaanbaatar.

Ginsburg, T. (1999), "Nationalism, Elites and Mongolia's Rapid Transformation", in Kotkin, S. and Elleman, B. eds. *Mongolia in the Twentieth Century, Landlocked Cosmopolitan,* New York: M.E. Sharpe.

Ginsburg, Tom. (1995), "Political Reform in Mongolia," *Asian Survey* 35: pp. 459-61.

__________(1998), "Mongolia in 1997: Deepening Democracy." *Asian Survey* 38 (1): pp. 64-68.

Globe International (2004), Democratic Elections and Media Project: Evaluation Survey Report. Ulaanbaatar.

__________ (2005), First Report on Media Coverage of the 22nd May Presidential Election. Ulaanbaatar.

Gopal, H.D., (1999), "The Development Perspective on Mongolia," *Asian Survey,* 39 (4): pp. 633- 655.

*Government of the Russian Federation, *Russia-Mongolia Relations*, 13th May 2009. Available at: http://www.premier.gov.ru/eng/visits/world/105/info/2852.html.

Green, Elizabeth E. (1986), "China and Mongolia: Recurring Trends and Prospects for Change," *Asian Survey* 26 (12): pp. 1337-1363.

Green, M. (2001), 'What We Talk about When We Talk about Indicators: Current Approaches to Human Rights Measurement', *Human Rights Quarterly*, 23 (12): pp. 1062-1097.

Heaton, William R. (1992), "Mongolia in 1991: The Uneasy Transition", *Asian Survey*, 32 (1): pp. 50-55.

Helliwell, J.F. (1994,) 'Empirical Linkages between Democracy and Economic Growth', *British Journal of Political Science*, 24: pp. 225-48.

Huntington, S.P. (1993), "The Clash of Civilizations". *Foreign Affairs,* 72 (3).

Josselin, D. and Wallace, W. (2001), *Non-state Actors in World Politics: A Framework*, UK: Palgrave Publishers.

Kapolonski, C. (2005), "Truth, History and Politics in Mongolia", *Critical Asian Studies*, 37 (2): pp. 323-337.

Keohane, R.O. (1986*), Neo-realism and its Critics,* New York: Columbia University Press.

__________and Nye, J.S. (1989), *Power and Interdependence: World Politics in Transition.*

Klug, F. Starmer, K. and Weir, S. (1996) *The Three Pillars of Liberty: Political Rights and Freedom in the United Kingdom*, London: Routledge.

Kopstein, J. and Reilly, D. (2000), 'Geographic Diffusion and the Transformation of the Post-Communist World', *World Politics*, 53 (10): pp. 1-37.

Kotkin, Stephen and Bruce Elleman, eds. (1999), *Mongolia in the Twentieth Century: Landlocked Cosmopolitan*, Armonk, NY: M.E. Sharpe.

Landman, T. (2003), *Issues and Methods in Comparative Politics: An Introduction*, Second Edition, London: Routledge.

__________(2005a), 'Democracy Analysis' in International IDEA, *Ten Years of Supporting Democracy Worldwide*, Stockholm: International IDEA, pp. 19-27.

__________(2005b), 'Review Article: The Political Science of Human Rights', *British Journal of Political Science*, 35 (July): pp. 549-572.

__________ *et al.* (2005), "State of Democracy in Mongolia", Paper prepared for 'Democracy Development in Mongolia: Challenges and Opportunities', National Conference, Ulaanbaatar, Mongolia (30th June to 1st July 2005).

Lasater, M. L. (1988), US Policy towards China's reunification: the Reagan years: 1980-1986.

Lebow, R. N. and Rissen K. T. (1995), International Relations Theory and the end of the Cold War. New York: Columbia University Press.

Lee, J. (2002) 'Primary Causes of Asian Democratisation: Dispelling Conventional Myths,' *Asian Survey*, 42 (6): pp. 821-837.

Linz, J. J. and Stepan, A. (1996), *Problems of Democratic Transition and Consolidation: South America, Southern Europe, and Post-Communist Europe*, Baltimore: Johns Hopkins University Press.

Lipset, S. M. (1959), 'Some Social Requisites from Democracy: Economic Development and Political Legitimacy', *The American Political Science Review*, 53(10): 69-105.

Little, R. (2001), "International Regimes" in J. Baylis and S. Smith (eds), *The Globalisation of World Politics: An introduction to international relations.* (2nd ed.) Oxford: Oxford University Press.

Liu Xiaoyuan (2006), *Reins of Liberation: An Entangled History of Mongolian Independence, Chinese Territoriality, and Great Power Hegemony,* Stanford: Stanford University Press.

Malcolmson, D. (2001), "Foreign Policy Aligned at Heads of Mission Conference", *Global Dialogue*, 5 (2), pp. 5-6.

Mearsheimer, J. (1994), "The False Promise of International Institutions", *International Security,* 19 (6), pp. 5-49.

Ministry of Defence of Mongolia, *Mongolian Defence White Paper, 1997-1998*, Ulaanbaatar, 1988.

Ministry of External Relations of Mongolia, *Mongolian Foreign Policy Blue Book*, Ulaanbaatar, 2000.

Ministry of Foreign Affairs (2006), "Concept of Mongolia's Foreign Policy," *Diplomatic Bluebook 2006*. Ulaanbaatar: Ministry of Foreign Affairs.

Moiseev, Leonid (2001), "Relations between Russia and Mongolia are warming", *Far Eastern Affairs*, 1: p. 12.

Morgenthau, H. J. (1973), *Politics among Nations. Fifth edition*, Revised. New York: Oxford Univ. Press.

Nachin, D. (2005), "Foreign Direct Investment: Trends in the World and in Mongolia". Yukiyasu Arai (ed). *Internal and External Factors on Economic Cooperation and Development in Mongolia and Northeast Asia*, Ulaanbaatar.

Nachin, D. (2005), "Foreign Direct Investment: Trends in the World and in Mongolia", in Yukiyasu Arai, ed., *Internal and External Factors on Economic Cooperation and Development in Mongolia and Northeast Asia*, Ulaanbaatar.

Neuman, S.G. (1998), *International Relations Theory and the Third World.* London: Macmillan.

* National Human Rights Commission of Mongolia. (2003), Human Rights and Freedoms in Mongolia: Status Report 2003. Ulaanbaatar.

Noerper, S., (2007) "Mongolia in 2006: "Land of the Rising Khan", *Asian Survey*, 47 (1): pp. 74-79.

Nye, J. (2003). *Understanding International Conflicts.* 4th ed. London: Longman.

Olzvoy, K. (1996), "A Mongol's View of Economic Development and Cooperation in Northeast Asia", *The Mongolian Journal of International Affairs*, 3: 13-24.

Peiran Wang *(2009),* "Mongolia's Delicate Balancing Act", *China Security*, 5(2).

Pomfret, R., (2000), "Transition and Democracy in Mongolia", *Europe-Asia Studies*, 52 (1): pp. 149-160.

Pomfret, Richard. (2000), "Transition and Democracy in Mongolia," *Europe-Asia Studies* 52 (1): pp. 149-60.

Przeworski, A. and Limongi, F. (1993), 'Political Regimes and Economic Growth', *Journal of Economic Perspectives*, 7 (3): pp. 51-69.

Przeworski, A. *et.al.* (2000), *Democracy and Development: Political Institutions and Well-Being in the World, 1950-1990*, Cambridge: Cambridge University Press.

Putnam, Robert. (1993), *Making Democracy Work: Civic Traditions in Modern Italy*. Princeton: Princeton University Press.

Reus Smit, C. (2005), "Constructivism" in S. Burchill, *et.al. Theories of International Relations* (3rd ed.) Houndsmills: Palgrave Macmillan.

Richard Pomfret, (2000): Transition and Democracy in Mongolia, *Europe-Asia Studies*, 52:1, 149-160.

Robert E. Bedeski (2008), Genghis Khan, Mongolia and the Theory of Human Security, *China and Eurasia Forum Quarterly*, 6 (4): pp. 81-102.

Rose, R. (1998*), Democracy and Its Alternatives.* Baltimore: Johns Hopkins University Press.

__________ and Mishler, W. (1994), "Mass Reactions to Regime Change in Eastern Europe," *British Journal of Political Science* 24 (2): pp. 159-182.

Rossabi, Morris (1992), "Mongolia: A New Opening" *Current History,* 91 (566): pp. 278-283.

__________ (2005), *Modern Mongolia: From Khans to Commissars to Capitalists,* Berkeley: University of California Press.

Ryokichi, H., (1992), "Mongolia's Struggle to Create a Market Economy", *Japan Review of International Affairs,* 6 (2): pp. 107-123.

Sabloff, P. (2002), 'Why Mongolia? The Political Culture of an Emerging Democracy', *Central Asian Survey,* 21 (1): pp. 19-36.

Sabloff, Paula L. W. (2002),"Why Mongolia? The Political Culture of an Emerging Democracy," *Central Asian Survey* 21 (1): pp. 19-36.

Sanders, Alan (1997), "Mongolia: Looking to the Sea", *Geopolitics,* 2 (1): pp. 134-152.

Sanders, A. (1997), "Foreign Relations and Foreign Policy", in Bruun, O. and Odgaard, O. eds. *Mongolia in Transition: Old Patterns, New Challenges,* UK: Routledge Curzon.

Sanders, Alan J.K. (1988), "Mongolia in 1988: Year of Renewal". *Asian Survey,* 29 (1) pp. 46-53.

__________(1992), "Mongolia's New Constitution: Blueprint for Democracy", *Asian Survey,* 32 (6): pp. 506-520.

Schmitz, H.P. and Sikkink, K. (2002), "International Human Rights" in W. Carlsnaes, T. Risse and B. A. Simmons, *Handbook of International Relations,* London: SAGE Publications.

Severinghaus, S. (2001), 'Mongolia in 2000: The Pendulum Swings Again', *Asian Survey,* 41 (1): pp. 61-70.

Severington, S.R, (2000), "Mongolia in 1998 and 1999: Past, Present and Future at the New Millennium", *Asian Survey,* 40 (1): pp. 130-139.

__________(2002), "Mongolia in 2001: The Pendulum Swings Again", *Asian Survey,* 41 (1): pp. 61-70.

Sharma, R.C., Warikoo K.,M. Haider and Sh. Bira, eds. (1992), *Mongolia: Culture, Economy and Politics,* New Delhi: Khama Publishers.

Sheldon R. Severinghaus (1995), Mongolia in 1994: Strengthening Democracy, *Asian Survey*, 35 (1): pp. 70-75.

Shin, D. and Wells, J. (2005), 'Is Democracy the Only Game in Town?' *Journal of Democracy*, 16 (2): pp. 88-101.

Smith, K. (2006), "International Organisations" in P.J. McGowan, *et.al.* (eds). *Power, Wealth and Global Equity: An International Relations,* (2nd ed). Cape Town: UCT Press.

Smith, S. (1995), "The Self-Images of a Discipline: A Genealogy of International Relations Theory" in K. Booth and S. Smith. *International Relations Theory Today,* Cambridge: Polity Press.

__________(1996), "Positivism and Beyond" in S. Smith, *et.al.* (eds). *International Theory: Positivism and Beyond*, Cambridge: Cambridge University Press. pp. 11- 46.

__________(2000), "The discipline of International Relations: Still an American Social Science?" in *British Journal of Politics and International Relations* 2 (1), pp. 382-3.

__________(2001), "Reflectivist and constructivist approaches to international theory" in J. Baylis and S. Smith (eds). *The Globalisation of World Politics: An introduction to international relations.* (2nd ed.) Oxford: Oxford University Press.

Soni, Sharad K. (2006), "Mongolia between Russia and China: Emerging Equation," in *Mongolica, An International Annual of Mongol Studies*, 17 (38): pp. 252-268.

__________(2006), "Mongolia between Russia and China: Emerging Equation," in *Mongolica, An International Annual of Mongol Studies*, 17 (38): pp. 252-268.

__________(2000), *Mongolia between China and Russia: An Historical Overview,* Kolkata: Maulana Abdul Kalam Azad Institute of Asian Studies.

__________(2001), "Mongolia and the Soviet Union: A Study of Political Relations (1921-1999)", in *Asia Annual 2001*, Mahavir Singh, ed., Delhi: Shipra Publications, pp. 41-61.

________(2001), "Mongolia's Foreign Policy Priorities", *Himalayan and Central Asian Studies"*, 5 (1): pp. 11-14.

________(2002), *Mongolia-Russia Relations: Kiakhta to Vladivostok,* New Delhi: Shipra Publication.

________(2003), *Mongolia between Russia and China: Emerging Equation,* Kolkata: Maulana Abdul Kalam Azad Institute of Asian Studies.

________(2005), "Mongolia's Security Concerns in the Post-Cold War Period", in Mahavir Singh, ed., *Building A New Asia*, Delhi: Shipra Publications, pp. 282-294.

________(2006), "Mongolia's Security Thinking and Outside World: A Reappraisal", *Bimonthly Journal of Mongolian and Tibetan Current Situation*, 15 (6): pp. 27-39.

________(2006), *Mongolia-China Relations: Modern and Contemporary Times*, New Delhi: Pentagon Press.

________(2006), "India's New Role in East Asia; Implications for Mongolia", *Mongolian Journal of International Studies,* no 13: pp. 32-41

________(2008), "Post-Cold War Identity of Mongolia: Strategic Concerns", in P.L. Das (ed.), *Emerging Asia in Focus: Issues and Problems,* Delhi: Academic Excellence, pp. 415-432.

________(2009), China periphery Policy: Implications for Sino-Mongolian Relations, *India Quarterly: A journal of international affairs,* 65: p. 251

Stallybrass, E. and C. R. Bawden (2001), "The Final Years", *Asian Affairs*, 32 (1): pp. 48-50.

Steiner-Khamsi, Gita and Ines Stolpe (2004), "Decentralisation and Recentralisation Reform in Mongolia: Tracing the Swing of the Pendulum", *Comparative Education*, 40 (1): pp. 29-53.

Stobdan, P (1998), "Mongolia and the US: Redefining Inner Asia", *Strategic Analysis*, 22 (1): pp. 198-252.

Sveringhaus, Sheldon. (2001) "Mongolia in 2000," *Asian Survey* 41 (1): pp. 61-70.

Telford Sarah (2004), "To What Extent Does Post–1990 Mongolia Pursue an Independent Foreign Policy?" Research *Unit on International Security and Cooperation (UNISCI)*, Spain: Madrid.

The Asia Foundation (2009) "Mongolia – Voter Education Survey", Ulaanbaatar, p. 44.

Thomas, S. (1996), *The Diplomacy of Liberation: The Foreign Relations of the ANC since 1960.*

Ts. Batbayar, (2002), *Mongolia's Foreign Policy in the 1990s: New Identity and New Challenges. Regional Security Issues and Mongolia,* Vol. 17, Ulaanbaatar, Institute for Strategic Studies.

__________ (2003a), "Foreign Policy and Domestic Reform in Mongolia". *Central Asian Survey*, 22 (1), pp. 45–59.

__________(2003b), "Mongolian-Russian Relations in the Past Decade". *Asian Survey*. 43(6), 950-970.

Tumurchulum, G. (1999), "Mongolia's Foreign Policy Revisited: Relations with Russia and the PRC into the 1990s", in Stephen Kotkin and Bruce Elleman, eds., *Mongolia in the Twentieth Century: Landlocked Cosmopolitan,* New York: M. E. Sharpe, pp. 277-289.

__________(2001), "Mongolia, Russia and China: The Geopolitical Perspectives", *Himalayan and Central Asian Studies*, 5 (1): pp. 33-44.

Tuya, N. (2005), 'Mongolia in 2004: Testing Politics and Economics', *Asian Survey*, 45 (1): pp. 67-70.

*United Nations Development Program (2003), *Human Development Report 2003 Millennium Development Goals: A Compact Among Nations to End Human Poverty.* Oxford: Oxford University Press.

*United Nations Food and Agriculture Administration (2003), *The State of Food Security in the World*, New York: United Nations Food and Agriculture Administration.

*United Nations General Assembly, 55th Session, *Report of the Secretary-General on Mongolia's International Security* *and Nuclear - Weapon - Free Status*, document no. A/55/166, 20 July 2000.

*US Department of State, Bureau of East Asian and Pacific Affairs, (2009), *Background Notes: Mongolia*, August 2009. Available at: http://www.state.gov/r/pa/ei/bgn/2779.htm.

*US State Department (1998) *Country Report on Human Rights Practices*, Washington DC: US State Department.

United States (1984). *China-Mongolia Boundary, International Boundary Study No. 173*. Washington, D.C.: Department of State, Office of the Geographer, Bureau of Intelligence and Research, August 14, 1984, 12, citing J.V.A. MacMurray, *Treaties and Agreements with and Concerning China, 1894-1919*. Oxford University Press, 2: pp. 992–993.

Vanhanen, T. (1997), *The Prospects of Democracy*, London: Routledge.

Viotti, P.R., and Kauppi, M.V. (1993) International relations theory: realism, pluralism, globalism. New York : Macmillan, 1993.

Wachman, Allan M. (2009), *Mongolia's Geopolitical Gambit: Preserving a Precarious Independence While Resisting "Soft Colonialism"*, EAI Fellows Program Working Paper Series 18, Seoul: The East Asia Institute.

Waltz, K. N. (1979), *Theory of International Politics*, California: Addition-Wesley Publishing Company.

Waltz, K.N. (2000), "Realist thought and neo-realist theory", in Andrew L. *International Relations: Critical Concepts in Political Science (vol. IV).* London and New York: Rutledge.

Weir, S. and Beetham, D. (1999), *Political Power and Democratic Control in Britain: The Democratic Audit of The United Kingdom*, London: Routledge.

William Heaton R. (1992) "Mongolia in 1991: The Uneasy Transition", *Asian Survey*, 32(1): 90-95.

William Heaton R. (1991), Mongolia in 1990: Upheaval, Reform, But No Revolution Yet, *Asian Survey,* 31 (1): 50-56.

__________(1987), "Mongolia in 1986: New Plan, New Situation", *Asian Survey*, 27(1): pp. 75-80.

Williams, M.C. (2005), *The Realist Tradition and the Limits of International Relations*, UK: Cambridge University Press.

Worden R. L. and Savada A. M. (1989), *Mongolia: A Country Study*. Washington: GPO for the Library of Congress.

Youla C. (2009), *the foreign policies of Mandela and Mbeki: A clear case of idealism vs. realism?* Dissertation for degree of arts, *South Africa:* Stellenbosch University.

Zakaria, F. (2003), *The Future of Freedom: Illiberal Democracy at Home and Abroad*, New York and London: W. W. Norton.

Zehfuss, M. (2005), *Constructivism in International Relations: The politics of reality*, Cambridge UK: University Press.

Zhang Zhirong. (2004), *Contemporary China Diplomacy: A New Interpretation*. Hong Kong: Lizhi Press.

WEBSITES

http://www.bayefsky.com

http://www.bbc.co.uk

http://www.humanrightsdata.com

http://europa.eu.int/comm/external_relations/mongolia/intro/index.htm

www.freedomhouse,org

www.heritage.org

http://opensocietyforum.mn

http://uk.reuters.com/article/2008/07/01/mongolia-idUKPEK27460920080701

http://www.bgipu.org/past/mongolia-report-september 2009.htm

http://www.duke.edu/web/diem/reports/IRI/Mongolia2000.pdf

http://www.idea.int/democracy/upload/sodMongolia05.pdf

http://www.internetworldstats.com/asia/mn.htm

http://www.isop.ucla.edu

*http://www.mongoliatoday.com/info/country_briefs.html

http://www.un.int/mongolia/Archives/2000/p-5sta~1.htm

http://www.usaid.gov/policy/budget/cbj2004/asia_near_east/Mongolia.pdf(accessed 04/04/12).

International IDEA (2002), 'Democracy Assessment: The Basics of the International IDEA Assessment Framework', Stockholm: International IDEA. International Press Institute; http://www.freemedia.at (accessed 07/01/12).

Japanese Ministry of Foreign Affairs, Mongolia briefing: http://www.mofa.go.jp/ region/asia-paci/mongolia/ (accessed 14/04/12).

Japan-Mongolia Summit Meeting, December 4, 2003: http://www.kantei.go.jp/foreign/koizumiphoto/2003/12/04mongol_e.html (accessed 14/04/12).

*Mongolian Ministry of Foreign Affairs. (2003). *Statement by Mr Nambaryn Enkbayar, Prime Minister of Mongolia at the 13th Conference of the Heads of State or Government of the Non-aligned Movement. 25 February 2003.* [Online] Available at http://www.mofa.go.jp/region/asia-paci/mongolia/telegram0301.html.

*National Center Against Violence. Center for Human Rights and Development, and CEDAW Watch Network Center. (2002), Violence against Women and Legal Framework in Mongolia. www.owc.org.mn/mones. (accessed 04/01/12).

Rossabi, M.(2000). *China Seeks to Bolster Its Economic Profile in Central Asia.* [Online] Available at http://www.eurasianet.org/departments/business/articles/eav081400.shtml (accessed 09/05/12).

www.forum.mn

www.transparency.org

ubpost.mongolianews.mn

http://www.undp.mn

*United Nations Development Programme (New York); http://www.undp.org.

*US Agency for International Development; http://www.usaid.gov.

US Department of State, Mongolia briefing: http://www.state.gov/r/pa/ei/bgn/2779.htm (accessed 04/04/12).

US Department of State. (2004), *Joint Statement on Bilateral and Regional Cooperation between Mongolia and the United States of America, January 31st 2004.* [Online] Available at http://www.state.gov/p/eap/rls/prs/2004/29143.htm (accessed 04/04/12).

USAID, (2004), *Mongolia.* [Online] Available at USAID, Mongolia briefing http://www.usaid.gov/locations/asia_near_east/ countries/mongolia/mong_brief.html (accessed 04/04/12).

World Bank; http://www.worldbank.org

www.freedomhouse.org.

www.ipu.org/parline-e/reports/2219_e.htm

Index

D

E

F

G

H

I

J

K

L

M